Switzerland–EU Relations

This book offers an up-to-date assessment of the state of Switzerland–EU relations with the aim of drawing lessons from the Swiss experience to shed light on the challenges facing the UK post-Brexit and, more broadly, on how non-member states can adapt to "integration without membership".

The book covers the main issues in the Swiss experience of dealing with the EU over the last 30 years. These include the determinants of the 1992 vote, the architecture of the bilateral agreements signed since then, the economic interests at stake, the role played by immigration, the impact on the country's federal system, the political, social, and cultural factors shaping attitudes to integration, and how the "Swiss model" has featured in the discourse about Brexit. The concluding chapter identifies the key lessons that Switzerland's experience offers for the British debate on the country's relations with the EU post-Brexit.

This book will be of key interest to scholars and students of European Union politics, European politics, Swiss politics, British politics, Brexit, and, more broadly, international relations.

Paolo Dardanelli is Reader in Comparative Politics at the University of Kent, UK.

Oscar Mazzoleni is Professor of Political Science at the University of Lausanne, Switzerland.

Dealing with Europe

This mini-series offers books which respectively examine the potential modes of affiliation adopted by key countries with the EU, systematically assessing the potential suitability of each arrangement as a viable EU affiliation post-Brexit model for the UK against the revealing backdrop of the domestic political context of each country. It clarifies which actors and factors are supportive of such arrangements in each country; which actors and factors are the main challenges; what form of balance there is and how precarious that is. Finally, each country case study considers what would happen should the UK try to adopt such a model.

Series editors: *John Erik Fossum, University of Oslo, Norway, and Christopher Lord, University of Oslo, Norway.*

Switzerland-EU Relations
Lessons for the UK after Brexit?
Edited by Paolo Dardanelli and Oscar Mazzoleni

Switzerland-EU Relations

Lessons for the UK after Brexit?

Edited by Paolo Dardanelli and Oscar Mazzoleni

Routledge
Taylor & Francis Group
LONDON AND NEW YORK

First published 2021
by Routledge
2 Park Square, Milton Park, Abingdon, Oxon OX14 4RN

and by Routledge
52 Vanderbilt Avenue, New York, NY 10017

Routledge is an imprint of the Taylor & Francis Group, an informa business

British Library Cataloguing-in-Publication Data
A catalogue record for this book is available from the British Library

Library of Congress Cataloging-in-Publication Data
A catalog record has been requested for this book

ISBN: 978-0-367-48205-3 (hbk)
ISBN: 978-0-367-49804-7 (pbk)
ISBN: 978-1-003-03871-9 (ebk)

Typeset in Times New Roman
by Deanta Global Publishing Services, Chennai, India

Contents

Figures

Tables

Contributors

Clive H. Church is Emeritus Professor of European Studies at the University of Kent. He is the author of numerous works on Switzerland, including *The Politics and Government of Switzerland* (Palgrave Macmillan, 2004), *A Concise History of Switzerland* (Cambridge University Press, 2013 – with Randolph Head), and *Political Change in Switzerland – From Stability to Uncertainty* (Routledge, 2016).

Paolo Dardanelli is Reader in Comparative Politics at the University of Kent. His research explores the causes and consequences of the territorial structure of political systems. He is the author of *Restructuring the European State – European Integration and State Reform* (McGill-Queen's University Press, 2017) and *Between Two Unions: Europeanisation and Scottish Devolution* (Manchester University Press, 2005), and co-editor of Routledge's Studies in Federalism and Decentralization series.

Blaise Fontanellaz is post-doctoral researcher in European politics at the University of Geneva. He is the author of *Entre* Sonderfall *et intégration – Les partis politiques suisses à l'épreuve de l'Europe, 1989–2014* (Academia/L'Harmattan, 2019).

Sabine Jenni is a research associate at the Liechtenstein-Institut, co-editor of EFTA-Studies.org, and author of *Switzerland's Differentiated European Integration: The Last Gallic Village?* (Palgrave Macmillan, 2016). Besides research, Sabine works in education and project management, mainly with Demokrative – Initiative für politische Bildung and the Historical Archives of the European Union.

Georg Kreis is Emeritus Professor of Modern History at the University of Basel. He is the author and editor of numerous works on Swiss and European history, including the landmark *Die Geschichte der Schweiz* (Schwabe Verlag, 2014).

Oscar Mazzoleni is Professor of Political Science and Director of the Research Observatory of Regional Politics at the University of Lausanne. He is the author of numerous works on Swiss and comparative politics in English, French, German, and Italian. He also co-edited *Regionalist Parties in Western Europe* (Routledge, 2017) and *The People and the Nation: Populism and Ethno-territorial Politics in Europe* (Routledge, 2020).

Sean Mueller is a Swiss National Science Foundation-funded Assistant Professor in political science at the University of Lausanne. He is the author of numerous works on Swiss and comparative politics, including *Schweizerische Demokratie: Institutionen, Strukturen, Prozesse* (4th ed., Haupt, 2017, with Wolf Linder) and *Swiss Democracy* (4th ed., Palgrave, 2021, with Wolf Linder).

Sergio Rossi is Professor of Economics at the University of Fribourg, where he holds the Chair of Macroeconomics and Monetary Economics, and Senior Research Associate at the International Economic Policy Institute at Laurentian University in Canada. He has authored and edited numerous works on macroeconomics, including an encyclopaedia on central banking. He has recently been ranked among the 40 most influential Swiss economists by the *Neue Zürcher Zeitung*.

René Schwok is Professor of Political Science at the University of Geneva. His research focusses on European integration, Swiss foreign policy, and international relations and security. He is the author of numerous works on Switzerland–EU relations, including *Suisse-Union européenne: L'adhésion impossible?* (Presses polytechniques et universitaires romandes, 3rd ed., 2015).

Pascal Sciarini is Professor of Political Science at the University of Geneva and President of the Swiss Political Science Association. He has authored and edited numerous works on Swiss politics.

Tobias Theiler is a lecturer in Political Science at University College Dublin. He is the author of several works on Swiss politics, European integration, and the EU including *Political Symbolism and European Integration* (Manchester University Press, 2005), 'The Origins of Euroscepticism in German-speaking Switzerland' in the *European Journal of Political Research* and 'Does the European Union Need to Become a Community?' in the *Journal of Common Market Studies*.

Guillaume Vallet is Associate Professor of Economics at the University of Grenoble. He has authored several works on the Swiss economy, including 'The Role of the Swiss Franc in Switzerland's European Stance' in *Research in International Business and Finance*.

Abbreviations

AUNS	Aktion für eine unabhängige und neutrale Schweiz/Action pour une Suisse indépendante et neutre/Azione per una Svizzera neutrale e indipendente [Campaign for an independent and neutral Switzerland]
CCG	Conference of Cantonal Governments
CJEU	Court of Justice of the European Union
CVP	Christlichdemokratische Volkspartei der Schweiz/Parti Démocrate-Chrétien/Partito Popolare Democratico [Christian Democratic Party]
DAA	Dublin Association Agreement
ECB	European Central Bank
ECHR	European Convention on Human Rights
ECSC	European Coal and Steel Community
EEA	European Economic Area
EEC	European Economic Community
EFTA	European Free Trade Association
EPC	European Payment Council
EU	European Union
FDP	FDP.Die Liberalen/PLR.Les Libéraux-Radicaux/PLR.I Liberali [Liberal Democratic Party]
FMPA	Agreement on the Free Movement of Persons
IFA	Institutional Framework Agreement
NEBS	Neue europäische Bewegung Schweiz/Nouveau movement européen Suisse/Nuovo Movimento Europeo Svizzera [New European Movement Switzerland]
OEEC	Organisation for European Economic Co-operation
SEPA	Single European Payment Area
SAA	Schengen Association Agreement
SNB	Swiss National Bank
SNP	Scottish National Party

SP	Sozialdemokratische Partei der Schweiz/Parti socialiste suisse/ Partito Socialista Svizzero [Socialist Party]
SVP	Schweizerische Volkspartei/Union démocratique du centre/ Unione Democratica di Centro [Swiss People's Party]
UKIP	United Kingdom Independence Party
WTO	World Trade Organisation

1 Introduction

Oscar Mazzoleni and Paolo Dardanelli

Although each national context is to some extent unique, countries can and often do learn from each other. At a crucial time for the Brexit process in the United Kingdom (UK), it is helpful to draw insights from other countries with a history of difficult relations with the European Union (EU).[1] Switzerland stands out as a potentially interesting case in this regard, as a country very open economically but at the same time highly protective of its national identity and sovereignty (e.g. Steinberg 2015; Church 2016). Deep societal cleavages, a polarising party system, delicate trade-offs facing diplomats and governments, and a long period of uncertainty: all of these aspects are also prominently on display in Switzerland. Indeed, no country outside the EU has had to face the challenges of integration more than the Swiss Confederation.[2] Switzerland has had to continuously and extensively deal with European integration while remaining outside the EU since the early 1990s. Although Swiss citizens have never been asked directly whether or not their country should join the EU, Swiss–EU relations have been high on Switzerland's political agenda over the last 30 years. This has been facilitated by the existence of instruments of direct democracy that are unparalleled in terms of a range of opportunities and frequency of use elsewhere in Europe, and indeed the wider world. The debate on European integration has been intense and has affected many issues, involving political, economic, social, and cultural dimensions. The European question has shaped the agenda of government and parliament, parties, and public opinion, affecting domestic and foreign policy, diplomatic relations, economic relations, and ideological divides. "Europe"[3] has been a salient issue, directly or indirectly, in all federal elections since the 1990s, and has profoundly influenced party competition (e.g. Hutter et al. 2016).

Between independence and integration

The history of Swiss–EU relations over the past 30 years has been punctuated by a series of crucial federal referendums: from a referendum on the European Economic Area (EEA) in December 1992 to a referendum "Against Mass Immigration" in February 2014 through various votes on bilateral agreements between 2000 and 2009. After Germany's re-unification and the acceleration of European integration at the turn of the 1990s, Switzerland faced a crucial dilemma:

continue on a *Sonderfall*, or special case, path, whereby the country, jealous of its political independence and spared from the destructions of World War II, aligned itself with the Western democracies but without joining NATO or the UN; or take a new path, that of European integration, not least to retain the competitiveness of its economy, which is highly dependent on European and world markets. The 1992 EEA referendum revealed a degree of polarisation unprecedented on a foreign policy issue and produced a shock defeat for the Federal Council – Switzerland's federal executive – and the wider political establishment, which had almost unanimously supported ratification.

After the people's decision on the EEA – widely seen as a stepping-stone to joining the EU – a new phase opened and Switzerland sought to conclude a set of wide-ranging agreements with the EU. Marked by challenging negotiations and punctuated by frequent popular votes, this bilateral approach developed from the second half of the 1990s onwards. The last phase in these bilateral relations, ongoing since 2018, concerns the adoption of an Institutional Framework Agreement (IFA), which would bring together the existing agreements and provide an umbrella for all future ones. Like its predecessors, ratification of this agreement is also subject to approval by the Swiss people and the cantons; in Switzerland, popular votes of constitutional significance require a double majority of the electorate as a whole, and of the cantonal electorate in a majority of the cantons. The last in the series of such popular votes concerned a proposal to end the free movement of persons with the EU, which was turned down by a large majority on 27 September 2020.

Even more so than previously, Swiss–EU relations are thus at a crucial juncture in their tortuous evolution, characterised by deep uncertainty. It is thus a propitious moment to review these relations looking for insights Switzerland's experience of dealing with Europe has to offer to the UK and more widely.

Aims and questions

Over ten years since another edited book covered a similar ground (Church 2007), the present volume offers an up-to-date assessment of the state of Swiss–EU relations with the aim of drawing insights from the Swiss experience that could shed light on the challenges facing the UK post-Brexit and, more broadly, on how non-member states can adapt to "integration without membership" (on this concept, see Vahl and Grolimund 2006). The book covers the main issues in the Swiss experience of dealing with the EU over the last 30 years. These issues include the determinants of the 1992 vote; the architecture of the bilateral agreements signed since then; the economic interests at stake; the role played by immigration; the impact on the country's federal system; the political, social, and cultural factors shaping attitudes to integration; and how the "Swiss model" has featured in the discourse about Brexit. The concluding chapter identifies the key insights that Switzerland's experience offers for the British debate on the country's relations with the EU post-Brexit.

In sum, the main questions addressed are: how did the proposal to join the EEA come about and why was it rejected in the 1992 referendum? What are the economic interests at stake? Why and how has the path of bilateral agreements developed and why is an overarching IFA currently on the table? Why has migration become a central issue in Swiss-EU relations? How has Switzerland's federal system been affected by "integration without membership"? How have the Swiss parties positioned themselves on Europe and what impact has the integration question had on the party system? What are the factors explaining citizens' vote on European issues and, in particular, how can we explain regional variations? Finally, to what extent has the "Swiss model" featured in the Brexit debate in the UK and how likely is the latter to be willing to look at Switzerland's experience to guide its own future relations with the EU?

The chapters

From different disciplinary backgrounds, the contributors to this volume seek to give an answer to these questions in their chapters. In the first part of the book, the authors provide an overview of the context within which Switzerland's European policy has been formulated, in its historical, economic, social, political, and institutional dimensions. From a historian's perspective, Georg Kreis takes a look back at the past, revisiting the path that led to the fateful vote of 6 December 1992 on Switzerland's membership of the EEA. Kreis shows how the roots of the rejection of the EEA are to be found in the legacy left by 50 years of post–World War II isolationist foreign policy inspired by a belief in Switzerland's *Sonderfall.* It highlights significant parallels with the UK's Brexit vote of 2016 and the crucial role played by appeals to history and identity in the respective campaigns. In their chapter, the economists Sergio Rossi and Guillaume Vallet discuss the economic factors underlying the relations between Switzerland and EU. They highlight the role played by a long-term guiding thread of Swiss European policy, namely the desire to benefit from economic integration while at the same time avoiding as much as possible institutional and political constraints, which has led the country towards a path of "integration without membership". The chapter points out that prominent aspects of the Swiss economy, such as the importance of the financial sector, have clear parallels in the UK. Hence, Switzerland's experience in handling the trade-off between economic benefits and political costs could have potentially fruitful lessons for the UK. René Schwok outlines the evolution of the architecture of bilateral agreements between Switzerland and the EU concluded since 1992. Schwok assesses the strengths and weaknesses of this bilateral approach and argues that, although it has served Switzerland reasonably well so far, it falls short of offering a stable basis for the future. The impasse in which Switzerland currently finds itself over an IFA, negotiated under pressure from the EU to replace the various sectoral agreements with a single framework agreement, illustrates the fragility of the bilateral approach and the uncertainties surrounding its future. If Switzerland's bilateral approach is unlikely to offer a ready-made model for the UK, the issues the former has had to deal over the past 30 years are bound to constitute significant obstacles on the future path of the latter as well.

In contemporary Swiss politics, the most controversial agreements are those concerning the free movement of persons, immigration, and asylum. Sabine Jenni studies these in detail, stressing similarities and differences between the Swiss legal framework and European standards, particularly with regard to restrictions on the social rights of migrant workers. She also discusses the effects of these agreements on the Swiss labour market and the unemployment rate, showing that free movement has not had a negative effect overall but its impact has been more significant in certain sectors and regions. Drawing parallels with the role that immigration has played in the Brexit debate, the chapter highlights the importance of the economic and social consequences of how immigration flows are distributed across a country. In the last chapter of this first part, Paolo Dardanelli examines another important aspect: the impact of integration on Switzerland's federal system, assessing in particular the tensions between fragmentation and centralisation. In addition to being a fundamental institutional feature of the Swiss political system, federalism has also become an important element of Swiss identity and has close links with direct democracy. It is therefore exposed in various ways to the effects of integration and, in turn, has a significant influence on the country's European policy. Noting that integration primarily has had a centrifugal effect in the UK, the chapter argues that the policy response called for is nonetheless a similar one: the need to strengthen communication channels and co-decision fora between levels of government.

A second set of contributions are devoted to more explicitly political aspects, such as party strategies, citizens' attitudes, and voting behaviour. Blaise Fontanellaz and Paolo Dardanelli map the positions that the main Swiss political parties have adopted on European issues, how these have changed over time, and the factors that have driven their evolution. Their analysis illustrates the internal tensions parties have faced over Europe and how competition over these issues has been a key factor in the reshaping of the party system over the last 30 years. The chapter highlights several aspects where the experience of the Swiss parties echoes that of their UK counterparts, thus shedding light on some likely future trajectories of the European question in British party politics.

Pascal Sciarini provides an extensive analysis of the factors that determined the results of federal referendums and popular initiatives from 1992 to 2014. Using the so-called VOX surveys, opinion polls conducted after each vote, Sciarini assesses the effects of a range of socio-demographic and attitudinal factors, highlighting the crucial role played by education, language, urban-rural location, and trust in the federal government. These factors broadly mirror those identified by analyses of the 2016 Brexit vote in the UK and indicate that citizens' attitudes to international co-operation are driven by some deep-seated factors impervious to short-term government action. The other three chapters in this part investigate cultural and territorial drivers of political mobilisation around EU issues. In his chapter, Sean Mueller offers a complementary look at the factors that determine citizens' votes on EU matters. Based on an analysis of the results at the municipal level of the ten referendum and popular initiatives, Mueller seeks to identify how far these factors are linked to territorial dimensions. In doing so, he stresses variation in terms of regional context, highlighting the interaction between border location and economic situation. His findings closely match the conclusions of research on Brexit drivers in the UK and confirm that policies directed at tackling these forms of territorial and social disadvantage may be the most effective ones in shaping citizens' attitudes to Europe.

Tobias Theiler addresses the contrast between French-speaking and German-speaking Switzerland, the main linguistic and cultural divide in Switzerland, whereby the former has consistently displayed more pro-EU orientations than the latter. On the basis of a linguistic-cultural analysis, the author argues that the roots of the different attitudes in the two language regions are to be found in their respective cultural-linguistic situation, within Switzerland and in relation to France and Germany, respectively. Theiler highlights the similarities with the way that English cultural identities have featured in the Brexit debate, thus calling for greater scholarly attention to the role played by cultural and identity factors. Oscar Mazzoleni explores another striking territorial pattern in Swiss voting on EU issues, the special case of Ticino, the main Italian-speaking canton, where opposition to European integration has been at its strongest. Discussing both the strategies of political actors and citizens' voting behaviour, the chapter stresses the crucial role that the conflation of regionalism and Euroscepticism has played in forging Ticino's divergent path.

Finally, Clive Church argues that although Switzerland's experience of dealing with the EU is potentially valuable to the UK in charting its own future European policy, the "Swiss model" has only fleetingly featured in the Brexit debate; it has often been poorly understood and is unlikely to have much influence on UK policy. This is primarily because the ideology underpinning Brexit has been inward-looking and narrowly focussed on "getting out", thereby not predisposing the UK to seeking to learn from other countries. While it is too early to assess its impact, the COVID-19 pandemic may further complicate UK–EU as well as Swiss–EU relations by deepening uncertainty and making economic challenges even more severe. The concluding chapter weaves together the various threads developed in the preceding chapters and distils the key takeaways from the Swiss experience.

Notes

1 We are grateful to Christopher Lord and John Erik Fossum for having read the entire manuscript and offering helpful comments and suggestions.
2 Although Norway has also had close interactions with the EU since the early 1970s, its status in relation to the latter has been highly stable since the foundation of the EEA in 1994. Switzerland's status, by contrast, has been continously renegotiated throughout the last 30 years.
3 We use "Europe" as shorthand for the EU and its predecessor organisations.

2 Looking back

1992 as a critical juncture

Georg Kreis

In Switzerland, advocates of an arms-length relationship with the EU often look to the United Kingdom for a confirmation of their own position. From this perspective, the Swiss rejection of the EEA in 1992 and the British rejection of EU membership in 2016 can be related. Such a comparison does not imply the two events are equivalent, but may shed new light on each of them.

Switzerland and the United Kingdom: An initial comparison

Some similarities between the two cases are striking: the outcome of the two referendums was very close (50.3% against participation in the EEA in Switzerland and 51.9% for leaving the EU in the UK) and in both countries it created deep divisions in society and sharpened differences. There was also a similar divergence across regions: the French-speaking minority in Switzerland, mirroring Scotland and Northern Ireland in the UK, had a much more positive attitude to Europe than the majority, German speakers in the former and the English in the latter. The urban-rural divide is likewise similar in the two cases, as are the differences in attitudes based on education and income (see chapters by Sciarini and Mueller, this volume). In both countries the majority of the business community favoured moving closer to the European Economic Community (EEC) or remaining in the EU. And if you saw outraged or depressed young people in front of television cameras after the Brexit vote in 2016, you could imagine the young people in Switzerland who were shocked in February 2014 at the acceptance of the mass immigration initiative that threatened their student mobility in the EU – but who had previously taken little interest in the campaign.

On the other hand, several significant differences come to mind: in Switzerland, the decision concerned the question of whether the country should be further integrated into the EEC/EU; in the UK, it was a question of whether the accession that had taken place over 40 years previously should be reversed. The rejection in Switzerland was in line with the course that had been followed for years and could be described – without implying any value judgement – as consistent. The British No vote in 2016, on the other hand, could be described as inconsistent, since the 1975 referendum had given a resounding yes, and EEC membership at that time already implied subscribing to an "ever closer union". In the UK, the plebiscite was primarily the result of a decision taken by a prime minister wanting to discipline his party by calling on the voters, although a commitment to it had been included in the 2015 Conservative manifesto. In Switzerland, the referendum was a standard procedure under the country's system of direct democracy. In addition, it could be added that in Switzerland the long practice with referendums brings with it a certain quality of decision making, whereas in the UK only two nationwide referendums, formally non-binding, have ever been held. In Switzerland, however, there is also a more limited practice of referendums on major foreign policy issues and it is difficult to take account of the essential differences between the subject matters: while domestic policy decisions are entirely "homemade" and can easily be reproposed, somewhat modified, in the event of rejections, foreign policy decisions are generally the result of agreement negotiated at the diplomatic level with other countries and are therefore difficult to change.

The party alignment was also very different: in Switzerland, there was widespread agreement between the moderate right and the Socialist party in favour of EEA membership and rejection was limited to the right-wing nationalist Swiss People's Party (SVP) and the leftist Greens. In the UK, the dividing line between Leave and Remain ran through the two major parties and the referendum called by Conservative Prime Minister David Cameron had the primary function of disciplining his own party and eliminating the perceived threat represented by the United Kingdom Independence Party (UKIP) – a gamble that, as it turned out, spectacularly misfired.

The media, which have a significant influence on voting behaviour, operated in Switzerland in 1992 in a markedly different way from that in the UK in 2016: in the former they were in favour of joining the EEA, in the latter many (the tabloids especially) were in favour of "leave". In addition, in 2016 the effect of electronic manipulation (such as the involvement of Cambridge Analytics) had to be factored in, something that did not yet exist in 1992. If this instrument had been available in Switzerland in 1992, the No campaign would have been even more successful, just as, conversely, without such manipulation, "Remain" may have prevailed in 2016.

The rejections in both cases were rooted in the same oppositional attitudes against "unlimited" immigration and against supranational courts, grounded in attachment to national identity and sovereignty. In both cases, those who took this kind of defensive stance could easily refer to existing historical experiences and to historical imagery that emphasised the nation's "special path". The fact that both countries were spared occupation during World War II and could claim to have defended their independence more or less single-handedly may have been of some significance. In the Swiss case, the Nazi years cast a negative shadow over supporters' argument that Switzerland should "join" the EEA by evoking parallels with the *Anschluss*, i.e. Nazi Germany's annexation of Austria. In both cases, Germany appeared to be the most problematic entity within the EEC/EU. In the Swiss anti-Europe discourse, "Brussels" was equated with "Berlin" and a purported "Fourth Reich" with the "Third Reich". In the UK, a deep-seated

Germanophobia (as expressed in the derogatory term "the Krauts"), dating back to World War I, might also have played a role.

In the small Alpine state, located in the centre of the European continent, there was also the real political concern of being overrun by a tide of heavy goods traffic as a result of its integration into the large EU internal market. In both cases, concerns about the effects on the labour market were probably ambivalent: in the Swiss variant, protection against cheap immigrant labour was intended to prevent a rise in unemployment; in the UK variant, there was the fear that going it alone would trigger an economic recession and cost jobs.

The other major difference is that, all in all, the EEC/EU was very attractive in 1992, so much so that even after the turn of the century the Swiss moderate right parties still advocated full membership. But the wider context had changed significantly by 2016, both Europe-wide and globally. The attractiveness of the EU had declined sharply and nationalism experienced a sharp resurgence as a result of globalisation.

Background

Before we look at Switzerland's "historic" decision in 1992 not to join the EEA, we need to appreciate the historical background to that decision. The years 1945–1989 are part of a longer "prehistory", i.e. the phase in which Switzerland's official doctrine and the corresponding pronouncements to the citizens repeatedly fuelled the notion of a "special case" and made pursuing a solitary path a national task. This included the distinction between desired forms of cooperation, which were classified as technical, and undesired forms, which were classified as political. In this sense, in 1948 Switzerland was allowed to cooperate in the Marshall Plan structure of the Organisation for European Economic Co-operation (OEEC), but for a long time it was prohibited from participating in the Council of Europe, founded in 1949 (Wyder 1999). Over time, however, this distinction became more questionable given that supposedly technical issues became increasingly political and political issues became increasingly economic and technical.

When in the mid-1950s the United Kingdom opposed the EEC project and launched, under the direction of Minister of Supply Reginald Maudling, the counter-project of a large free trade zone, its most zealous ally was Switzerland, which also disliked the planned customs union of the six founding states (Maurhofer 2001: 49–79). Switzerland, of course, also followed the British course when the latter in 1960 set its sights on at least a smaller free trade area, the European Free Trade Association (EFTA). After the UK, the main pillar of EFTA, abandoned it to join the EEC in 1972-73, the other EFTA members, including Switzerland, each sought to conclude their own bilateral free trade agreements with the EEC. Switzerland's agreement proved uncontroversial and was easily approved by the people. As widely expected, on 3 December 1972 an overwhelming majority of 72.5% and all 22 cantons (Jura had not yet come into existence) voted in favour, on a 53% turnout. Mobilisation, as measured by turnout, was much lower than in the EEA vote 20 years later (Linder 2010: 319-21).

The expectation that the agreement would be easily approved, tempted the politicians to submit it to a mandatory referendum – which in Switzerland is subject to a double majority, of voters and of cantons – even though doing so was not constitutionally required. This created a precedent for the EEA vote in 1992. The arguments of the No campaign, which attracted half a million votes, were to a large extent the same as those that would be put forward, more successfully, in 1992 (Guerber 1995). The winners of the 1972 referendum were satisfied with their success, possibly on the understanding that the free trade agreement was a permanent solution that would not to be followed by any further steps towards integration.

From 1972 to 1988, Swiss European policy bobbed along without any serious discussion of future options. This was mainly due to the fact that with the 1972 agreement Switzerland had essentially obtained what it wanted. Not much more was needed, and above all, not much more was desired. Added to this was the fact that there was not much forward movement in the EEC during these years. In April 1984, however, EEC and EFTA ministers met in Luxembourg to discuss how the two organisations could be brought closer together. A number of bilateral and multilateral agreements followed which were known as the "Luxembourg process". Although these were concluded without the need to make use of the development clause included in Switzerland's free trade agreement, they should have alerted the country to the fact that the world had not stopped in 1972 (Freiburghaus 2009: 161ff.).

Delayed departure

In 1989, at long last, Switzerland entered what we could term the "closer prehistory" of the 1992 vote. As in 1972, it was not the only country to do so, but was again part of the group of EFTA members. In 1989, the reason for this was that in January of that year, European Commission President Jacques Delors proposed an interim solution, which was to be given the name EEA and which, in its original idea, aimed less for close involvement in the European integration project than to offer an intermediate stopover to members aspiring to join the EEC. It was also a question of finding a solution for the "EFTANs" which would allow them to participate in the forthcoming deepening of the EEC internal market. For almost two years, from January 1988 to December 1991, it remained open whether the EFTA members in the EEA were to be given decision-making rights in contentious European law issues. Delors had originally envisaged this. Finally, the Court of Justice of the European Union (CJEU) insisted on the sole right of interpretation (Kreis 2018a: 34).

It is no coincidence that at the beginning of the 1990s, but only after three years of preparation, a substantial book was published, aptly titled *Switzerland: Breaking the Deadlock* (Widmer 1991). In times of accelerated change, a cautious approach, often seen as a typical Swiss habit and even as a national virtue, was increasingly perceived as difficult and problematic. In any case, it was remarkably late for Switzerland to turn its attention to the increasingly important European question only in the late 1980s.

At that time, Switzerland was exposed to a number of mutually reinforcing dynamics from which it was hard to escape. The fall of the Berlin Wall in 1989 had certainly had a major impact. However, it was in part only the consequence of a broader-based change that had started already in the mid-1980s and led to new beginnings in both East and West. In the East, *perestroika* (i.e. reconstruction, reorganisation, restructuring) had been set in motion. At about the same time, around 1985, political efforts began in the West to complete the EU internal market by the end of 1992. In the late 1980s, the economic upturn and the optimism stimulated by the single market programme also had a dynamic effect. Finally, the prevailing mood of optimism in the EEC was transferred to the EFTA members: as early as February 1988, there were rumours – including in the Swiss media – that Austria could apply for membership of the EEC. Austria's formal application followed in July 1989, once a Soviet veto was no longer expected. The step was praised in the Swiss press as courageous and exemplary (e.g. *Der Bund*, 18 July 1989). Sweden followed in July 1991, Finland in April 1992, and even Norway, which had first said no in 1972, joined the round dance in November 1992. As a result, the opinion that things were in motion and that you could miss something if you did not move too, was also reinforced in Switzerland.

Under these conditions, the domestic debate on European policy that arose in Switzerland towards the end of the 1980s was hardly the result of impulses emanating from the federal parliament but rather arose from the perception that a corner had been turned in the European integration process.

As Pascal Sciarini has shown, it was only in the years 1988–1990 that there was a real awakening – "réveil de caractère réactif" – in parliament concerning relations with the EEC (Sciarini 1991: 417). There are numerous other indications that the so-called "European debate" experienced a take-off in the spring of 1988. The European single market was a much-discussed topic, for instance, at the Swiss national fair of that year. Also in March 1988, Federal Councillor Delamuraz announced in the National Council that, with immediate effect, all legislative proposals would explicitly mention the corresponding EEC regulation (Official Bulletin, 15 March 1988: 306). And in the same month, the Swiss Foreign Policy Association, together with the University of Fribourg, which was particularly attentive to European issues, held a conference at which European integration was at least addressed as a "challenge" (Universität Freiburg 1989). The initiative for this conference came from the Swiss Society for Foreign Policy, which had been founded in 1968, a period marked by an attitude of liberalisation and opening.

Procrastination and hesitations

It was not until the autumn of 1988 that the federal parliament issued a detailed, albeit rather vague, statement. The last major European report had been published 17 years earlier, in 1971, in the run-up to the free trade agreement of 1972. In this report, the Federal Council launched the slogan that Switzerland should become or remain "Europe compatible". It stated: "In the improvement of Switzerland's

European capability lies an important key to mastering our future" (BR 1988: 131, author's translation). This meant competitiveness, a certain degree of legal adaptation and an approach that would make Switzerland's concerns known at the European level. However, it was not said at that time that the aim was also to move away from inappropriate ideas of Switzerland's uniqueness. "European capability" – this was little more than a rhetorical phrase which had the function of sweetening the harsher core statement "that no fundamental reorientation of Swiss integration policy is required at the present time" (BR 1988: 3). The word "required" revealed the fundamental reluctance with which the Federal Council reacted to the need for reorientation.

This stasis was in a sharp contrast to the dynamism of the international environment, but it also did not match the perception expressed by the Federal Council itself. Indeed, the first sentence of the Federal Council's report read: "Western Europe is in a phase of upheaval". The Federal Council even went so far as to say that the Swiss public was asking itself "the legitimate question" of what position Switzerland should take "in this rapidly advancing development of European cooperation and integration" and whether the country would succeed in participating in the necessary comprehensive way in the "building of Europe" (ibid.: 2). Federal Councillor René Felber, who was in charge of foreign policy, spoke at length on several occasions, lamenting the lack of awareness concerning Europe, but at the same time made it clear that everything would continue as before, that cooperation would simply have to be intensified somewhat so that Switzerland would not be left on the sidelines (Felber 1988).

Berne was not in a hurry on the question of European integration. Initially, the National Council was scheduled to discuss the integration report in its December 1988 session – but it was postponed to spring 1989 (Kreis 2012). The parliamentary deliberations confirmed the willingness to consider new options. In the National Council, more than 60 speakers debated for nine hours. The result was that the Federal Council was instructed to report annually to parliament on the status of the integration process. Christoph Blocher, the future leader of the right-wing national resistance, marked his firm opposition to possible accession to the EU and received particular media attention. In its report on the debate, for instance, the *St. Galler Tagblatt* of 2 March 1989 included a single photo, depicting a young Blocher in his typical posture with raised arms and clenched fists.

In the ensuing debate in the Council of States in the summer of 1989, even *realpolitik* experts such as Bruno Hunziker, a business lawyer from Aargau and president of the Liberal party (FDP), warned that the current position was "fatally offside". It was not enough to come to terms with foreign economic policy as well as possible and to continue to celebrate "the Helvetic special case". Concrete steps must be taken at an early stage, in particular by adopting EEC law. Hunziker called for extensive education of the citizens: "In order to awaken the necessary understanding of the complex problems of integration, a much broader debate is needed than we can have here in parliament. Our people must be made familiar with it, so that they can express their opinion *en connaissance de cause* on the course our country must take in the future, both in Europe and worldwide"

(National Council minutes, 21 June 1989: 366; author's translation). Two other major integration reports were to follow in 1990 and 1991. However, the so-called "European question" did not become a priority issue. In surveys on the forthcoming federal elections in autumn 1991, it ranked fourth behind environmental protection, social security and the question of foreigners (Brückenbauer 36, 4 September 1991).

Aggravating circumstances and a fatal request

The EEA agreement, with its 129 articles, 49 protocols, 22 annexes, 30 joint declarations, and 39 other declarations, was only signed on 2 May 1992. This was linked to the expectation that by the end of the year the federal parliament together with its counterparts in the other EFTA states would grant ratification authorisation so that the agreement could enter into force on 1 January 1993, as with other EEA members.

The "rapprochement" with the EEC, which had been demanded or recommended by almost everyone since the beginning of the 1990s, ran counter to the idea that the Swiss special case was incompatible with the European integration project. Even in the years 1989–1992 there were some voices that tried to relativise these traditional reservations. But they were not sufficient to neutralise the notion of incompatibility that had been nurtured by the political elite for decades. In 1992, these old burdens could not be quickly eliminated and, on the contrary, even formed an intact reservoir that the EEA opponents could tap. In retrospect, from the point of view of the EEA supporters, it must be said that it would have been good if, long before the campaign started in the summer of 1992, the deep-seated reservations against closer involvement in the European integration project had been addressed more decisively. This could have been done via declarations going beyond general expressions of solidarity and by manifesting a willingness to compromise on direct democracy, federalism, and neutrality in order to gain market access, in the case of EEA membership, and full decision-making rights, in the case of EEC accession.

Not only did this not happen, but the path towards ratification was made more difficult by several aggravating circumstances:

1. The tight schedule alone had a negative impact, because it created a hectic pace unusual in Switzerland.
2. Added to this was the fact that the people were called upon to vote on an issue originating from abroad, rather than from the internal democratic process.
3. It was also disadvantageous that the ministers responsible for the matter, Economy Minister Delamuraz and Foreign Minister Felber (who also held the country's rotating presidency in 1992), both came from French-speaking Switzerland and therefore did not exactly have a strong influence in the more sceptical German-speaking part of the country (see also chapters by Sciarini, Mueller, and Theiler, this volume). The fact that on 21 October 1991 the two Federal Councillors announced to the Swiss people from abroad – the

press room of the European Commission in Luxembourg – that they were now seeking to join the European Union may also have had a negative effect, by reinforcing the perception integration was being imposed on Switzerland from the outside (Freiburghaus 2009: 260).

4. A further, homemade complication was that, as already noted, the bill was submitted to a double majority, i.e. of the cantons as well as of the people, without a constitutional requirement to do so. Because the free trade agreement of 1972 had already been subject to a mandatory referendum with a double majority (as a result of a hasty promise made in 1962-63, see Hausherr 1980 and Zbinden 1992), it would have been difficult to treat the EEA agreement differently (Germann 1990; Kreis 1995).
5. In addition, the Federal Council was divided and the campaign was not conducted in a professional manner (Goetschel 1994).
6. The habit of always presenting Swiss foreign policy as being entirely committed to continuity was an aggravating factor. As early as 1972, when the fervently desired free trade agreement with the EC was first discussed in parliament and later before the people, those responsible for shaping the country's foreign policy were at pains to emphasise that the agreement did not represent a break with the past. Thus, Federal Councillor Ernst Brugger stressed in the National Council in September 1972: "The agreement does not represent a reorientation of Swiss foreign policy in the sense of a unilateral turn towards Europe, for example" (National Council minutes, 21 September 1972: 1480, author's translation). This reassurance made it clear that a different policy, which could be described as a "unilateral turn towards Europe", would have been something deeply worrying.

In a further integration report in November 1990, the Federal Council at least dared to state that the then developments in Europe indicated "that the time may come when Switzerland, as a member of the EEC, would de facto be in a better position to protect its interests than if it remained outside". Nevertheless, it reiterated its reassurance that the situation had not changed since the previous report of August 1988 (BR 1990: 59ff.). Two years later, EEA supporters believed they could once again promote the agreement with the reassuring message that the EEA was nothing new and that the whole exercise was just a continuation of the policy pursued since 1948 (Jolles 1992). However, this was neither able to convince the opponents, nor could it sufficiently mobilise those who would have liked something new.

Part of the continuity discourse revolved around the notion that Switerland should only ever pursue closer economic integration and avoid any political entanglement. Instead of "economic" one could also have said "technical", in accordance with the distinction introduced in 1948, which classified this type of institutionalised cooperation as unproblematic, while "political cooperation" appeared highly problematic. Hence the slogan: economic integration without political participation (Tanner 1990; Jost 1999: 157ff.). The EEA was therefore sold as a purely economic matter, the political dimension was actually suppressed

(Goetschel 1994: 269, 276). There are echoes here of the way EEC membership was presented to the British people in the 1975 referendum, i.e. as a primarily economic arrangement as opposed to pursuing an "ever closer union" (e.g. Butler 1996).

The EEA could have been an acceptable solution to the dilemma facing Switzerland as a middle-of-the-road option between the kind of bilateralism practised hitherto and the looming prospect of full membership. It would have left Switzerland the room for manoeuvre it needed for its own foreign economic policy with other countries (given that it implied no customs union with the EEC/EU), and moreover, participation was not open-ended. But it came at a price that was initially said never to be acceptable: the rapprochement process had been based on a premise that soon proved to be an illusion and thus led to a feeling of disillusion. It had initially been expected that a common court would decide in the event of differences of interpretation. However, the EEC took the position that in EEA matters only its court, the CJEU, had jurisdiction. The EEC judges in Luxembourg thus became the "foreign judges" that had "always" been fought against, especially in the 1970s in connection with accession to the European Convention on Human Rights (Kreis 2018a: 25). This led to some disappointment in Switzerland and was another reason for the rejection of the EEA. And it was an important point, full membership with co-decision rights would be more attractive than the EEA if the latter meant automatic acceptance of European law and CJEU jurisprudence. The same issue has featured prominently in the UK debate, where Leavers have touted the end of CJEU's jurisdiction over the country as one of the key benefits of Brexit.

The most consequential mistake was the government's decision, by a narrow four to three majority, on 18 May 1992 to send a request to Brussels to open negotiations on full membership (BR 1992). The Federal Council wanted Switzerland to participate in the accession negotiations which were also about to begin with the other EFTA states. But the move came as something of a surprise, seemed almost arbitrary, and was widely blamed retrospectively for the failure of the EEA proposal. The application for accession negotiations remained on the table for several years afterwards, but was eventually withdrawn in the summer of 2016 following a motion of the SVP parliamentary group in 2014 and wider pressure from right-wing nationalists.

The letter to Brussels did not come out of the blue, it had a longer history. Federal Councillor Jean Pascal Delamuraz had already spoken out in 1989 in the Council of States, i.e. publicly, that one should keep an eye on the option of EEC membership "every day" (Council of States minutes, 22 June 1989: 375). The foreign policy committees of the two chambers of parliament also urged the Federal Council to submit a request for negotiations (Kreis 2018b: 60–70).

As Martin Beglinger shows in his convincing account of the events surrounding the request for negotiations, EEC accession moved from the bottom to the top in the Federal Council's integration reports within just under four years: "In 1988 it was still not an issue, in 1990 it became an 'option', in May 1991 already a 'primary option' and in October 1991 definitely a 'strategic goal'" (Beglinger

2016). In March 1992, the Federal Council was urged by the Council of States to take this step "without delay" by means of a petition. In the third integration report of 18 May 1992 (after the second report of November 1990), the Federal Council also consistently spoke out in favour of accession to the EEC, albeit conditionally: "If we want to participate in the formulation of rules and policies which will have an ever greater impact on us (…), there is no other way than accession to the EC" (NZZ 1992).

From then on, the EEA agreement was perceived even less than before as an option in its own right, but only as either an accepted or rejected stepping-stone to EEC membership. The Federal Council thus offered additional opportunities for attack to those actors that were against any further rapprochement with the EEC. Christoph Blocher had, of course, already launched his campaign against the "threat of EEC dirigisme and the supremacy of the 'Etatists' there". Against the normal practice of starting campaigning only after parliamentary deliberations, Blocher already opened the anti-EEA campaign with the Albisgüetli speech of January 1992 (Kreis 2018b: 31ff.) Advocates of the EEA were forced to emphasise more and more what the EEA agreement did not mean, rather than what it was for: no loss of sovereignty, no encroachment on the asylum system, no regulations in social policy, no customs union, no effects on taxes, no changes in agricultural policy, no threat to neutrality, no ties in military and security policy – and, in particular, no automatic transition to EEC membership.

Growing opposition fuelled by appeals to Swiss history and identity

The mood remained confident in 1990–1991, even if the initial enthusiasm probably lost some of its strength. As the decisive phase drew nearer and the questions became more concrete, the generic argument that had been expressed in a spirit of friendly exchange since 1988 rapidly gave way to deepening polarisation on the core question of EEC membership. In the autumn of 1992, the *Neue Zürcher Zeitung* (NZZ), the main Swiss newspaper, noted a "clear change of mood" to the disadvantage of the pro-integrationists, which was probably true, but at the same time further reinforced what had been diagnosed (NZZ, 4 September 1992). According to the retrospective VOX analysis (Kriesi et al. 1993: 14ff.), the chances that the EEA would be supported by a majority were still reasonably good in September 1992 (with 51–52% "rather yes" voting intentions versus 34–35% "rather no" ones). This was apparently the result of a positive effect of the parliamentary deliberations on the EEA agreement. In the final vote on 9 October 1992, the federal parliament had clearly expressed its support for the EEA agreement: the National Council by 127 votes to 64 and the Council of States by 39 votes to four.

In the previous phase, at the end of July/beginning of August 1992, the early campaign of the EEA opponents had led to an initial decline in approval (with only 40–41% "rather yes" versus 38-40% "rather no" intentions). The uptick in approval in September 1992 could not, however, be maintained despite approval, with 63.6% in favour, of a transit plan across the Alps, which was regarded as indirect approval of the provisions regarding cross-Alpine traffic (see Schwok, this volume).

The adaptation of the Swiss legal system to that of the EEC (the so-called Eurolex project) in preparation for accession to the EEA in October 1992, although enormously complex, went remarkably smoothly, also thanks to the temporary suspension of the right of referendum in that field (Freiburghaus 2009: 244ff.). Renamed Swisslex, it was subsequently completed despite the EEA setback. This pragmatism did not, however, relativise any dogmatism surrounding traditional notions of sovereignty, which were still claimed to be highly valid. The rapid adaptation of Swiss legislation to the EEA standard with the adoption of the Eurolex package with its more than 80 proposals does not appear to have had a major impact on the attitude towards the EEA.

In the final phase of October and early November 1992, the political and economic establishment was cautious and left the field open to the opponents of the EEA, which again led to a decline in support among voters (by then tied on 42–43% between "rather yes" and "rather no"). Not even the hectic advertising that began towards the end of the voting campaign was able to change much of this. The VOX report also contains information on the frequency of discussions ("among friends"); this only increased significantly in October–November. The campaign quickly took on the characteristics of an unequal struggle: on one side, the apparent might of the establishment, with increasingly frequent interventions by the Federal Council, "top diplomats swarming all over the country", and an enormous public relations effort. On the other side, the supposedly isolated fighters against the political establishment, giving voice to the silent majority (*Weltwoche*, 28 May 1992). This constellation alone caused an increase in support for the underdogs and growing reservations about the "superior power" of the establishment. In this constellation, the fact that symbolic figures of the moderate right parties (e.g. Vreni Spoerry, Gilles Petitpierre, Carlo Schmid, and Markus Kündig) stood up for the EEA helped the Yes camp to a limited extent only and actually encouraged some among their rank-and-file to turn against it for this very reason (*Tages-Anzeiger*, 15 June 1992).

The dispute intensified dramatically on 20 November 1992 when, in a "sacred place" – namely the Federal Charter Archives, where copies of the original treaties that gave birth to the Swiss Confederation are held – the main television channel held an event on the EEA, side by side to the ancient treaties but also in the presence of a large number of colourful figures dressed in shepherd shirts and carrying big cow bells. Federal Councillors Arnold Koller and Adolf Ogi were repeatedly interrupted in their speeches by grumbling, booing and shouting. In the tumultuous scene, shouts of "Hitler" and "Saddam Hussein" could be heard before the microphones were turned off. The Schwyz folk musician Dominik Marty launched himself into a crude diatribe against the Federal Council because of the choice of venue – for which the television channel was responsible – and was escorted out of the museum by security guards. The NZZ complained that the questions posed by the interviewers were "almost entirely taken from the right-wing populist arsenal of opponents such as Christoph Blocher" and that "existing (but also inflamed) worries and fears, but also a vast amount of false or distorted information" had been voiced. The final comment of the NZZ was thus: "To be a good Swiss, it is not enough to put on a *Sennechutteli* [shepherd shirt]. One must also behave as a Swiss" (NZZ, 23 November 1992).

As the analysis that follows shows, the question was decided on the emotional front. Emotions were tapped primarily by the opponents, who, led by SVP National Councillor Christoph Blocher, appealed to old defence instincts with archaic slogans referring to the battle of Marignano (1515) and Brother Klaus (1481) summarised in the claim: "The EEA is unworthy of a free Switzerland". The term "colonial treaty" might have come up later, but the assessment of the EU as a "misconstruction" already existed then. They also stressed the lack of information and potential threats to the environment deriving from the increase in cross-Alps heavy goods traffic. Supporters, by contrast, employed primarily rational arguments centred on economic utility. Although they also stressed opening up, broadening horizons, and safeguarding the future, they did not try, unsurprisingly given the "prehistory" discussed above, to portray embracing integration as being in line with Swiss identity.

"Black Sunday": 6 December 1992

There are moments in the long course of history that are only referred to – positively or negatively – with a shortened date. A positive short date in the Swiss case is "1st August", which celebrates the first confederal agreement of 1291. A negative date for some – but by no means for all – is "6th December", which Federal Councillor Jean Pascal Delamuraz branded, in unusually stark terms, as a *dimanche noir*, or black Sunday, for Switzerland (*Journal de Genève/Gazette de Lausanne*, 7 December 1992). Participation in the EEA was rejected by 50.3% of voters and 16 out of 23 cantons on an unusually high turnout of 78.7%.

With the vote on the EEA, a decision of greater significance was taken. It has had far-reaching and long-lasting consequences, which in turn can be assessed positively or negatively. In any case, the decision taken in the weekend of 4–6 December 1992 had a complex genesis, which we will briefly discuss below, with the aim of explaining why the result was what it was. The effect of the EEC membership application is controversial. Given the narrowness of the popular majority, several factors could have been decisive, such as, for example, the Greens' call, later revised, for a No vote. The rejection of the Maastricht treaty in a referendum in Denmark in June 1992 and the narrow approval of the treaty in a subsequent referendum in France in September 1992 may also have had a negative influence. In any case the clear No of the cantons could not have been avoided.

The high voter turnout was largely the result of the mobilisation of the populist right and thus probably benefited their cause. The majority of the German-speaking region rejected the EEA, the French-speaking areas clearly agreed with it, while Italian-speaking Switzerland (especially the canton of Ticino) also rejected accession to the EEA despite counting Flavio Cotti, its representative in the government, among the supporters. With 61.5% No votes, Ticino's rejection was above the national average. Five other cantons, however, were even more clearly opposed, for example Canton Grisons with 67.6% of No votes. Ticino's rejection of closer relations with the EEC/EU would become even more pronounced in the following years (see chapters by Sciarini, Mueller, and Mazzoleni, in this volume).

French-speaking Switzerland was in favour of the EEA agreement by a large majority: Neuchâtel with 80%, Vaud with 78.4%, Geneva with 78.2%, Jura with 77.2% as well as the bilingual cantons of Fribourg and Valais, with 64.9 and 55.9%, respectively. The VOX analysis aptly observes that the *Romands*, "in view of their more outward-looking perspective and their prospective value attitudes", have long since developed an awareness of Europe and have done so much more clearly. However, the analyses that emphasise the linguistic and cultural divide tend to overlook the fact that most German-speaking cities, not only Basel and Zurich but also Lucerne and Winterthur, but not St. Gallen, agreed to the proposal. One possible factor was that in the French-speaking region the EEA was expected to reduce unemployment, whereas some in the German-speaking region expected the EEA actually to increase unemployment, which was lower in the latter case.

After 6 December, the task was to find an alternative solution through bilateral agreements. However, in order not to be perceived as disregarding the verdict of 6 December, these had to be below the level of integration entailed by the EEA. From the EU's point of view, the bilateral agreements resulting from the subsequent negotiations lasting several years were merely an interim solution which was made available to the supposed future EU member Switzerland in a spirit of accommodation (see Schwok, this volume). The EEA model itself was repeatedly mentioned in the following years, particularly in 2012–2013 – for instance by the former Secretary of State Franz Blankart (NZZ, 2 May 2012) – when, in the context of the "20 years after" debate, discussions focussed on how to overcome the impasse in the bilateral approach.

Conclusion

The EEA proposal posed a completely new challenge to Switzerland. Dealing adequately with it would have taken more time than was available – and also than was actually used. In the early phase of change, in 1988–1989, supporters of closer relations with the EU should have striven to address the long-held reservations about integration. Instead, they largely adopted a wait-and-see approach, looking for opportunities to arise. What else could have been done?

In hindsight, it would have been wise to explain from the outset that there is a trade-off between the economic gains to be derived from access to the European market and the political costs attached to it in terms of reduced national autonomy. The latter should be understood not as a questioning of Switzerland's sovereignty but as a call for a judicious reform of federalism and direct democracy.

In 1990–1991 the idea, or rather the illusion, of being able to participate in the emerging EEC/EU internal market without having to adapt to the latter's legal order remained, however, in the foreground. This was so because proponents stuck with generic notions such as "European capability" and "rapprochement" and did not think things through. Had they done so, they would have inevitably realised that there can be no privileged access to the EU market without recognition of the legal system it is founded upon. In the light of the current challenge posed by the draft IFA (see Schwok, this volume), we wonder whether anything has changed in the meantime.

What does a comparison with Brexit suggest? As we have seen, the Swiss decision of 6 December 1992 was binding, but that does not mean it is once and for all; under a direct democracy system people can vote again and change their mind if they so wish. In Switzerland, for instance, the introduction of proportional representation was voted on three times and the introduction of female suffrage twice. There will not be a second vote on British EU membership in the foreseeable future, although double votes would be a good thing: a first time on a negotiating mandate and a second time on the result achieved. This is especially the case for delicate votes on international treaties, for Switzerland and the UK alike.

Brexit carries an expectation of entering a completely new era and is partly also linked to the hope of returning to "past greatness", i.e. to the good old days. How is this to be achieved? The alternative to multilateral EU membership consists of concluding a large number of bilateral free trade agreements. Switzerland, with its small size, tries to obtain both: the greatest possible participation in the EU internal market and yet global trade freedom. Given its small size and its central location on the continent, Switzerland can to a certain extent expect to have somewhat special arrangements with the EU. The UK – much larger, with a very different location, and a past as former member – will find the circle more difficult to square and is unlikely to be offered a special treatment by the EU. Willy-nilly, it will have to find, for better or worse, its own way but can at least look at Switzerland's experience for early warning of some the challenges it is likely to face in the future.

3 The economic dimension

Sergio Rossi and Guillaume Vallet

The economic relationships between Switzerland and the EU provide several insights that the UK could consider with respect to its future relations with the EU, particularly as regards trade and the labour market, considering also the likely economic consequences of the COVID-19 pandemic in the long run. This reflection also provides an opportunity to question the drivers of European integration in light of the theory of regional integration, considering the merits and shortcomings of the Swiss peculiar stance in this regard. As a matter of fact, the difficult and time-consuming Brexit negotiations have revealed a number of issues about the dynamics of European integration, which has enfolded over more than 60 years. Interestingly, during these negotiations, the UK contemplated adopting the kind of relationship that Switzerland and the EEC/EU have had since 1957.

Indeed, Switzerland historically belongs to the so-called "reluctant Europeans" (Gstöhl 2002). Located at the heart core of Europe both geographically and economically, Switzerland has favoured – since the signature of the Treaty of Rome in 1957 – an integration approach with the EU that is fundamentally different from the enlargement-and-deepening dynamics suggested by the theory of regional integration summarised in the next section.

In fact, the Swiss stance towards European integration over the last 60 years has aimed at being sufficiently integrated into the EEC/EU on economic grounds while postponing any form of political integration, as we explain in the second section (see also Kreis, this volume). The third section provides an overview of the state-of-the-art with regard to the current relationship between Switzerland and the EU, and the fourth section presents some reflections in this regard, taking into account also the likely consequences of the COVID-19 pandemic, thereby offering a number of points that could also be relevant for the future relationship between the UK and the EU, after Brexit. The conclusion summarises the two major points that stand out with regard to the nature of the bilateral agreements between Switzerland and the EU, which could inspire the UK in designing its own future relationships with the EU as a whole.

The dynamics of regional integration in the European context

The seminal idea encapsulated in the Treaty of Rome (which established the EEC in 1958) expected the countries joining this framework of regional integration to create various ratcheting-up effects (in both the economic and the political spheres), which would increasingly tie up member countries with each other over time. Furthermore, these effects were meant to be irreversible: once a step forward in the integration process is accomplished, it should be impossible to go back to the previous stage.

This dynamic refers, on the one hand, to the enlargement process, which is ongoing, because the EU will likely enlarge to other countries in the future (particularly those in the Balkan area). On the other hand, it also implies a deepening process: EU membership is supposed to create a closed web, which has an economic and political cohesion, as its member countries' mutual relationships are much denser than those with the rest of the world. A number of specific interdependencies exist and expand over time among these countries, whose bilateral relationships affect the whole set of member countries eventually. This amounts to saying that direct relationships – that is, economic relations between two countries – as well as indirect relations (namely, the links between direct relationships that affect all countries eventually) are affected by regional integration.

These relationships within the closed web become stronger as economic integration develops and the web density increases, to wit, as the intensity and volume of economic transactions increase. These cohesion effects also make regional integration more viable *ex post*, since the positive effects of a country's membership are reaped once the economic links are established. In this framework, being a member of this area stimulates all kinds of economic transactions.

This is why the enlargement of the EU and the deepening of the relationships between its member countries mutually reinforce each other: network effects and membership effects can become negative for non-member countries, inducing firms that export to the latter countries to exert pressure on their own country's political authorities for enlargement. This dynamic, then, gives rise to further enlargements, particularly for non-member neighbour countries. The economic web formed by regional integration derives its strength from the density of transactions within it as well as from its capacity to expand in one way or another as time goes by.

Now, Brexit shows that the European integration process does not work according to this double logic anymore: there are actually different degrees of integration within the same process (which questions the unity and uniqueness of the EU), and the UK case shows that it is possible to leave the integration process described above.

The question in this regard concerns the costs and benefits of leaving the EU. In other words, is it viable to come out of the dynamics of regional integration? Is it possible not to be an EU member state but to remain linked to it institutionally? Even though the EU does not have the best economic growth perspectives in the world at present, it has in any case a huge and attractive single market, to which any European country would like to be linked in some way. The Brexit negotiations have clearly shown that. Let us turn to the Swiss case to explain this interest in practice.

Sixty years of Switzerland's "integration without membership"

As already mentioned, Switzerland has adopted a particular stance towards European integration. This started with the country not signing the treaty establishing the European Coal and Steel Community (ECSC) in 1951. The idea of delegating part of national sovereignty to a supranational institution was problematic for Switzerland already at that time. The same occurred when the European Economic Community (EEC) was established in 1958 (see also Kreis, this volume).

However, it is important to point out that Switzerland does not refuse any form of regional integration, quite the contrary. Being dependent on foreign markets – owing to the small size of its domestic market, to its geographical location, and to its production specialisation (we will come back to this later) – Switzerland needs to be integrated internationally, which makes its economy also heavily exposed to the consequences of the COVID-19 pandemic.

In fact, although Switzerland did not agree with the philosophy of regional integration espoused by the EEC (the forerunner of the EU), it was a founding member of EFTA, which was established in 1960. Bringing together Austria, Denmark, Norway, Portugal, Sweden, Switzerland, and the UK, EFTA aimed to promote free trade across Europe as an alternative to the EU. Unlike the latter, EFTA did not aim to set in motion an economic dynamic based on ratcheting-up effects as described by Balassa (1961), whereby the achievement of an integration step leads to another step being taken (along the following path: free-trade area, customs union, single market, monetary union, and political union eventually).

EFTA member states feared that these ratcheting-up effects would imply an increasing transfer of national sovereignty to some supranational institutions, a fear particularly strongly felt in Switzerland: "accession to EFTA leaves our national independence intact, allows us to fully honour our neutrality obligations in times of war and does not impinge on our neutrality policy aiming for that" (Gstöhl 2002: 78).

Indeed, from a political perspective, Switzerland fears that its "national identity triangle" (which consists of neutrality, federalism, and direct democracy) may be jeopardised as a result of transferring some sovereign powers to the EU supranational institutions (Vallet 2010). According to many Swiss politicians, this triangle is historically a "founding utopia" of both national cohesion and identity. It is also linked to some specific institutions intended to provide a balance between the federal and cantonal levels of government in both the economic and the political spheres (Schweitzer 1991; Obinger 1998).

Nevertheless, Switzerland had to adapt itself to the evolution of European integration after the setting up of both the EEC and EFTA. The crucial development was that, in the course of the 1970s and 1980s, the EEC became more attractive than EFTA, inducing some important member states of the latter to revise their European stance: Denmark and the UK, for instance, joined the EEC in 1973, thereby affecting EFTA's economic dynamics negatively.

In this context, without questioning its own philosophy, Switzerland tried to develop closer links to the EEC. A first step was taken in 1972 with the signature of bilateral agreements between Switzerland and the EEC, in order to stimulate trade of industrial and some agricultural products (see also Kreis, this volume). These agreements allowed Switzerland to align itself more closely to the EEC economically, without being obliged to become a member, something that satisfied the Swiss authorities in terms of procedures, implications, and objectives.

The successful deepening of the EEC in the 1980s – with the perspective of creating a huge single market as well as a single currency – together with its further enlargement (Greece in 1981, Spain and Portugal in 1986) led to the fear of a chasm developing between "in" and "out" countries such as Switzerland. This gave rise to the idea of creating a European Economic Area, that is, a large free-trade area including both EEC and EFTA member states,[1] without offering the EFTA countries the same decision-making rights enjoyed by EU members. In spite of this institutional asymmetry, Switzerland was one of EFTA member states most in favour of creating an EEA, because the latter matched to its own philosophy very well.

Table 3.1 shows the economic determinants of such an interest by providing data concerning the increasing dependency of the Swiss economy on the EEC, which put pressure on the former to reconsider its institutional relations with the latter.

Some Swiss industrial activities, very important for the domestic economy, were heavily dependent on the EEC, as its member countries absorbed a very large share of Swiss exports, such as the industrial machines and equipment sector (45% of the total exports in the 1980s).

Switzerland's problem was that its economic and political leaders were largely in favour of adhering to the EEA whereas the Swiss people voted against it in 1992 (see Kreis, this volume). This decision put Switzerland in an uncertain position, because the day after the results of the referendum were published, Switzerland had no preferential access to the single European market – which damaged its exports significantly.

In 1994, Switzerland asked the EU to enter into further negotiations, stressing the need to proceed "step by step" and consider each case separately. Its aim was to try to find a new way to economic integration, one that would be profitable for Switzerland even if it entailed greater concessions to its counterpart. Switzerland was not in a strong position during these negotiations. The EU negotiators knew that a Swiss membership was unlikely to occur but also that the country could not be indefinitely excluded from the European single market (Schwok 2006). Furthermore, EU politicians were at that time more focussed on integrating the then new member states (Austria, Finland, and Sweden) and laying the ground for the introduction of the euro in 1999.

Table 3.1 Swiss exports to the European Economic Community (1984–1992)

Year	*Export ratio (Swiss exports to the EEC as a percentage of total Swiss exports)*	*GDP ratio (Swiss exports to the EEC as a percentage of Swiss GDP)*
1984	50.6	14.4
1989	56.5	16.4
1992	58.9	16.0

Source: Authors' elaboration based on Gstöhl (2002: 150).

Hence, the EU authorities accepted the Swiss proposal of entering into bilateral agreements, but on some conditions: some important issues for Switzerland (such as taxation of foreign savings) had to feature at the core of the negotiations, and the Swiss authorities would be involved in future decisions about these bilateral agreements. As a result, Switzerland has only a passive role at the institutional level in this framework (see also Schwok, this volume). Also, any kind of agreement has to be renegotiated systematically, which implies each time a new source of uncertainty for Switzerland. The famous "guillotine clause" illustrates this uncertainty: for a number of issues at stake in the negotiations, the EU demanded that the whole package of bilateral agreements would be discontinued if either party decides to withdraw from any one of them.

In spite of this clause, Switzerland accepted to sign two "packages" of bilateral agreements in 1999 and 2004, concerning a variety of areas and having different economic implications (see Schwok, this volume). These agreements satisfy Switzerland, even though the country remains in an asymmetrical position vis-à-vis the EU, particularly at the institutional level as explained above. These agreements allow Switzerland to access the European single market, even though they are not considered a stepping stone to joining the EU. Their nature and objectives are different from those agreements that the EU has signed with other non-member countries. They provide for a particular brand of "integration without membership", or a third way between membership and isolation, that is rather peculiar to Switzerland (Vallet 2010). Even though it is a weak form of integration, it is the most appealing solution to Switzerland and could also be seen as an option for the UK after Brexit.

From the EU viewpoint, these bilateral agreements can be considered from two different perspectives. On the one hand, they maintain the stability of economic relations with a partner country whose purchasing power is high and has a trade deficit with the EU. On the other hand, the official recognition of these bilateral agreements reinforces the lack of unity and uniqueness of regional integration across Europe as mentioned above: these bilateral agreements are part of the so-called "spaghetti bowl" in Europe, as Baldwin (2006) put it (see Vallet 2016). This refers to the web of relations across Europe and the rest of the world, that the EU has created, which have however also made the operation of the EU itself more complex if not more difficult. These relations sustain the viability of "ad-hoc integration", which Switzerland is pursuing and that the UK may be interested in emulating.

It is therefore worth exploring this issue more deeply, focussing on the current relations between Switzerland and the EU: how much is Switzerland integrated into the EU? Is this integration really enough to preserve its "integration without membership"? We expand on this in the next section.

The current state of Switzerland's "integration without membership"

As explained above, Switzerland has no choice but to keep close relations with its neighbours, which are all EU member states. In terms of product specialisation and standards of living, Switzerland and the EU form a "natural trading block" (Krugman 1991), in which the incentives to trade with each other are high. The very different size of the two economies also implies that the European single market is very attractive for Switzerland (Vallet 2012). These gravitational effects mean that Switzerland cannot afford to cut itself off from the EU: the European single market is an unavoidable export market for the country.

Indeed, it is worth recalling that one-third of all jobs in Switzerland depends on its exports to the EU, and Switzerland is the second most important country (after the United States) for EU exports. Table 3.2 confirms the Swiss dependency on the European single market, because the most important trading partners of Switzerland induce large gravitational effects for the latter.

Also, about 45% of Swiss foreign direct investments (FDIs) go to the EU, and the EU is the source of around 50% of FDIs into Switzerland.

Nevertheless, the European market is not the only important one for Switzerland. The country has strong economic relations also with non-EU member countries around the world. For instance, the United States is the second most important economic partner of Switzerland after Germany. Also, Switzerland has developed its relations with emerging economies: its specialisation in "old economy" sectors such as industrial machines, chemical products, and watches has enabled it to find new markets in these countries, in particular with regard to precision instruments and luxury goods (Table 3.3).

The roots of Switzerland's preference for "integration without membership" are also to be found in the financial sector. Switzerland is highly specialised in

Table 3.2 Switzerland's commercial dependence* (1995–2018)

	1995	*2000*	*2005*	*2010*	*2015*	*2018*
France	10.78	10.01	9.51	8.54	8.26	8.33
Germany	29.27	25.58	26.09	26.37	27.04	27.22
Italy	9.17	8.51	9.59	9.73	9.69	9.54
Spain	1.67	1.97	3.14	2.27	1.98	1.78
Portugal	0.59	0.39	0.34	0.30	0.24	0.25
EU	73.34	68.82	71.36	66.96	65.89	65.85
Eurozone	63.77	59.61	61.95	59.25	58.97	58.95

Source: Authors' calculation based on Swiss National Bank data.
Note: *Percentage of exports to individual countries out of total exports.

Table 3.3 Trading volume of Switzerland with some of its major partners

	Billions of CHF in 2018	*Rate of growth (2009–2018)*
EU countries	302	5%
China	44	18%
India	30	23%

Source: Authors' calculation based on Swiss National Bank data.

banking and financial activities, which, together, contribute about 10% of the country's gross domestic product. Beyond the quality of its banking and financial services, Switzerland has a legal, political, and monetary stability that inspires investors' confidence and therefore attracts foreign capital. In this regard, two points should be noted:

- Swiss legislation is attractive to investors seeking to diversify risks and maintain information security. For instance, even though Switzerland had to abandon banking secrecy (which had been introduced in 1934) vis-à-vis the rest of the world, the EU in particular, this secrecy remains largely in place for Swiss residents. Also, the Swiss financial sector remains a world leader in the fields of derivatives on raw materials and wealth management. In the latter field, for instance, Switzerland managed US$2tn in 2014, ahead of the UK, with US$1.7tn, and the US, with US$1.4tn (Deloitte 2015).
- The Swiss financial sector can rely on an internationally-recognised currency whose value is preserved over time by the monetarist-inspired policy of the Swiss National Bank (Laurent and Vallet 2014; Rossi 2019).

Given the abundance of financial capital, the Swiss economy is able to profit from an interest rate "bonus" (Kugler and Weder 2002) insofar as Swiss real interest rates are lower than abroad. This reduces the upward pressure on the Swiss franc exchange rate in normal times. In this regard, being integrated with the EU financial markets is necessary for Switzerland in order to maintain positive capital flows.

Hence, since 2010 Switzerland has been a member of the Single Euro Payments Area (SEPA), which represents a significant step towards establishing a single European market for payments. More precisely, the SEPA provides the foundations for an infrastructure allowing a fully automated and standardised processing of payments, thus transforming the largely fragmented eurozone markets into a single European market. More than 4,000 financial institutions participate in the SEPA across Europe. As a result, since 2009, European banks can offer to their clients some SEPA withdrawal services denominated in euros, which are established on common principles across Europe. As regards credit card payments, the SEPA allows bank clients to use their cards across the whole SEPA, without any technical, legal, or economic problems – both at automated teller machines and in retail shops.

Non-EU member countries that are highly integrated with the euro area, given their dependence on loans and payments denominated in euros, are affected more or less directly by this process. European monetary union enables all participating financial systems to operate in the same currency and avail themselves of new opportunities concerning the settlement of transactions on the goods markets as well as with financial investments and foreign exchange transactions. The attraction effects generated can lead to a full integration, particularly if some non-EU member countries feel themselves discriminated. Not by chance, all EEA countries are integrated into the European single market for financial services, even though their national central banks are not in a position to obtain liquidity from the Eurosystem on a regular basis. Such a possibility, however, exists in case of need but requires an ad-hoc agreement between the European Central Bank (ECB) and the relevant national central banks of the affected non-EU member states.

In the case of Switzerland, particularly because a large share of its foreign trade is denominated in euros,[2] it is important for it to have access to payment instruments across the eurozone. This also applies to all banking and financial transactions between the two areas given the high volume of EU-Switzerland cross-border financial transactions. The Swiss financial sector has been in the SEPA since 2006, because Swiss banks and banking associations participate in the European Payments Council (EPC). The EPC is tied to the SEPA: when EU authorities sought to deepen monetary and financial integration, they were looking for a contribution by the banking sector through the development of electronic payment instruments denominated in euros.

Swiss banks fully participate in the EPC on the same footing as those domiciled in EEA countries: since the EPC is based on private law agreements signed with banks, Swiss banks may be member of the SEPA in the absence of public law agreement. This is why the EPC works according to its own logic, to wit, its operations play no role in the adoption of EU laws by its participating countries. This set-up could also be attractive for the UK, and particularly for the City of London.

Since 2006, more than 300 Swiss banks of different kinds may carry out their clients' payment orders denominated in euros through the SEPA – hence beyond Swiss borders – as simply and cheaply as domestic payments. These banks gather more than 90% of the Swiss payments traffic denominated in euros. Indeed, a platform created with EuroSIC (the department of the Swiss payments system that carries out payment orders denominated in euros) enables Swiss banks to obtain euros, not only in Switzerland but also in the eurozone, via the SEPA. Hence, EU banks are in a position to transfer euros to Switzerland, which is also quite beneficial to their business. Switzerland is actually one of the most important players in the SEPA: with regard to the number of financial institutions within it, Switzerland ranks seventh among the 31 participating countries. The management of SEPA – where the ECB leaves much room to self-regulation – corresponds to the workings of Swiss financial markets and to the attitude of the Swiss National Bank (SNB) regarding payments traffic.

In this area, Switzerland is thus fully integrated into the European financial system, on a level playing field with EU and EEA countries. Like banks and non-bank financial institutions, Swiss firms also benefit from this integration. Even for those that do not export to the eurozone, the SEPA has a positive impact for their transactions denominated in euros, which typically account for a high proportion of the total. The SEPA, however, does not cover all payments; hence non-EEA countries such as Switzerland are still somewhat at a disadvantage compared to member states. This is because the EU directive on payment services covers a wider spectrum than the SEPA, given that it includes all electronic payments (the

SEPA only covers non-urgent payments, withdrawals, and credit cards) and all European currencies (the SEPA only covers the euro).

However, Switzerland is not required to comply with EU regulations and directives, hence its financial integration with the EU is only partial. This allows Switzerland to reap the benefits of a major collective good – thanks to the goodwill of the European authorities, who consider Switzerland's inclusion to produce positive network effects (notably with regard to additional banking activities) and a higher level of financial stability in Europe – without having to surrender too much autonomy in this subject matter. The setting-up costs of the SEPA for Switzerland (around CHF100m) will be largely paid off over the medium run, thanks to the harmonisation of European payments systems. All in all, the partial reduction in autonomy deriving from Switzerland's participation in the SEPA is a price the country is happy to pay given the significant benefits it derives from it. A similar argument would apply to the UK, if the latter remains in the SEPA after Brexit.

Conversely, the real interest rate "bonus" of Switzerland could disappear if the latter joined the EU, and the eurozone in particular. Indeed, since joining the EU implies joining the eurozone eventually, this would be likely to align Swiss interest rates to those of the eurozone, even if the "country risk" differential still favoured Switzerland. This prospect represents a threat for the competitiveness of the Swiss economy as a whole. The Swiss banks also fear that joining the EU would force them to abandon banking secrecy even within the country, potentially inducing significant capital flight.

Switzerland's "model" of financial integration with the EU can be seen as either a form of "ad-hoc" integration with the EU or as actually an alternative form of integration to that pursued by the latter. Its significance thus goes beyond Swiss–EU relations and is particularly relevant to the post-Brexit UK.

Banking and financial activities are as important to the UK's economy as they are to Switzerland's and in both cases international financial transactions are at the heart of the sector. Before Brexit, the UK played a key strategic role regarding financial activities in Europe, since it possessed the "European financial passport" – allowing a bank or a non-bank financial institution based in London to offer its services across the whole EU – and hosted the clearing house for euro-denominated transactions.

The introduction of the euro thus benefitted London's foreign exchange market at the expense of those smaller European financial centres that specialised in transactions of their former national currencies. Although the London International Financial Futures and Options Exchange (LIFFE) was purchased by Euronext in 2002, the City of London has been able to capture about half of all daily financial transactions on derivatives (Economist 2006). It is therefore likely that losing these advantages as a result of Brexit will affect the City of London negatively (Table 3.4).

For some activities, though, losses could be limited: the income reduction could be of £2bn a year (2% of its total business turnover), the loss of tax income could be of £500m a year, and 4,000 jobs could be lost (Wyman 2016). The impact depends on the depth and internationalisation of London-based financial activities (The CityUK 2014).

Table 3.4 Examples of ecosystem impacts and risks as a result of Brexit

Area	*Ecosystem impacts and risks*
Sales and trading	**Ecosystem impacts**: Fragmentation of liquidity, reduced capital efficiency and cost duplication as EU related activities are separated from non-EU related activities. **Risks**: Reduction in non-EU clients and related activities that had come through the UK.
Market infrastructure	**Ecosystem impacts**: Loss of netting and compression benefits in clearing between euro-denominated derivatives and other currencies. **Risks**: Clearing of all currencies relocates away from the UK to retain capital efficiencies.
Asset management	**Ecosystem impacts**: Loss of proximity to the sell-side, and the associated skills and liquidity. **Risks**: Value of delegating portfolio management to the UK is reduced, leading to reduced assets under management.
Financial technology	**Ecosystem impacts**: Less activity and fewer people and businessmen in the UK for firms to sell their products to and develop new technologies alongside. **Risks**: Slower rates of improvement in the services provided to clients, and alternative hubs emerge across Europe that benefit from future growth opportunities.
Specialty insurance	**Ecosystem impacts**: Loss of depth in the marketplace as EU activities shifted out of the UK. **Risks**: Fewer international business coming to the UK to take advantage of the scale in the marketplace.
Cross-cutting (talent)	**Ecosystem impacts**: Erosion of UK as a centre for internationally mobile financial service professionals. **Risks**: Fewer international businesses set up in the UK as its competitive advantages versus other locations are eroded.

Source: Wyman (2016: 8).

Also, data in Table 3.5 show that the UK and Swiss financial markets are neither fully nor exclusively linked to those in the EU. The correlation coefficients in Table 3.5 indicate that some strong interconnections exist also with non-European financial centres. The dynamics of the UK and Swiss financial markets also depend on their autonomy: there is a "cluster effect" that operates across them, notably since the development of some activities attracts other activities, thereby creating a cluster including all of them eventually.

Similar to commercial transactions, Switzerland is situated "between two worlds" in the banking and financial spheres. The Swiss strengths in this field make sense for the country to seek to maintain extensive financial transactions with other countries. In any case, Switzerland is very well placed to benefit from the internationalisation of the renminbi (the Chinese currency). Switzerland's support to the internationalisation of the renminbi enables the country not only to compete with the largest world's financial markets, but also to profit from the

Table 3.5 Correlation coefficients between stock market indices in London and Zurich and indices of other world financial markets (1999–2018)

	FTSE 100	*STOXX 50*	*DOW JONES*	*NIKKEI 225*	*SMI*
SMI	0.87	0.69	0.71	0.78	–
FTSE 100	–	0.62	0.75	0.66	0.87

Source: Authors' calculation based on SNB data.

diversification of Chinese investments and of China's surplus savings. As a major financial market, Switzerland has an interest in developing investment opportunities for the renminbi. In December 2012, the Swiss Federal Council approved Switzerland becoming a hub for developing renminbi transactions through its financial markets. This was aimed at increasing the supply of related services, and further the internationalisation of the Swiss financial centres, to help them take on global players such as London or New York. A particular area for growth is the development of "dimsum bonds" (SBA 2015).

All in all, financial issues illustrate Switzerland's interest in keeping its situation of "integration without membership" vis-à-vis the EU. Two points stand out in this regard:

- The key question concerning Swiss foreign economic policy is about establishing some commercial and financial relations with the EU member countries, while at the same time retaining a number of essential economic and political assets. The philosophy underlying this strategy is to postpone full integration into the EU as long as the transactions with the rest of the world remain a major component of its economy.
- This outlook is shared by other European countries who are also "reluctant" towards European integration, notably by the UK, whose own strategy for Brexit displays strong parallels with Switzerland's.

These two points may suggest that Switzerland is fully autonomous in deciding the shape of its relations with the EU, and that "integration without membership" provides benefits without any costs. This, however, would be incorrect. The viability of this strategy depends on a crucial variable, namely, the stability of the exchange rate of the Swiss franc against the euro. Bearing in mind Switzerland's heavy dependence on the European markets, a structural instability of this exchange rate would severely damage cross-border transactions between the two parties, forcing Switzerland eventually to reconsider its European strategy. Let us turn to this issue now.

Is "integration without membership" viable?

The principal structural constraint facing Switzerland is the fact that its national currency tends to appreciate over time against other major currencies, including the euro. This results from the structural surpluses of the Swiss current account as well as from the international role of the Swiss franc. Historically, the latter has played a "safe heaven" role (Vallet 2012): in times of crisis (of various origins) in the global economy, there is a sudden and strong demand for Swiss franc denominated assets. Because of the relatively small size of Swiss financial markets, which limits assets supply, their prices increase and the exchange rate of the Swiss franc appreciates. Recently, this occurred as a result of the great recession that followed the global financial crisis of 2007–2008. In particular, the public debt difficulties experienced by several European countries produced a very strong demand for Swiss franc denominated assets, leading to a strong and rapid appreciation of the Swiss franc on foreign exchange markets. A similar effect could be observed in relation to the COVID-19 pandemic: after the ECB announced its €750bn pandemic purchase programme in March 2020, the Swiss franc appreciated against the euro. A global shock of this magnitude shows how difficult it is for a country situated just across the EU border (in this case, Switzerland) to react to this difficult situation without being involved in EU decision-making seeking to address the effects of this shock in a co-ordinated fashion. The UK could find itself in a somewhat similar situation in a not-too-distant future.

If Swiss firms, owing to both their product specialisation and their long experience with it, have learned to cope with the appreciating trend of the Swiss franc, their problem is that once a certain threshold level in the Swiss franc/euro exchange rate is attained, their competitiveness is highly affected. Due to its heavy reliance on export-oriented firms, this in turn negatively affects the entire economy. This could be observed during the great recession: the eurozone's public debt crisis triggered such a strong appreciation of the Swiss franc against the euro that the SNB decided in September 2011 to introduce a minimum exchange rate in this regard, namely, CHF1.2 for one euro. This exchange-rate floor – which was kept from 6 September 2011 until 15 January 2015 – reveals that Switzerland's European stance, as well as its export-led economic growth model, are rather fragile and highly related to the Swiss franc exchange rate against the euro. The SNB had already introduced a similar floor against the Deutschmark in 1978–1979, although without much success.

Furthermore, the SNB's interventions to stabilise the exchange rate of the Swiss franc against the euro give rise to a number of internal costs for the Swiss economy. For instance, having been criticised for its minimum exchange rate vis-à-vis the euro, the SNB replaced it with a negative interest rate from 22 January 2015. In spite of strict regulations in this domain, negative interest rates incentivise borrowing to finance speculative investments in real-estate and financial markets. By so doing, the SNB helps speculation crowd out productive investment, with negative effects for Switzerland's financial stability (Rossi 2019).

Nevertheless, one should not overlook the fact that, in some periods, the Swiss franc also depreciates against other major currencies (the euro and the US dollar in particular). Considering Switzerland's relatively low interest rates, a positive interest rate differential between foreign interest rates and Swiss ones is likely to induce a series of "carry trades": as a matter of fact, the Swiss franc also plays the role of financing currency across the global economy, which contributes to destabilising its exchange rate and impacts Swiss monetary policy negatively (Gubler 2014).

All in all, Switzerland must succeed in redesigning its future relationships with the EU in order to strengthen its position over the long run. In the next section, we elaborate on some prospects for the future relations between Switzerland and the EU, which may be of interest to other countries that for different reasons cannot or do not want to engage in "total" integration with the EU.

Swiss–EU relations: Some prospects

The priority for Switzerland in its future relations with the EU consists in consolidating its bilateral agreements, an ad-hoc solution tailored to the country's needs (Federal Council 2016: 525). In this section we first explore Switzerland's prospects along this path and then discuss how the Swiss "model" could be adopted elsewhere, for instance by the UK.

The bilateral approach: Between opportunities and uncertainty

In pursuing the bilateral approach, the optimal solution for Switzerland consists in negotiating a single institutional agreement, which should have wider coverage, a simpler structure, and a more secure legal basis than the existing bilateral agreements. A particular priority for Switzerland would be to increase its decision-making rights: the country should have more than merely the right to be consulted regarding the evolution of European legislation. At present, Switzerland passively transposes European laws into domestic legislation, using a procedure that is very slow in adopting the changes.

A number of policy domains are not sufficiently covered by the existing bilateral agreements. For instance, this concerns the environment, industrial regulations, financial services, agricultural products, health care, electricity, and wage levels. Both Switzerland and the EU, therefore, have an interest in engaging in negotiations regarding these fields.

Such negotiations, however, face severe obstacles. To illustrate this, let us consider a problematic issue at the core of them, that is, the free movement of persons, in particular EU workers across Swiss borders (see chapters by Schwok and Jenni, this volume). The EU would like the existing agreement in this domain to be respected without any discrimination, while Switzerland tries to maintain various measures to protect its own labour market.

Swiss citizens' acceptance of a popular initiative aimed at limiting and controlling immigration, on 9 February 2014, reflects fears the influx of EU workers would lead to a downward pressure on wages and a worsening of working conditions.

Now, if no nationwide substitution effect has been observed as a result of cross-border workers (see Jenni, this volume), there are significant effects in several sectors. Unskilled and low-skilled workers are very much impacted, and the risk for them of becoming working poor is rather high, even more so in the wake of the COVID-19 pandemic and the resulting dramatic slowdown of economic activities. At the time of writing, there are 140,000 working poor in Switzerland, and 570,000 individuals live under the poverty line (CHF2,247 per month for a single person; CHF3,981 per month for a couple with two children). This concerns 7.5% of the population (to wit, 600,000 individuals), and the risk to fall under the poverty line in Switzerland concerns 14.7% of its residents, compared to 13.6% in France, 14.1% in Austria, and 17.3% in the EU as a whole.

The Federal Council is aware of these issues and is ready to make some concessions, as a high number of Swiss firms depend on foreign workers to remain competitive in the global economy. It is therefore in the interest of the Swiss authorities to find an institutional solution respecting both the people's decision of 9 February 2014 and the bilateral agreement concerning the free movement of persons.

In the same vein, company taxation and banking secrecy will be at the core of Switzerland's European agenda. The EU often accuses Switzerland of engaging in a form of fiscal dumping to attract multinational corporations, which then export their goods to the EU, thus making Switzerland a "fiscal hub". For this reason, the Swiss government is ready to make some concessions, as suggested with regard to some fiscal reforms that were first rejected by Swiss voters in 2017 but then eventually accepted in 2019.

Another issue concerns the energy independence and security of Switzerland. After several discussions that began in 2011 (which led to the enactment of a federal law in 2018), Switzerland adopted an "Energy strategy 2050" (Schneider and Vallet 2019). While the country already has rather high environmental standards (for instance, it has the lowest carbon intensity among the 30 member countries of the International Energy Agency), its Achilles' heel is represented by its very high dependency on imports of fossil fuel (Schneider and Vallet 2019: 7).

Considering that hydroelectric production is already at its peak, Switzerland must find a different energy mix to satisfy its economic needs, bearing in mind also environmental challenges. In this regard, it is important to recall that the Swiss power market is interconnected and highly dependent on its neighbours' markets. This is the reason why Switzerland proposed to the EU a bilateral agreement on electricity supply in 2012, negotiations over which failed, however, in 2014. Nevertheless, achievement of the "Energy strategy 2050" targets will necessarily require the conclusion of such an agreement, as recommended by a variety of international institutions such as the International Energy Agency. Such an agreement would complete the existing one for transports, because both are key to reducing greenhouse gas emissions (Schneider and Vallet 2019).

Last but not least, the legal issue is not fully solved yet: Switzerland would like to create an arbitral tribunal to solve any conflicts, while the EU insists that (as for any European laws) the CJEU addresses these conflicts (see Schwok, this volume). Switzerland also draws a "red line" at adopting European legislation that forces it to integrate into its national laws aspects of European citizenship.

All in all, at the institutional level, the future relations between Switzerland and the EU are far from being clearly established. If both parties agree on the signature of an IFA between them, this will not provide an answer to all issues on the table. In the short run, it is actually highly probable that Switzerland will continue to passively adapt its own laws after the constantly evolving European legal framework. In light of the above, could other countries, particularly the UK, adopt this model? Let us turn to this issue in the remainder of this chapter.

The bilateral agreements between Switzerland and the EU: A viable model?

The long-run viability of the bilateral approach outlined in this chapter, and its extension to other countries, largely depend on the EU's willingness to accept it, in a period of reduced economic activities and foreign trade owing to the COVID-19 pandemic. On the one hand, in its neighbourhood perspective, the EU has an interest in stabilising its relations with non-member countries: either because economic or political issues prevent them from joining the EU (as in the case of Switzerland), or because some countries could hope that a bilateral approach would lead them to join the EU eventually (the case of Ukraine might be relevant in this regard). Hence, for the EU the bilateral approach includes a number of models whose results and implications could be very different over time and across space.

Furthermore, the EU does not necessarily intend to enter into negotiations on new agreements that could put its unity at stake by institutionalising "ad-hoc" forms of integration. The negotiations with the UK over the latter's withdrawal agreement showed it very clearly: in the short run, the UK's decision to leave the EU has weakened both parties, as it gave rise to a period of high uncertainty. For the EU, the challenge is to reduce this uncertainty by turning this decision into an opportunity to strengthen the unity among the remaining EU member states over the long run. To be sure, the 2009 eurozone crisis showed the need to focus on the deepening of the EU rather than its widening. The COVID-19 pandemic underlined this even further.

It is therefore unlikely that the EU is prepared to display the same type of institutional pragmatism with the UK that it was willing to accept vis-à-vis Switzerland in the 1990s. Hence, although the Swiss "model" has been touted by some UK politicians as a possible option post-Brexit, its viability for the UK must be open to question. The UK could also seek to forge an alliance with Switzerland to co-ordinate their strategies vis-à-vis the EU but so far there is little indication of a willingness to do so (see Church, this volume). Beyond these legal and institutional issues, the bilateral agreements between Switzerland and the EU do not appear entirely to fit the UK's aims, be it with regard to accessing the single market, the free movement of persons, contributions to the EU budget, and, particularly, financial transactions.

The above points show the complexity of Switzerland's form of "integration without membership" and by implication its problematic replication by other countries such as the UK. Indeed, the EU's insistence on treating its "four freedoms" (of goods, services, capital, and persons) as a whole will force the UK to make some difficult choices given its own priorities:

- Either favouring the trade dimension (like Switzerland) and being prepared to make some concessions on immigration. With regard to the latter, the Irish "backstop" illustrates the point well. This expression refers to the necessity to provide a commercial safety net to avoid the reintroduction of a border between the Republic of Ireland and Northern Ireland. This could consist in a transitional period during which both will continue to be part of the same customs union. Second, the immigration issue will arise with regard to the need to keep the UK attractive for high-skilled workers, particularly as regards both banking and financial activities, but also with respect to teaching and research in higher education. In any case, this dilemma will have some political and economic implications for the UK, notably as regards public spending. The choices that will be made could lead to a fragmentation of the UK, be it with respect to social classes (as clearly demonstrated by the Brexit vote) or the territorial unity of the country (should Scotland's independence be put again on the agenda).
- Or privileging controlling migration but at the expense of having a less privileged access to the European single market. In such a scenario it may be difficult for the EU to recognise divergent UK norms (Farrand 2017). This would have significant trade implications given that around half of UK exports go to EU countries, and that even exports to countries beyond Europe can be impacted negatively by both Brexit and the COVID-19 pandemic. Third countries may decide not to accept specific UK norms, while there are many EU norms already recognised worldwide. Swiss producers' widespread adoption of EU regulations preserves the viability of "integration without membership" by avoiding a marginalisation of the Swiss economy.

Swiss–EU relations will also be impacted by the kind of agreement struck between the UK and the EU. Switzerland could indeed benefit from Brexit if the UK loses its "optimal" institutional position from an economic and financial point of view. When the UK was in the EU (but not in the eurozone), it benefitted from the "European financial passport" allowing a foreign institution based in London to carry out, without discrimination, any banking or financial transactions with any EU country. According to Goetz (2017), about 20% of the British banking sector was directly linked to the existence of such a "European financial passport". Since the UK lost this "passport" with Brexit, Swiss financial centres could experience an increase in their competitiveness. As Table 3.6 shows, British financial activities are linked to the EU to a large extent.

Also, euro-denominated clearing operations have hitherto been carried out in London. If some of these transactions move to continental financial centres, Switzerland could attract a share of them. Although the current bilateral agreements between Switzerland and the EU do not cover the financial sector, some

Table 3.6 Share of the United Kingdom in European financial transactions (%)

Savings managed by hedge funds	85
Foreign exchange transactions	78
Transactions on derivatives concerning interest rates	74
Insurance for sea freight	65
Investment funds management	50
Stock market capitalisation	30
Bank loans	26

Source: Authors' elaboration based on Chavagneux (2017).

links exist between the two parties, such as Eurex on derivatives. Now, more financial transactions between Switzerland and the EU mean stronger links between the two parties, thus underpinning Switzerland's "integration without membership". The SNB and the ECB could in particular adopt a common supervisory framework and cooperate more closely in the event of a symmetric financial shock (notably through swaps agreements).[3]

Furthermore, Switzerland could benefit from the development of renminbi-denominated transactions, as pointed out above. The country could eventually become a major hub for these transactions, displacing the UK, which currently controls 60% of the renminbi-denominated transactions beyond China, signed an RMB200bn swap agreement in 2013, and has been hosting a renminbi clearing bank since June 2014. Switzerland also aims to compete with Luxembourg, which hosts three of the largest Chinese banks and has been issuing the first dimsum bonds for a European firm outside China.

Brexit also raises questions as to its impact on the UK economy over the long run, also in light of the negative effects on foreign trade produced by the COVID-19 pandemic. This uncertainty could affect Switzerland given its national currency's role as a "safe heaven". The Swiss franc could therefore be put again under pressure, and its appreciation could be exacerbated in case of further uncertainties as regards the dynamics of European integration or a prolonged period of economic stagnation at the global level owing to the COVID-19 pandemic.

Conclusion

The analysis presented in this chapter shows that the economic relations between Switzerland and the EU are important, complex, and challenging. After more than 60 years of "integration without membership", the Swiss economy cannot but continue being highly interconnected with the EU's economic and financial systems, owing to its geographic proximity and mutual interdependence. The UK is in a somewhat similar situation, which makes the Swiss experience potentially of interest.

Two major points stand out with regard to the nature of the existing bilateral agreements between Switzerland and the EU:

- These agreements are certainly attractive for Switzerland, because they provide many economic advantages while being in line with the political stance the country has taken towards European integration, but they are also rather fragile in their institutional architecture, especially so because the EU wants to replace them with an overarching IFA.
- These bilateral agreements are specific as regards the relationship that has been established between the two parties over more than 60 years, and cannot be transposed without major changes to other countries such as the UK, notably because the situation and the perspectives of the global economy at the time of writing are very different from those prevailing in the second half of the 20th century.

In light of both the theory of regional integration and the practice of the Swiss–EU economic relationships there are several advantages in concluding bilateral agreements between relevant stakeholders. Once the number of these agreements goes beyond a given threshold, however, the dynamics of regional integration becomes so complex and interconnected that the participating countries need a "quantum leap" to be able to continue benefitting from the type of "integration without membership" epitomised by the Swiss case. A properly designed IFA would represent a crucial step in the right direction, but only if it manages to satisfy the key objectives of the two partners.

Notes

1 Not all economic transactions are concerned, because some industrial and agricultural products, as well as some services, are excluded from free trade across the EEA.
2 In 2019 the euro was the second invoicing currency for Swiss exports (the Swiss franc being the first) and the first invoicing currency for Swiss imports: 30.8% of Swiss exports and 44.6% of Swiss imports were denominated in euros (Federal Customs Administration and Federal Department of Finance 2020).
3 Nevertheless, because the ECB mandate does not imply for it to worry about the monetary situation in non-EU countries, this kind of agreement does not feature in the political agenda.

4 The bilateral approach

Achievements and limitations[1]

René Schwok

Following the rejection of the EEA in the December 1992 referendum, Switzerland and the EU decided to put in place sectoral bilateral agreements. The aim was to prevent Switzerland from being marginalised, especially economically, in relation to the EU, while not actually aspiring to membership (Cottier and Kopse 1998).

This period of bilateral relations can be divided into three phases. The first phase began in 1993 with negotiations on a first series of bilateral agreements, the so-called Bilateral Agreements I (BA I). These were signed in 1999. Negotiations were extremely difficult and diplomats were able to find compromise solutions only after a long time. These agreements were not based on a pre-established model and were not intended as a long-term solution. Throughout this phase, the negotiations were jeopardised on several occasions by popular votes on land transport (road and rail) issues. Eventually the negotiations were concluded, and a majority of the Swiss electorate voted in favour of the agreements in 2000.

In the 1990s, Switzerland's negotiating position was different from that of the UK today. Switzerland was then in a process of increasing integration, while the UK is today engaged in a process of disintegration from the EU. In addition, the EU of the 1990s was not the EU of the 2020s. It had only 15 member states and was less subject to centrifugal forces (populism, Eurosceptic leaders, recurrent crises). This limits the comparisons that could be drawn between the two cases.

The second phase was characterised by the consolidation and extension of the bilateral approach. It started in 2002 with the implementation of the BA I set of agreements and the signing of a series of new bilateral agreements, the BA II. The main one pertains to Switzerland's participation in the Schengen Area and the Dublin system. This phase was also punctuated by several referendums on the abolition of the free movement of persons, in which the majority of voters rejected the abolition.

The third phase is marked by fragility and uncertainty. It began in 2014 with the success of the popular initiative, launched by the SVP, against "mass immigration", which threatened the bilateral agreement package as a whole. At present, relations between the EU and Switzerland are in an impasse because of the Swiss government's refusal to sign an IFA its diplomats spent years negotiating.

Bilateral Agreements I

After the rejection of EEA membership, Switzerland and the EU engaged in extended and laborious talks which led to a first package of bilateral agreements (CS 1999). Signed on 21 June 1999 in Luxembourg, the agreements were adopted by the Swiss electorate on 21 May 2000 and entered into force on 1 June 2002 (Schwok 2006).

The package includes seven distinct agreements (see Box 4.1). From a legal perspective, they are linked to each other, in that were Switzerland to fail to honour any of them, all the others could also fall. This is known as the "guillotine clause" (denunciation clause, art. 22) (CS 1999).

Box 4.1 The Seven Bilateral Agreements I

1. *Air Transport.* Swiss airlines are put on an equal footing with their European competitors.
2. *Public Procurement Markets.* Reciprocal opening of local public procurement markets.
3. *Participation of Swiss universities in the EU research programmes.*
4. *Agriculture.* Prescriptions for veterinary medicine and plant protection are recognised as equivalent. There is also a reduction of customs duties and quotas on some agricultural products.
5. *Elimination of Technical Barriers to Trade.* Introduction of mutual recognition of conformity assessments: certificates, authorisations, evaluations, and inspections.
6. *Land Transport.* Consent on free circulation of lorries above 28 tonnes.
7. *Free Movement of Persons* (free choice of residence). Elimination of restrictions for EU citizens to settle in Switzerland and vice versa.

Five of the agreements concerned relatively minor matters. The other two – free movement of persons (or, more accurately, free choice of residence) and land transport – by contrast, gave instead rise to intense controversies.

Land transport

At first sight, the issue of land transport appears to be straightforward. The agreement aims principally to allow lorries of more than 28 tonnes to circulate through Switzerland. This agreement however did lead to heated discussions in Switzerland, with no fewer than four popular votes held on the subject during the 1990s! As a result, a colossal new railway tunnel was built under the Gotthard.

Negotiations had to resolve the following dilemma. On the one hand, the EU wished to step up north-south road transport across Europe. Moreover, it wanted to limit the amount of highly polluting traffic through France and Austria generated by the Swiss 28-tonne ceiling. On the other hand, the Swiss government had limited room for manoeuvre as it did not want to alienate the environmentalists or the population living in the Alpine regions. Most importantly, the Federal Council had committed itself, pursuant to a constitutional initiative adopted by the electorate on 20 February 1994, to transferring goods transport from road to rail within ten years (the so-called "Alps Initiative").

The solution found to break the deadlock was mainly to channel as much as possible of the Alps traffic to rail transport, under the so-called "piggyback" policy. So, on the one hand, the agreement allowed European lorries above 28 tonnes to circulate freely in Switzerland. But, on the other hand, a complex quota and duty system was set up and new tunnels were constructed through the Alps. The railways tunnels concerned are the Lötschberg and, above all, the new Gotthard railway tunnels, whose construction began in 1996 and was completed in 2016. The base tunnel was at time of its construction the longest in the world (57 km), at places reaching a depth of 2,300 metres! With the opening of this tunnel, a kind of "railway highway" has been put in place, which offers a realistic alternative in terms of cost and speed to road transport.

The four "European" referendums on land transport

The intensity of the 1990s controversy over freight transport through the Alps is only a distant memory today. At the time, though, it generated heated discussions and triggered no fewer than four referendums. In the first referendum, held on 27 September 1992, the Swiss were asked to vote on a federal resolution concerning the construction of two new trans-Alpine railways lines due to their exorbitant cost and the uncertainty surrounding the feasibility of transferring heavy goods vehicle traffic from road to rail. The Federal Council's proposal was supported by 63.6% of the electorate. This consultation, nevertheless, had no concrete outcome as it had preceded the EEA vote of December 1992 and the entire European question was revisited after the latter.

On 20 February 1994 a majority of the people and the cantons accepted the constitutional initiative on "the protection of Alpine regions from transit traffic". Under this initiative goods transiting through the Alps were required to be transported by rail. This initiative was adopted by 51.9% of all voters. Only seven cantons, mainly the French-speaking ones, opposed it. This initiative had been launched by environmentalist groups, left-wing parties, and local governments in central Switzerland. It had been opposed by the Federal Council, right-wing parties, and business organisations.

On 27 September 1998 the Swiss (57.2% of the electorate) rejected a referendum that had been launched by the Swiss Road Transport Association. The lobby of lorry drivers opposed the federal law that established the above-mentioned fee for heavy vehicle traffic. On 29 November 1998, 63.5% of the voters adopted the federal decree on the Implementation and Funding of Public Transport Infrastructure. This very general proposal on transport included the construction of new tunnels through the Alps, above all the Gotthard tunnel.

Free movement of persons (free choice of residence)

The agreement on free movement of persons enables any citizen of an EU member state to settle in Switzerland. It has subsequently been extended to include EFTA countries. It is applied, on a basis of reciprocity, to any Swiss citizen wishing to settle in an EU country. The agreement also outlaws any discrimination on the labour market. National preferences are removed, with the exception of occupations linked to national security. This agreement on persons was the most difficult to conclude (see also Jenni, this volume), as it faced the following dilemma. On the one hand, the EU demanded that freedom of settlement be automatically granted to its citizens. On the other hand, the Swiss government refused to accept this request due to its concerns about xenophobia. This agreement prompted numerous and highly emotional popular votes.

Before going into details, it is important to clarify that we prefer to use the expression free choice of residence rather than free movement of persons. This is because we feel it important to avoid the common confusion with the free movement as per the "Schengen" agreement (see below). Moreover, this agreement does not do away with border checks. Therefore, this is indeed an agreement on freedom of settlement and removal of national preferences in the labour market rather than on freedom of movement.

Such freedom of settlement, however, is conditional. Eligible persons must be able to prove they have a work contract or are financially self-sufficient. Under the agreement there is a partial and time-limited liberalisation (maximum 90 days) of the service sector. Domestically, the Federal Council, employers' associations, centrist and right-wing parties had to grant concessions to left-wing parties and trade unions. The left had threatened not to support the Bilateral Agreements I if this were not the case. Switzerland, therefore, introduced flanking measures against wage and social welfare dumping: (1) streamlined and partial extension of collective labour conventions, (2) plans to introduce minimum wages in border cantons, (3) measures against workers posted in Switzerland by a foreign company (see Jenni, this volume).

It is important to note that the implementation of the freedom of settlement did not have a significant impact on the unemployment rate, which fell sharply between 2003 and 2008, from 4% to 2.4% in September 2008. After spiking up as a result of the autumn 2008 economic crisis, in early 2020 and before the Coronavirus crisis, it was back to a rate around 2.2%, which is very low compared to other European states (see Jenni, this volume).

The free movement of persons has been an important condition for Switzerland's economic growth because the competitiveness of companies depends to a large extent on their ability to hire an adequate workforce in sufficient quantity. The

Swiss labour market is not able by itself to provide sufficiently qualified personnel due to a lack of specialists. The principle of freedom of residence has enabled Swiss companies to find employees in the EU that they could not find in Switzerland. This has encouraged them to stay in Switzerland and create jobs there. The free movement of persons is also very attractive for foreign companies setting up in the country. Multinational companies would hesitate to come if they could not easily recruit their specialists from across Europe. However, the most significant consequence of this agreement on freedom of settlement has been a very high level of immigration.

Referendum on the Bilateral Agreements I – 21 May 2000

The Swiss people endorsed the Bilateral Agreements I on 21 May 2000 with a comfortable majority of 67.2%. Why did voters endorse the Bilateral Agreements I, after rejecting the EEA? What was it that triggered this swing in public opinion? This question concerns the German-speaking part of Switzerland more than the French-speaking one, which remained true to its pro-EU orientation.

First of all, discussion on the Bilateral Agreements I managed to sidestep the confusion reigning in 1992 on the issue of accession to the EU (see Kreis, this volume). In contrast to what happened with the EEA vote, the government and its supporters had clearly distinguished between the sectoral bilateral agreements and full accession to the EU. In 2000 there was no ambiguity like that surrounding the EEA referendum, when the Federal Council had muddled matters by applying for membership of the EU in the course of the campaign.

Moreover, it also important to bear in mind that Switzerland's formal sovereignty is better preserved in the Bilateral Agreements than in the EEA. The Bilateral Agreements do not contain any supranational elements such as the European Surveillance Authority or oversight by the CJEU. Nor do they provide for automatic transposition of new EU legislation in the field. All this reassured those most attached to Switzerland's formal sovereignty. It is also undeniable that the decision by Christoph Blocher, the SVP, and the Campaign for an Independent and Neutral Switzerland (AUNS) not to campaign against the Bilateral Agreements I reduced the number of opponents. That decision neutralised the radical wings of the SVP and AUNS, fanatical defenders of sovereignty, who did not rally to the opposition. A final point should be highlighted: the unambiguous commitment of the establishment. The Federal Council, the mainstream political parties, and the economic and labour associations all closed ranks in a communication campaign that was much more effective than that of 1992.

Referendum on the extension to the new member states – 25 September 2005

On 25 September 2005, a 56% majority of voters came out in favour of extending the agreement on the free movement of persons to the ten countries that had joined the EU in 2004. In the event of a refusal, the entire package of Bilateral Agreements I would have been under threat, due to the "guillotine clause" mentioned above.

Referendum on the cohesion fund for east-central Europe – 26 November 2006

Switzerland promised to contribute CHF 1bn (ca. €620,000) to a cohesion fund for the new member states that had joined in 2004. This sum was above all intended for the eight countries located in east-central Europe. In legal terms, there is no link between the so-called "Cohesion Billion" and the extension of the Bilateral Agreements I to these eight countries. The EU had, in fact, given up its demand to link the two so as not to give those in the "no" camp any additional ammunition in the campaign for the 2005 referendum. Notwithstanding, there was clearly an informal tie between the two issues. In the 26 November 2006 vote, a 53.4% majority of voters came out in favour of this "Cohesion Billion".

Referendum on the renewal of the free movement of persons and its extension to Romania and Bulgaria – 8 February 2009

Renewal of the free movement of persons agreement, as well as its extension to the EU's two newest members, Romania and Bulgaria, were presented to the electorate in one single package in February 2009 as a result a referendum challenge launched by the SVP and its allies.

The arguments deployed by opponents were familiar ones, having been well rehearsed in the referendum campaigns of 2005 and 2006. They invoked images of Switzerland being invaded by a crowd of undesirables. Their rhetoric degenerated into pure xenophobia and they also waved anti-Roma sentiment, misleadingly tarring all Romanians with the same brush. In the supporters' camp, a broad coalition stressed Switzerland's international commitments and its tradition of openness. This camp included parties from both the right and the left of the political spectrum, plus employers' associations and trade unionists, intellectuals and journalists. Their main argument was focussed on reminding voters that, if they voted against the free movement of persons, the EU would be perfectly within its legal rights to rescind the entire package of bilateral agreements with Switzerland ("guillotine clause").

In the vote held on 8 February 2009, 59.6% of the electorate voted in favour of renewing the free movement of persons and extending it to Bulgaria and Romania. French-speaking Switzerland continued to show greater enthusiasm for these agreements, with, for example, a 70.2% of "yes" vote in the canton of Vaud. It should be noted that the urban regions of German-speaking Switzerland also showed a clear approval.

SVP popular initiative "Against Mass Immigration" – 9 February 2014

Having failed in its strategy of holding referendums against agreements or laws, the SVP chose to use popular initiatives instead. Thus, through an initiative on "limiting mass immigration",[2] this party has successfully managed to undermine the free movement of persons with the EU, since its proposal was adopted by popular vote, albeit on a very narrow majority of 50.3%, on 9 February 2014.

This initiative requires the federal government to limit the number of residence permits awarded to foreigners, by means of annual quotas, and to introduce the principle of national preference. The text of this initiative has been included as a new article, Article 121a, in the Federal Constitution.

The SVP craftily led the people to believe that the text of the initiative only targeted non-European foreigners, whereas, in fact, it could only be relevant to EU (and EFTA) citizens since they were the only foreigners who were not already subject to quotas and the national preference principle (see Jenni, this volume).

The referendum once again showed a gap between the different linguistic regions of the country, and between the more urban and less urban areas. Thus, a majority of Swiss Germans and, even more so, of Swiss Italians voted in favour of this limitation of foreign immigration, while French-speaking Switzerland voted against it (see Theiler and Mueller, this volume). However, German-speaking Swiss cities such as Zurich, Berne, and Basel rejected the proposal, while some suburbs, small towns and rural areas in French-speaking Switzerland voted in favour. The positive vote of the Swiss people was a response to concerns about Switzerland's population, which increased by 14% between 2000 and 2013. By the end of 2013, net migration had risen to 89,500 people (due to the free movement of persons, around 70% of them are immigrants from the EU). Relative to a Swiss population of 8.2 m, and to the rate in other European countries, this represents significant population growth.

After this vote, bilateral relations between Switzerland and the EU became a real political headache. It took almost three years to get out of what seemed to be an irresolvable dilemma.[3] On the one hand, Switzerland could not impose quotas on immigrants and a national preference rule on nationals of EU countries since the agreement on the free movement of persons formally prohibits it. But, on the other hand, the new Article 121a of the Federal Constitution had to be applied, hence quotas on immigrants and a national preference rule against citizens of EU countries had to be implemented.

Tension reached a new peak when the EU imposed sanctions restricting Swiss universities' participation in European scientific research programmes, following the Federal Council's refusal to grant free movement of persons to Croats, in accordance, precisely, with this new constitutional article. Dozens of compromise solutions were then envisaged and negotiations were also conducted in an attempt to convince the EU to soften its position, but the latter refused to budge, even slightly, on the principle of the free movement of persons.

Finally, the Federal Parliament decided to adopt legislation, in 2016, to implement this new constitutional article.[4] But this piece of legislation is, in fact, nothing more than window dressing in that the measures introduced do not set any immigration quotas nor do they enforce the principle of national preference. They only stipulate that, when seeking to hire, employers must consider the profiles of job seekers residing in Switzerland first, but without being forced to hire them. Moreover, this is only applied in the event of high unemployment in certain sectors or regions. Clearly, the SVP could not be satisfied with the way in which the

Swiss parliament had implemented (in fact had not implemented) its proposal to limit immigration. That is the reason why this party decided to launch a new popular initiative, which we discuss below.

The Bilateral Agreements II

The EU and Switzerland signed a second series of Bilateral Agreements (BA II) on 26 October 2004. These agreements cover nine fields (see Box 4.2), each of which took effect on a different date (Kaddous and Jametti Greiner 2006). From a legal perspective, these agreements are not linked to each other. Contrary to the Bilateral Agreements I, they do not include a "guillotine clause". Switzerland could have refused any one of them without the others being called into question.

Six of these agreements did not pose any problems and concern relatively minor issues. The three others, by contrast, were the subject of heated debate: Schengen/Dublin, the fight against fraud, and taxation of savings. We shall present only the most controversial agreement in further detail, the one on Schengen/Dublin.

Box 4.2 The Nine Bilateral Agreements II

1. *The Fight against Fraud*: Switzerland undertook to help the EU fight against fraud in customs duties and indirect taxes. It obtained further guarantees concerning its banking secrecy.
2. *Processed Agricultural Products*: Reduced customs duties on products such as soups, chocolate, biscuits, instant coffee.
3. *Statistics*: Switzerland joined Eurostat.
4. *Pensions*: Income tax exemption for the pensions of retired EU officials living in Switzerland. Only 50 persons were affected.
5. *The Environment:* Switzerland joined the European Environment Agency (EEA).
6. *MEDIA*: Swiss participation in MEDIA, an EU programme aiming to strengthen the European audio-visual industry.
7. *Education, Occupational Training, Youth*: Swiss participation in EU programmes aiming to encourage cross-border mobility of students, trainees, and young people.
8. *Taxation of savings*: Switzerland imposed a withholding tax on all income from savings of persons with residency in the EU. This agreement made it possible to preserve banking secrecy for around 15 years. However, it lost its relevance from 2018 and the introduction of automatic information exchange.
9. *Schengen/Dublin. Schengen*: Checks on persons at borders were abolished. Dublin: It was prohibited to request asylum in Switzerland if the request had already been made in another European state.

Schengen/Dublin

The Schengen agreement allows the free movement of individuals by removing border checks between countries that are parties to it. Switzerland has the right to participate in so-called EU decision shaping but lacks the right to participate in formal decision making. This resembles the mechanism provided for within the EEA. Switzerland may thus contribute to decisions that concern it, for example an amendment to visa law or asylums rights. Moreover, it may participate in the subsequent development of the Schengen *acquis* and is granted access to new instruments, for example SIS II, the second European electronic information system (see Jenni, this volume).

It should be noted that the Schengen agreement has not changed the actual situation on the Swiss borders as much as in the EU member states. The EU is a customs union, but Switzerland is outside that customs union and has only concluded a free trade agreement with it. In the case of industrial goods, the origin of products still has to be checked since Switzerland has not adopted the Common External Tariff. In addition, the agreement on agricultural produce is only partial. Checks at border crossings are therefore still necessary. Finally, Switzerland is not part of the indirect tax area of the EU. It can still check the payment of VAT and excise duties on entry into its territory.

The 5 June 2005 referendum on Schengen

In the 5 June 2005 vote, a 54.6% majority of the electorate came out in favour of the agreements. The large German-speaking cities such as Zurich, Basel and Berne as well as the French-speaking cantons approved Switzerland's participation in Schengen by majorities ranging between 57% and 70%. The rural areas of German-speaking Switzerland were much more hostile and rejected the agreement.

As on previous occasions, the campaign against the Schengen/Dublin agreement was mainly run by the SVP and AUNS and was extremely virulent. Their arguments emphasised Switzerland's loss of sovereignty, disappearance of border checks, an invasion by foreigners, free immigration of criminals, and submission to foreign judges. On the other hand, the remainder of the Swiss political forces as well as employers and labour associations closed ranks in order to secure Switzerland's entry into the Schengen /Dublin agreement.

SVP popular initiative against the agreement with the EU on freedom of settlement – 27 September 2020[4]

In September 2020, the Swiss people were asked to vote on the popular initiative "For moderate immigration" (limitation initiative). The reason for this initiative was related to the already mentioned frustration of the SVP, which considered that the outcome of its 2014 popular initiative "Against Mass Immigration" had not really been implemented. The party thus resumed its offensive by launching a new initiative, whose text, unlike the previous one, explicitly called for a prompt termination of the agreement on the free movement of persons with the EU[5].

Had this new SVP initiative been approved, a new Article 121b would have been inserted in the Federal Constitution. The article would have stipulated that no new international treaty providing for the free movement of foreign nationals may be signed by Switzerland. The text also specified that the Federal Council must negotiate with the EU with a view to terminating the current agreement on the free movement of persons within 12 months following approval by the people of a new constitutional article (Art. 197, 12). If this objective could not be achieved, the government would have had to terminate the agreement with the EU within 30 days.

According to the SVP, the free movement of persons has a negative impact on Switzerland. Since the agreement with the EU came into force, the resident population has increased by more than one million people: as of late 2019, Switzerland's population reached almost 8.5 m inhabitants, 25.1% of whom were non-citizens. For the SVP, Switzerland does not have the capacity to absorb such an influx of people. Moreover, the number of cross-border commuters is constantly on the rise: more than 320,000 EU workers cross the border daily to work in Switzerland. The political right argued that the free movement policy has led to overpopulation, strains on the environment and infrastructure, and exploitation of the social security system.

For the Federal Council, all the other mainstream parties, the business community, trade unions and civil society groups, the SVP initiative would jeopardise relations with the EU, Switzerland's main economic and politic partner. They believe that the free movement of persons is of crucial importance for the country. The abolition of the free movement of persons agreement would, therefore, have serious negative consequences. This would have meant the end not only of the freedom of movement of persons but also of the bilateral approach as a whole, because of the "guillotine clause" mentioned above.

Surprisingly, this new SVP initiative was rejected by 61.7% of voters. It won a majority only in three tiny German-speaking cantons and in Italian-speaking Ticino while the French-speaking part of the country unanimously rejected the proposal.

The result of this vote is astonishing because the text of the 2020 initiative broadly replicated that of the initiative accepted in 2014. So how can we explain this significant turnaround in the preferences of the electorate in just six years? The first reason is likely due to the wording of the 2020 text, which clearly mentioned the end of the free movement of people with the EU, as opposed to the more ambiguous 2014 version which did not explicitly refer to the EU. The second motive has probably to do with the fact that the number of people coming to Switzerland from other countries was much lower in 2020 than in 2014 and that immigration is no longer at the top of voters' concerns. The third reason may be due to the Covid-19 pandemic, as most Swiss did not want to add an additional crisis (with the EU) to the crisis generated by the virus outbreak.

The Institutional Framework agreement

In general terms, this agreement stems from the European Union's desire to modify its relations with Switzerland. In fact, such an agreement (DFAE 2018a) was originally proposed by the Swiss authorities and was only intended to consolidate the bilateral approach. However, in the course of the negotiations, the European Union changed its scope towards a form of institutional integration of Switzerland into the EU system (Muller 2020). Indeed, the EU considers the current bilateral agreements inadequate because they give Switzerland too much leeway to deviate from EU law and to undermine the integrity of the single market.

Switzerland's response to EU pressure has been mixed. The Federal Council would have preferred to maintain the existing approach. As a result, the Swiss government has, for years, pursued a policy of procrastination in an attempt to buy as much time as possible. In order to understand the Swiss position on this issue, it is important to note that the bilateral and sectoral agreements governing relations between Berne and Brussels are relatively unburdensome. Except for the Schengen and air transport agreements, they do not require Switzerland to adapt its legislation to developments in the so-called *acquis communautaire* relevant to those bilateral agreements. Nor do they confer upon a supranational institution such as the European Commission, the power to verify that Switzerland is applying EU law correctly. They do not oblige Switzerland to follow the jurisprudence of the CJEU, although, in practice, it increasingly refers to it. Finally, there is no mechanism for a judicial dispute settlement; there are only political mechanisms which senior officials of the two parties meeting in joint committees.

Finally, on 6 December 2018, after ten years of discussions, five years of effective negotiations and 32 rounds of meetings, the text of an "agreement facilitating bilateral relations between the EU and Switzerland" (which we have referred to as Institutional Framework Agreement or IFA) was published. But in an extraordinary turn of events, the Federal Council did not endorse it and did not put it forward to parliament. To buy time, it has undertaken a broad consultation with political parties, cantonal governments, and interest groups to find out their position. This resulted in 54 often very detailed reports and … even more confusion. To buy yet more time, the Federal Council has asked the EU for concessions that it knows Brussels does not want to make.

The main components of the draft IFA

The scope of the IFA is for the time being confined to five areas: the free movement of persons, land transport, air transport, technical trade barriers, and agriculture. Future agreements in other fields, such as for example electricity, could be included later.

As regards Switzerland's implementation of this agreement, the EU wanted it to be monitored by a supranational authority, such as the European Commission, the EFTA Surveillance Authority or by a new monitoring mechanism. But Switzerland was opposed to this. In the final compromise text (Articles 6 and

7) Switzerland remains alone responsible for the correct implementation of the agreement on its territory (two-pillar model). But the Commission can now monitor Switzerland's proper implementation of the agreement and can initiate a dispute settlement procedure in the event of suspected non-compliance.

Adjustment to developments in EU law

The EU wanted Switzerland to commit to almost automatically adjusting to developments in EU law, in areas relevant to the bilateral agreements, lest legal discrepancies, and therefore obstacles to trade, arise too often. However, the Federal Council would have preferred to keep the status quo, under which Switzerland has not yet adapted its legislation to the EU *acquis* relevant to the bilateral agreements (except for Schengen and air transport; see also Jenni, this volume). In practice, Switzerland almost always implements new EU law even if it is not formally required to do so.

The compromise reached consists of a "dynamic adoption" approach. Thus, both the static model wanted by Berne and the automaticity advocated by Brussels have been discarded. The advantage of the notion of "dynamic" over that of "automatic" is that Switzerland can decide on each legal development in accordance with the decision-making procedures established by its Constitution. Thus, the right to hold a referendum is respected. However, if Switzerland is unable to implement one development in EU law, the EU may initiate dispute settlement proceedings which would not leave Switzerland much room for manœuvre (see below). It should be noted that the EU has granted Switzerland one of its long-standing demands, namely to participate in "comitology" processes and to be systematically consulted in shaping developments of relevant EU law and thus to be able to present its concerns early on in the process ("decision shaping"). Switzerland has thus been granted the same status as EEA members Norway, Iceland, and Liechtenstein.

However a few concrete issues emerged during the negotiations that illustrate the difficulties that Switzerland would face if it were to adopt a dynamic adoption approach to EU law developments. These issues pertain to (1) posted workers, (2) the revision of the regulation on the coordination of social security systems, and (3) the directive on the protection of rights of EU citizens.

POSTED WORKERS

The EU considers some of Switzerland's flanking measures to be discriminatory towards EU citizens (see also Jenni, this volume). With this in mind, Protocol 1 of the draft IFA requires Switzerland to adopt EU Enforcement Directive 2014/67 and the amended directive 2018/957 concerning the posting of workers. This poses two main problems for the trade unions and the left-wing parties. First, Switzerland currently applies a rule, in some specific sectors, whereby EU companies must provide notification at least eight days prior to posting workers to Switzerland. But the EU wished to remove this restriction, which it considers contrary to its law, and discriminatory for its workers. Finally, a compromise was reached and a four-day rule was agreed upon.

Secondly, Switzerland currently requires a financial deposit from companies posting workers to Switzerland to ensure that they pay all the social security costs for their posted employees. But the EU considers that this, too, is discriminatory, and therefore contrary to EU law. Indeed, this condition is not required of Swiss companies. In the end, an agreement was reached. Switzerland has agreed to waive this guarantee requirement, but a financial guarantee may nevertheless be requested from EU employers previously convicted for failing to meet their financial obligations. This solution is, however, deemed unsatisfactory by the trade unions and the Socialist Party.

THE REVISION OF THE REGULATION ON THE COORDINATION OF SOCIAL SECURITY SYSTEMS

The EU is currently further revising Regulation No 883/2004 on the coordination of social security systems. A key issue concerns the change of responsibility for paying unemployment benefits to cross-border workers. In practice, it is currently the country of residence that pays benefits to a cross-border worker who has lost her/his previous job in Switzerland. It is envisaged that in future the state of employment (e.g. Switzerland) should pay such unemployment benefits.

The revision process is still ongoing. This is why the revision of the regulation is not mentioned in the IFA. But this revision may pose a difficulty for Switzerland and is an example of why the dynamic adoption approach is problematic for the country. Indeed, any dispute concerning Switzerland's future adoption of amended Regulation 883/2004 would have to be settled under the dispute settlement mechanism. Here it is not only the SVP, but also some employers' organisations and the right wing of the FDP who take a negative view of such a provision, which may prove costly for the federal government.

THE DIRECTIVE FOR THE PROTECTION OF EU CITIZENS' RIGHTS

At present, Switzerland does not fully apply this Directive 2004/38/EC on the right of EU citizens and their family members to move and reside freely within Switzerland (see also Jenni, this volume). For Brussels, this directive constitutes a further development of the agreement on the free movement of persons and must, therefore, be applied by Switzerland; this is contested by Berne. From a material point of view, this raises several concerns for those with a conservative outlook in Switzerland, related in particular to the extension of the social protection rights of EU nationals, the extension of their protection against expulsion, as well as their right of permanent residence in Switzerland after five years.

In the draft IFA, the EU waived the requirement that Switzerland explicitly commit to adopting the directive in question within a specified period. But some fear that Brussels might soon bring up the issue again. In this case, too, should a disagreement arise with the EU as to Switzerland's adoption of this directive, the dispute settlement mechanism provided for under the IFA would apply. This explains the concerns expressed by some, within the ranks of the SVP and also among sectors of the moderate right.

Dispute settlement

The main difficulty is related to the settlement of disputes (Article 10 and Protocol 3). Currently, in case of a dispute arising between the EU and Switzerland, the matter is brought before the joint committees comprising diplomats from the European Commission and from Switzerland. If they cannot agree, there is no legal mechanism in place to compel them to reach a solution. Switzerland would have liked to keep the status quo, but the EU has demanded that the CJEU be the final and binding arbitrator on disputes, to avoid deception on the part of Swiss actors.

At first sight, the compromise proposal set out in the draft IFA seems to favour the Swiss side, which has obtained the right to establish an Arbitral Tribunal, a prominent provision in the text of the agreement. The tribunal would be composed of an equal number of arbitrators appointed by Switzerland and the EU. The resulting decisions would thus be characterised by equanimity. But in practice, if the dispute concerns the interpretation or application of EU law, which is almost always the case, the Arbitral Tribunal will have to refer the matter to the CJEU, whose ruling would be binding on the Arbitral Tribunal and the parties!

The SVP argument mostly revolves around the threat represented by "foreign judges", i.e. those in the CJEU, who would have the authority to issue decisions binding on Switzerland and dismisses the Arbitral Tribunal, which it see as a sham tribunal. It should be noted that this issue has been the object of much debate among legal experts. Opponents of the IFA have argued that the Arbitral Tribunal would have almost no independence from the CJEU, whereas those who are more favourable to European integration tend to emphasise the broad leeway given to the Tribunal.

Note finally that, if Switzerland decided not to implement a decision made by the Arbitral Tribunal under guidance from the CJEU, or if the EU considered that the measures implemented by Switzerland contravene the ruling, the EU would be entitled to impose compensatory measures (retaliatory action). However, Switzerland has been able to ensure that any compensatory measure implemented by the EU must conform with the principle of proportionality. Should opinions differ on the subject, an Arbitral Tribunal may then examine the proportionality of these measures at Switzerland's request.

A political appraisal

In sum, four main reasons explain the lack of enthusiasm of the Swiss government for this draft IFA.

First, the Swiss negotiators have had to make concessions and to cross the red lines initially drawn by the Federal Council, for instance on the role of the CJEU. Second, the SVP has already announced that, should the text of the agreement eventually be approved by parliament, it will launch a referendum challenge against it. It is highly likely that SVP will have no difficulty collecting the 50,000 signatures required to force the government to submit the issue to a popular vote. Third, the Socialist Party strongly opposes the agreement's provisions concerning the flanking measures, which it believes would weaken the country's social protection system. Lastly, the centre-right parties hesitate to officially endorse the IFA. In any case, the latter only have three out of seven representatives in the government and are also in a minority in the National Council, i.e. the lower house of parliament.

Conclusion

The bilateral approach is currently weakened. On the Swiss side because, unlike the 1990s and 2000s, the political parties supporting it, and more broadly a willingness to compromise with the EU, are now in a minority in the lower house of parliament and in the federal government. The SVP is the largest party in the lower house and has two representatives in the government. The most consequential phenomenon has been the change of position by the Socialist Party (SP), traditionally an ally of the Christian Democratic Party (CVP) and Liberal Party (FDP) in support of the bilateral approach. Disappointed by the concessions made by Swiss negotiators on the flanking measures, it now refuses to support the IFA. Under these conditions, it is currently illusory to expect majority support for this agreement.

On the EU side, because pressure has become more intense, Brussels is more intransigent and wants to prevent certain Swiss sectors from not playing by the same rules of the game as their EU counterparts. These considerations have led the EU to push for an institutional agreement that reduces Switzerland's room for manoeuvre, particularly on the question of dispute settlement and the role of CJEU.

This stiffening on the part of Brussels can be explained by three main reasons. First, the EU became aware that the institutional dimension of the 1990s agreements was too favourable to Switzerland, perhaps because at the time they were conceived as a temporary solution. Second, Brussels has considered some Swiss economic policies as abuse, discrimination, or even cheating. Third, because any laxity towards Switzerland could have been claimed as a precedent by third countries that have also embarked on a bilateral approach with the EU. This is particularly the case for the United Kingdom and its Brexit negotiations, which delayed those with Switzerland and made Brussels' position more uncompromising. Indeed, the EU did not want to grant concessions to Switzerland that could be claimed by the UK later.

Finally, the question remains as to whether the Swiss model could be followed by other states such as the United Kingdom. Politicians such as the former German finance minister Wolfgang Schäuble (Waterfield 2017), as well as some experts mentioned this model as a source of inspiration (Schwok 2018). A careful reading of the European Commission negotiating mandate with the UK of February 2020 reveals that, indeed, the EU favours an approach fairly close to the Swiss bilateral and sectoral model, except that it does not include the free movement of persons.

The advantages of the Swiss model are as follows: (1) it offers better access to the EU internal market than the EU-Canada model; (2) it leaves the United Kingdom free to conclude international trade agreements, unlike a customs union such as the one that is binding Turkey and the EU, (3) it creates less dependence for the United Kingdom than the Eastern agreements (e.g. with Ukraine, Moldova, and Georgia) because the European Commission has fewer powers of control and of conditionality, (4) it involves fewer national legal constraints and less financial expenditure than EEA membership (aka the "Norwegian model").

Thus, in comparative perspective, the Swiss model could constitute an interesting reference point for the United Kingdom. But, at the time of writing, we must note that this is not the path that is favoured by the government led by Boris Johnson. On reading its negotiating mandate, it appears that its aim is solely a free trade agreement, i.e. one limited to the abolition of customs duties and leaving non-tariff barriers unaffected. This would be quite similar to the agreement that Switzerland concluded with the EEC in 1972 (in the context of the UK's departure from EFTA to join the EEC …).

Notes

1 A previous version of this chapter was published in *European Foreign Affairs Review* vol. 25, no. 2, 2020, pp. 159–176.
2 Popular initiative "Against Mass Migration". As it was approved, it was added to article 121a of the federal constitution, https://www.bk.admin.ch/ch/f/pore/vi/vis413t.html
3 A popular initiative to vote again in order to strike article 121a off the Constitution was significantly called "Out of the Dead End" [Raus aus der Sackgasse]. It had even collected more than the required 100,000 signatures, https://www.bk.admin.ch/ch/d/pore/vi/vis458.html.
4 Implementation of article 121a of the Swiss Federal Constitution: The Federal Council passes the amendments to ordinances, https://www.ejpd.admin.ch/ejpd/fr/home/aktuell/news/2017/2017-12-081.html#_blank.
5 Popular initiative "For Moderate Immigration" (limitation initiative), https://www.bk.admin.ch/ch/f/pore/vi/vis483.html.

Appendix

List of 18 popular votes in Switzerland about the European Union since 1992

27 September 1992: Referendum against the construction of trans-Alpine railways lines agreed with the European Union.

6 December 1992: Referendum against membership of the European Economic Area (EEA).

20 February 1994: *Alps* initiative, to prevent European heavy goods vehicles from crossing Switzerland.

8 June 1997: Lega initiative, to withdraw membership application.

27 September 1998: Referendum against new taxes on heavy vehicle traffic, to dissuade European traffic and to finance cross-Alpine freight haulage.

29 November 1998: Referendum on, inter alia, financing of Cross-Alps freight haulage.

21 May 2000: Referendum against the first Bilateral Agreements.

4 March 2001: NEBS initiative, to start membership negotiations.

5 June 2005: Referendum against Switzerland's participation in the Schengen/Dublin agreements.

25 September 2005: Referendum against free movement of nationals from the eight East-Central European countries which joined the EU in 2004.

26 November 2006: Referendum against a cohesion fund for the eight East-Central European countries which joined the EU in 2004.

8 February 2009: Referendum against the extension of free movement to nationals of Bulgaria and Romania, and renewal of the Bilateral Agreements I.

17 May 2009: Referendum against the introduction of biometric passports (indirectly against Schengen).

14 February 2014: SVP initiative "against mass immigration" (indirectly against free movement of nationals from the EU).

30 November 2014: *ECOPOP* initiative "overpopulation cap" (indirectly against free movement of nationals from the EU).

25 November 2018: SVP initiative on "Swiss law instead of foreign judges", a.k.a. "Initiative on self-determination" (indirectly against an IFA with the EU).

19 May 2019: Referendum supported by the SVP against the adoption of an EU directive regulating the possession of certain weapons more severely (indirectly against Schengen).

27 September 2020: SVP initiative on “Moderate immigration”, a.k.a. “Limitation initiative” (directly against free movement of nationals from the EU).

5 The question of immigration

A challenge to national identity and social cohesion

Sabine Jenni

Immigration and the country's relationship with the EU are among the biggest challenges for Swiss politics. Current developments in international and European politics arouse loud opposition led by the populist right. Consequently, the Swiss government has attempted to appease both sides, but this approach has become increasingly impractical in recent years. Nowadays, Switzerland is neither able to further develop its agreements with the EU, nor is it willing or able to fulfil the populist right's demands. The United Kingdom has found itself in a similar situation since the Brexit referendum in 2016 and can thus potentially learn useful lessons from the Swiss experience.

The impasse is also a consequence of the Swiss electorate's stance on immigration and the country's relationship with the EU being all but coherent. Opposition to both, that is immigration and a deepening relationship with the EU, stems partially from the same political groups led by the Swiss People's Party (SVP), the largest party in the national parliament. But at the same time, according to recent surveys, a high percentage of voters in favour of tougher limits on immigration are also in favour of access to international markets and the agreements with the European Union (e.g., Sciarini et al. 2015; Golder et al. 2017).

These preferences are difficult to translate into coherent policies as they are partly contradictory. The European Union is both the most important export market for Switzerland as well as the most important source of immigration. The vast majority of non-nationals entering the country today do so on the basis of the agreement on the free movement of persons (FMPA) between Switzerland and the EU. The EU has repeatedly defended free movement of persons as a non-negotiable part of Switzerland's access to the single market and has repeatedly threatened to abolish other crucial agreements if Switzerland does not respect the agreement.

The crucial role of immigration in the debate on European integration is common to both Switzerland and the United Kingdom. As this chapter shows, however, there are major differences between the two countries: they are related to the political system and the political culture, but also to migration history and policy. Nevertheless, the Swiss case offers a significant experience, which may be useful to a post-Brexit United Kingdom and other European countries with influential immigration-sceptic political parties.

In a first step, this chapter analyses the Switzerland–EU agreements that are related to immigration, comparing them to the scope of the respective policies in the EU. It shows that regarding free movement rights, Switzerland has preserved small but substantial limitations compared to the scope of the rights in the EU, protecting the domestic workforce and limiting social rights for EU citizens. These would be reduced were Switzerland to approve the institutional framework agreement (IFA) as drafted at the time of writing. Regarding Schengen and Dublin policies, Switzerland's association does not differ with regard to policies, but with regard to its institutional integration.

In a second step, the agreements with the EU related to immigration are analysed regarding their effect on Switzerland's immigration policies and on migration movements. The FMPA changed Switzerland's immigration policies, introducing a distinct and more favourable treatment of nationals from EU member states compared to immigrants from the rest of the world. The association to Schengen and Dublin, by contrast, required virtually no substantial policy changes, as Switzerland had already adapted its policies to international developments well before Schengen and Dublin became part of EU legislation.

With regard to migration movements, the FMPA had the strongest effect among the three immigration-related agreements. The FMPA and domestic policy changes had the effect that labour market-driven immigration today comes almost exclusively from the EU/EFTA states. The descriptive statistics analysed in this contribution indicate that the FMPA-related immigration is heavily influenced by the economic cycle and the development of the labour market, though with considerable regional differences. After unprecedented peaks in the years of the economic crisis in Europe, peaks that were also observable for example in the UK, yearly total net immigration has gone back since 2015 to the level of 1990.

The chapter concludes with an analysis of Switzerland's most important challenge when it comes to the future of its relations with the EU: the sources of domestic opposition to the agreements with the EU in the field of immigration and the role of direct democracy in the Swiss political system.

Swiss–EU relations and immigration

The relationship between Switzerland and the European Union is based on numerous sectoral agreements with different purposes and legal principles (see Schwok, this volume). Three of the most salient and controversial agreements deal with immigration policy: the Agreement on the Free Movement of Persons (FMPA), which entered into force in 2002, and the Schengen (SAA) and Dublin Association Agreements (DAA), which entered into force in 2008.

The immigration-related agreements are among the most important agreements between Switzerland and the EU and were the result of package deals. The FMPA was part of a package deal called "Bilaterals I" (see Schwok, this volume). It fulfilled both Switzerland's aim to secure sectoral access to the EU's single market, and the EU's wish that free movement of persons be part and parcel of market access (Dupont and Sciarini 2007). The Schengen and Dublin agreements were part of a package deal called "Bilaterals II" and were part of the deal at Switzerland's request, as the latter was concerned with its security (BR 1988, 1994) and the EU offered association to Schengen and Dublin in exchange for Switzerland's cooperation in other sensitive areas such as the taxation of savings (Lavenex 2006; Afonso and Maggetti 2007).

The plans announced by the British government for post-Brexit relations with the European Union show that the United Kingdom aims to have no, or minimal, common rules on immigration with the EU (HMG 2020). In the areas of border control ("Schengen") and asylum ("Dublin") this is nothing new, as the UK has had an opt-out in these areas. The Swiss and UK situations are rather different for practical reasons: Switzerland has land borders with four EU member states which have been very permeable for a long time before the abolition of border controls was even imagined at the European level, while the United Kingdom is an archipelago, which makes it much easier to control its borders autonomously.

The opposite is the case for the principle of the free movement of persons. Not only was the UK one of the EU member states with the most liberal stances on the free movement of persons – for example, contrary to most other old member states, it granted free movement rights to citizens from the new Eastern European member states without a transition phase in 2004 (BBC 2020). As the plans for UK–EU relations aim for tight economic relations, the Swiss case shows how these can be dependent on the free movement of persons. Accepting such free movement of persons was the most significant price Switzerland had to pay to develop economic relations with the EU more ambitious than a traditional free trade agreement for goods.

Until now, the free movement of persons principle is part and parcel of Switzerland's access to the EU's market. The FMPA is legally linked to the other agreements of the Bilaterals I package. If one of the seven agreements should be abrogated, the others would be automatically abrogated as well, a provision colloquially called the "guillotine clause". This clause targets the FMPA in particular, as it is the only Bilaterals I agreement to experience opposition since it entered into force. The guillotine clause is an early manifestation of the EU's stance that the free movement policy cannot be separated from sectoral access to its single market – a position it reaffirmed in recent years, demanding that the FMPA be covered by a new IFA agreement alongside other market access agreements.

Although the abolition of border controls is often interpreted as the perfect embodiment of the free movement of persons, Switzerland's association to Schengen is not legally linked to the FMPA (Ferraro 2013). The SAA and DAA are only legally linked with each other. While it is possible to pursue a free movement of persons policy outside the border-control-free Schengen space (e.g. Switzerland prior to 2008 or the United Kingdom until the end of the transitory phase after its exit from the EU on 31 January 2020), a border-control-free zone without free movement rights barely makes sense.

The Swiss–EU agreement on the free movement of persons

With the FMPA, Switzerland accepted almost completely the EU's free movement rights and policies. The free movement rights encompass the right of EU citizens to enter another member state, take up residence, accept a job or become self-employed without the need for permits. Migrants are protected against discrimination on the grounds of nationality, benefit from recognition of their professional qualifications and coordinated social security systems. These rights are also granted to family members. Only the "small print" of these rights reveals minor, but politically important, deviations compared to equivalent rights within the EU. There are two reasons that explain the differences.

One reason is that the FMPA is modelled on EU legislation in force at the time of signature of the FMPA. The most important legal development in the EU since the signature of the FMPA was the Union citizenship directive (2004/38/EC). The right to free movement finally lost its mainly economic character and became a basic right of all Union citizens. EU legislation is increasingly interpreted in a way that not only prohibits discrimination on the grounds of nationality, but also aims to minimise restrictions and deterrents to free movement. Most concretely, the directive automatically grants movers permanent residence rights after five years of legal residency, and, as a consequence, access to the social security system on the same terms as nationals (Baldoni 2003; Tomkin 2011).

The other reason is due to Switzerland's incomplete access to the EU's market. The difference regards posted workers. Posting of workers facilitates the cross-border provision of services, because some services can only be provided by deploying employees to the country of the service recipient. However, as in Swiss–EU relations the provision of services is not generally liberalised, but only facilitated in specific sectors or for specific purposes, the posting of workers too is limited (for an overview of the legal scope of Switzerland's market access, see Tobler et al. 2010).

The FMPA allows the posting of workers from an EU country to Switzerland, referring to the outdated 1996 directive on the posting of workers. The general EU principle that posted workers remain employed in their employer's country and consequently contribute to and receive benefits from the social security systems of their country of employment applies to postings from the EU to Switzerland and vice versa. But postings to and from Switzerland are limited to a maximum of 90 days per calendar year, while the 2018 EU directive allows postings of up to 24 months (2018/957/ EU).

Moreover, while transposing the now outdated EU directive on posted workers, Switzerland adopted various control and sanctioning measures to combat wage and social dumping known as "flanking" or "accompanying" measures. They were the trade unions' condition for their support for the FMPA, without which the agreement would not have been approved at the polls in 2000. The aim of these flanking measures is similar to a principle included in the amended 2018 EU directive on posted workers, namely that wages and working conditions of posted workers must correspond to those of local employees (e.g. Dauner et al. 2018).

The EU has repeatedly asked Switzerland to remove these differences between Swiss–EU free movement rights and internal EU rights. When the EU asked Switzerland to transpose the Union citizenship directive into the FMPA, mainly in order to automatically grant EU citizens a permanent residence permit after five years of legal residence, Switzerland refused, arguing that the FMPA covered only the free movement of workers (e.g. Epiney and Gammenthaler 2008).

Similarly, the EU has repeatedly criticised the flanking measures for imposing bureaucratic hurdles on posting firms that create deterrents to the free provision of services. But legal scholars argue that, unlike EU law, the FMPA only clearly prohibits discrimination, but not measures likely to restrict free movement without being discriminatory (e.g. Tobler et al. 2010).

In the absence of rules for the updating of the FMPA and a dispute settlement mechanism, Switzerland for a long time simply ignored the EU's requests. Situations such as this one were the reasons why the EU evaluated Switzerland's agreement-based access to the single market less and less favourably over time (CoEU 2012; 2014; 2016; 2017; 2019). As a solution, the EU and Switzerland negotiated an IFA. The Union citizenship directive and Switzerland's flanking measures were a core controversy in the negotiations (Epiney and Hehemann 2019; Tobler and Beglinger 2020).

A look at the British case shows some similarities and differences with the Swiss case. A similarity is the very general unease of some voters and politicians in both Switzerland and the UK to grant foreign nationals the same social security rights enjoyed by their own citizens. The limitation of welfare benefits to workers from the EU was one of the main aims, and negotiation successes, of David Cameron, when he re-negotiated the terms of UK's EU membership prior to the 2016 referendum (Weiss and Blockmanns 2016). It also lies at the heart of Switzerland's unwillingness to transpose the citizenship directive, which would extend the social rights of movers.

An important difference is that, after Cameron's negotiation successes to limit welfare benefits became obsolete because of the Brexit referendum, subsequent British governments clearly signalled their intention to abolish free movement, while maintaining not only the freedom to provide services, but even coordination of social security systems (HMG 2018; 2020). The coordination of social security systems is important for movers within the EU, because it ensures moving workers that periods of contributions to social security systems in other countries are recognised by the country of current employment and/or residence (e.g., Baldoni 2003).

An important difference between Switzerland's free movement regimes and the concessions Cameron obtained, concerns the flanking measures, as Switzerland has better managed to protect its domestic labour force from undue competition. The focus of the flanking measures is not to limit the rights of EU citizens (e.g. limiting access to welfare benefits), but to enforce their right to the same wages as local employees, which is of special importance for Switzerland, where salaries and living costs are much higher than in the surrounding countries.

The Schengen and Dublin Association Agreements

Unlike the UK, Switzerland is not an archipelago and feared that it would become a haven for asylum seekers and organised crime when surrounding European states started to cooperate in areas of border control, police coordination, related information exchange and asylum policy. The policies were adopted in the 1980s and 1990s as parts of separate agreements named after their cities of signature ("Schengen" and "Dublin" agreements) which are still used for the SAA and the DAA with Switzerland. In the EU, the policies today are assembled under Title V on the "Area of Freedom, Security, and Justice" of the Treaty on the European Union (Wüger 2013).

The Dublin policy consists of a handful of EU regulations, assigning responsibility for a person seeking asylum to the Dublin-signatory state where s/he was first registered by the authorities. A rejection of the asylum request is valid for all Dublin states. In order to implement this principle, the Eurodac database for the exchange of information on asylum seekers was established and several directives defining common standards for the treatment and support of asylum seekers, for asylum procedures, and for granting protection to persons not qualifying as refugees according to the Geneva Convention were adopted.

The DAA covers responsibilities regarding asylum procedures and access to the Eurodac database, including the EU's data protection legislation relevant for the treatment of asylum seekers' personal data. Switzerland's administrative cooperation with the European Asylum Support Office, an agency coordinating member states' policies and supporting them in implementing Dublin directives, is based on an additional agreement that entered into force in 2016 (Epiney et al. 2007; Wüger 2013; Tobler 2017).

The policies referred to by the name "Schengen" cover a lot more than a handful of legal acts, and also more measures than the Dublin policies. At the core of Schengen remains the abolition of systematic border controls between Schengen states. However, most policies associated with Schengen are measures mitigating potential security risks of a border-control-free area. In particular, they concern border security between Schengen and non-Schengen states (so-called "external border") and combatting organised crime, most importantly drug and weapons smuggling, and by measures such as police cooperation and legal assistance (Ferraro 2013: 1).

In practice, the association to Schengen means that Switzerland no longer systematically checks persons crossing its borders and must distinguish between Schengen and non-Schengen nationals at its airports, where it holds responsibility to protect the Schengen area's external border. Identity documents and visas issued by the Swiss authorities must correspond to Schengen standards (e.g. biometric data). Tourist visas issued by any Schengen state are also valid for Switzerland, as are tourist visas issued by Switzerland for the whole Schengen area. Longer-term visas remain a national matter, but third-state nationals still have the right to make short-term trips to other Schengen states without obtaining additional visas (Epiney et al. 2007).

Switzerland is virtually a full-fledged member of the Schengen and Dublin country group. Unlike in the case of free movement, there are no substantial policy differences between Switzerland and the EU member states. What arouses controversies and criticism in Switzerland, and what is instructive for the UK post-Brexit, is Switzerland's obligation to transpose new EU legislation without having the right to vote in the EU decision-making process. This is an important difference compared to the FMPA, and to other earlier agreements with the EU. Such an obligation challenges the democratic legitimacy of transposed Schengen legislation.

Such practical problems are related to the fact that Schengen nowadays covers a broad range of policies, and it is not always easy to establish whether a new EU legal act is relevant for Switzerland's Schengen association. The European Commission normally decides right at the draft stage whether a legal act is relevant for Schengen. Switzerland decides based on the legal basis of an EU act, the text of the SAA, and whether it participated in the elaboration of the act as foreseen by the SAA (Tobler 2017).

The challenge for democratic legitimacy is that Switzerland committed to transposing all new relevant legislation in exchange for participation, but not voting rights, in the elaboration of new legal acts (so-called "decision-shaping"). While the majority of legal changes fall within the competence of the government and are of minor significance, some are substantial, need approval by the Swiss parliament, and can be challenged by referendum. Respect for the domestic decision-making process is explicitly foreseen in the SAA and DAA, but the agreements can be terminated if Switzerland fails to transpose relevant new legislation. The freedom to say "no" to a Schengen act in parliament or in a referendum is thus limited, as a "no" always threatens to affect not only the act in question but the whole Schengen association (Jenni 2018).

While Schengen and Dublin policies may not play a central role in the planning of UK's post-Brexit relations with the EU, the institutional setting of Switzerland's Schengen and Dublin association is relevant. Switzerland already accepted similar institutional rules in areas such as custom security checks and the automatic exchange of information, which are closely related to the smooth functioning of trade, and in the near future it will have to accept overarching obligations to abide by changing EU legislation also for its basic market access agreements (Epiney 2018; Pirker 2019).

Immigration policies and migration movements

Statistics describe Switzerland as an immigration country, but this description neither resonates with the self-perception of many Swiss citizens, nor with Switzerland's immigration policies, at least until recently.

Switzerland has become a "guest worker" country since World War II, because of labour shortage and an economic boom. In order to meet the demands of its economy, it has pursued a liberal policy as far as access to its labour market is concerned. For a long time, though, immigration was perceived as a temporary phenomenon, justifying restrictive policies regarding permanent residency and social and political rights for immigrants (Afonso 2005).

According to population statistics, 35.9% of Swiss residents have foreign roots (2015 data, Sarrasin et al. 2018: 3) and 25% of Swiss residents do not have Swiss citizenship (2016 data, BfS 2018b: 4). While both point to past immigration movements, the latter is also a consequence of strict naturalisation rules: half of Swiss residents without a Swiss passport have lived in Switzerland for ten years or more (ibid.). Switzerland is the European country with the second highest share of foreign-born residents after Luxembourg (2016 data, BfS 2018b: 4).

Compared to Switzerland, the percentage of foreigners among the resident population in the UK started to increase much later – only in the last few decades of the 20th century (MW 2014). Also, with just short of 10% of non-citizens among the resident population, the UK ranks around the average for European countries (Eurostat 2019).

The agreements with the EU influenced Switzerland's immigration policy and migration movements. Most importantly, Switzerland started to treat non-nationals from EU/EFTA countries differently and more favourably compared to non-nationals from the rest of the world. As a consequence, immigrants from the European Union quickly and massively outnumbered immigrants from other countries. While immigration had served the needs of the Swiss economy throughout the 20th century, the labour market became even more decisive as the driving force of migration movements in the wake of the FMPA (SECO 2017).

The effects of the FMPA on immigration policies and numbers

For most of the 20th century, Switzerland's immigration policies were best described as part of its "politics of national identity" (Riano and Wastl-Walter 2006: 1). The Swiss–EU agreements changed the logic of these policies for EU and EFTA state citizens. They are no longer subject to the law on foreigners. Their rights to enter and work in Switzerland are granted by the FMPA.

Similar to the transition phases old member states could invoke after the accession of east-central European countries to the EU, Switzerland also maintained annual quotas, national preference rules and prior examination of contract and working conditions during transition periods after the entry into force of the FMPA in 2002. These transition periods expired in 2014 for the old member states and those which joined in 2004, in 2019 for Bulgaria and Romania, and will expire in 2027 for Croatia. For Swiss employers, it is almost as easy to hire an EU or EFTA national as a Swiss national. As seen above, the UK, as a then "old" EU member state, did not invoke any transitory limitations to immigration after successive enlargement rounds (BBC 2020).

The FMPA's focus on labour market-driven immigration does not run counter to Switzerland's immigration policy, as operated in the 20th century, which was primarily based, as we have seen, on the needs of the Swiss economy. But the way the FMPA enshrines this in law was new for Switzerland. It marked an end to sectoral and regional immigration quotas, as the FMPA grants the right to immigration automatically to any EU worker.

Before the FMPA, the Swiss government, based on the needs of the economy, defined each year immigration quotas for specific regions and economic sectors, and granted time-limited work permits to make sure immigrants would "rotate" and not put down roots in the country (D'Amato 2008). The FMPA thus challenged the economic and political logic of Switzerland's policy of liberal entry but restrictive rights.

Economically, the reluctance to grant immigrant workers longer-term or even permanent residency, coming with limited rights to family reunification, made the immigrants a "buffer" for the Swiss economy. When the economy needed less labour, permits were not renewed, and immigrants had to leave the country, thus keeping unemployment down. Politically, the reluctance to grant immigrants permanent residency and social rights fostered segregation between foreigners and Swiss citizens, supported the view of immigration as a temporary phenomenon, and appeased immigration sceptics (Riano and Wastl-Walter 2006).

In terms of immigrant rights, the FMPA required that Switzerland abolish short-term work permits (seasonal and annual permits) and participate in coordinating social security systems. However, EU and EFTA nationals' right to social security benefits in Switzerland remain linked to their economic activity. They are entitled to maternity or unemployment allowances or similar, but they do not have access to social assistance unless they have permanent residency.

Switzerland's migration statistics reflect the entry into force of the FMPA, its subsequent extension to new EU member states, as well as economic trends in Switzerland and in the EU. The effects of the FMPA are clearest with regard to the country of origin, the qualifications, and the labour force participation rate of immigrants. With regard to the number of immigrants, the effects of the FMPA must be considered alongside the economic cycle and labour market developments.

Figure 5.1 shows the net total of immigrants (immigrants minus emigrants) to Switzerland per year for the period 1991–2017. It distinguishes between the total number of immigrants per year (grey-shaded area), the number of immigrants from countries that belong to the EU or EFTA (solid line), and the number of immigrants from other countries (dashed line).

Figure 5.1 shows that the numbers of EU and EFTA immigrants fluctuate more than those for other countries of origin and that this difference becomes more pronounced after 2002, the year when the FMPA entered into force. While the FMPA facilitates labour market-driven immigration for nationals of EU and EFTA states, third-country nationals can enter Switzerland only if they are highly qualified professionals or refugees or family members of Swiss residents. The first category concerns a small group of people, while the second two are not labour market driven (Afonso 2005; D'Amato 2008; SECO 2018).

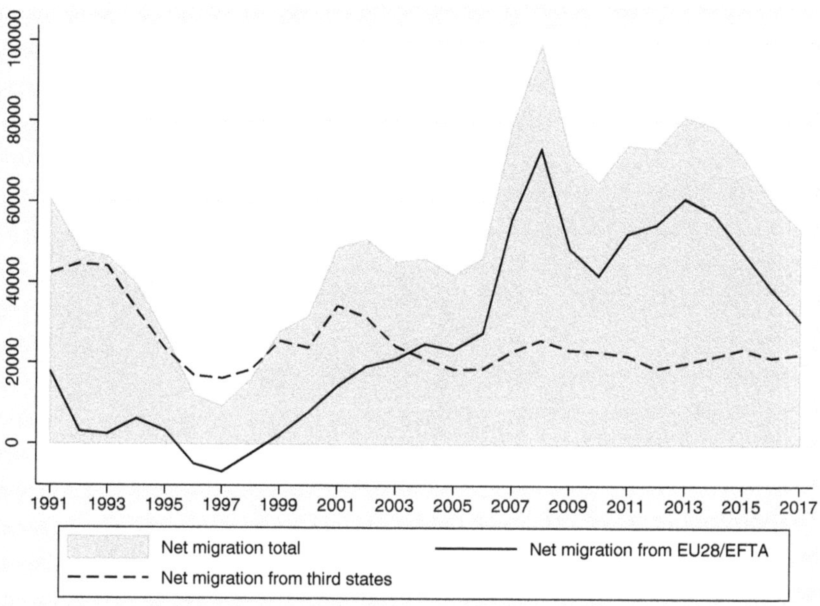

Figure 5.1 Net migration to Switzerland 1991–2017. Note: Net migration means the number of immigrants minus the number of emigrants. Source: Federal State Secretariat for Migration, ZEMIS; graph by the author.

Civil servants and some politicians agree that the number of immigrants has been influenced more strongly by Switzerland's economic cycle than by its immigration policies (Bühler 2018; Lampart et al. 2018). Research findings support these statements, as various measures such as quotas, national preference rules and similar did not lead to a significant reduction in the number of immigrants in the second half of the 20th century (Afonso 2014). Nor does Figure 5.1 show an upward trend following the end of the first FMPA transition period in 2014.

Migration movements must thus also be analysed in light of economic development and Switzerland's wealth. For most of the time since the turn of the 20th century, Switzerland's GDP per capita has been significantly higher than that of France and Germany – or the UK (Zürcher 2010: 11). This has made Switzerland attractive to immigrants.

The development of Switzerland's economy for the relevant period before and after the entry into force of the FMPA in 2002 is illustrated by Figure 5.2 (growth of Switzerland's GDP per capita 1991–2017) and Figure 5.3 (unemployment rate 1991–2017). In the 1990s, Switzerland experienced a slowdown. This slowdown was moderate compared to previous recessions in the 20th century (the GDP growth rate remained positives), but it was followed by an increase in unemployment to a level Switzerland had last experienced during the Second World War

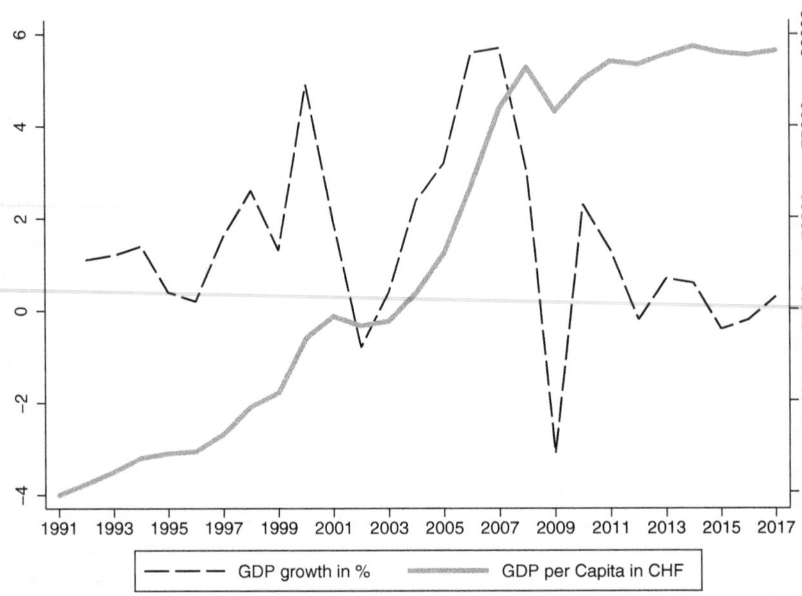

Figure 5.2 Development of Switzerland's gross domestic product 1991–2017. Note: Real GDP growth. Source: Federal Office for Statistics; graph by the author.

(D'Amato 2008: 181; Zürcher 2010). Figure 5.3 shows that unemployment rates increased from 2% in 1991 to almost 5% in 1997.

Unemployment rates increased so sharply because net immigration reacted less flexibly to the economic recession in the 1990s than, for example, in the 1970s. By 1990, 60% of non-Swiss nationals had acquired permanent residence permits (compared to 20% in 1970). Although the policy of short-term permits was still in place, it had lost some of its effect as a buffer for the labour market well before it was abolished with the FMPA (Afonso 2005). But net immigration still reacted to the worsening labour market situation in Switzerland. Figure 5.1 shows that the recession was followed by negative net migration numbers from the EU/EFTA states between 1995 and 1999, meaning that more people left than entered Switzerland (Figure 5.1). Overall net migration remained positive. Since 2000, net migration from the EU/ EFTA has remained positive (Figure 5.1).

The immigration peaks for EU/EFTA nationals in 2008 and 2013 are related to the financial and economic crisis, which affected Switzerland less severely and from which it recovered more quickly than other European states, making Switzerland an attractive destination for people from countries with rising unemployment. The decrease in net immigration after 2013 can be explained by the slowing down of the Swiss economy, related partially to the appreciation of the Swiss franc against the euro as a consequence of the eurozone crisis (SECO

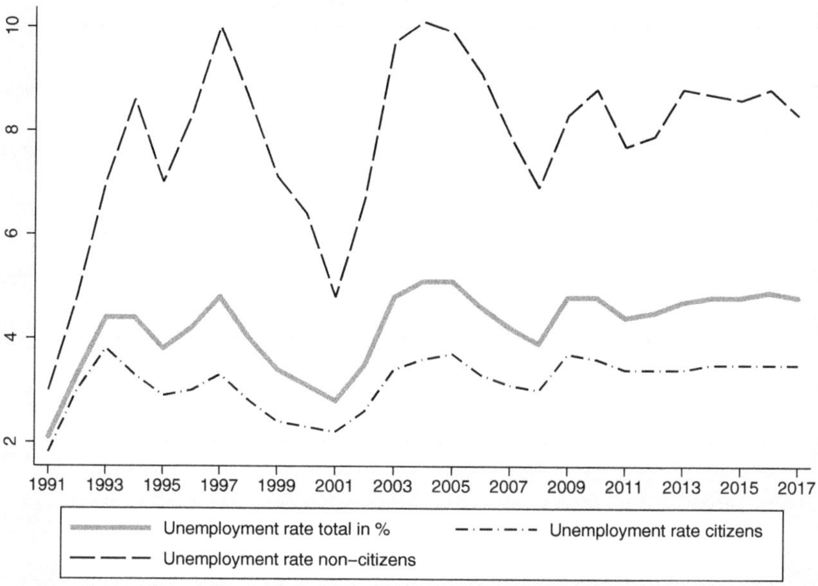

Figure 5.3 Unemployment rate 1991–2017. Note: Unemployment rate according to the definition of the International Labour Organisation ILO. These rates are between 1 and 1.5% higher than official unemployment rates, which count only persons registered as unemployed. Source: Federal Office for Statistics; graph by the author.

2018). In a very similar way, net migration numbers to the UK increased in recent decades in parallel with comparatively higher GDP growth (BBC 2020).

After the increase in the 1990s, average unemployment rates remained above 3% (except for 2000 and 2001) and have stayed above 4% since 2003 (Figure 5.3). This higher level of unemployment is mostly affecting non-Swiss citizens. Among them, unemployment rates are two to three times higher than among Swiss citizens. Among the non-Swiss, unemployment rates for third-state nationals are significantly higher than unemployment rates for EU/EFTA nationals (e.g., 8% for third-state nationals compared to 5.5% for EU/EFTA and 2.4% for Swiss citizens in 2016, see SECO 2018: 59). This points to immigrants from the EU and EFTA being better integrated into the labour market than third-state nationals, which again shows that FMPA-related migration is driven by the labour market.

The effects of the FMPA and the development of the labour market diverge across regions. The French- and Italian-speaking cantons experienced higher net immigration and higher unemployment rates than the German-speaking ones. Also, in the French- and Italian-speaking cantons EU and EFTA nationals more frequently work without actually immigrating. They do so mostly as cross-border commuters, but also as posted workers or short-term employees. These forms of employment are also considerably facilitated by the FMPA.

On the aggregate level, only 6.2% of the Swiss labour force consisted of cross-border commuters in 2017, but this reached a maximum of 28.4% in the Italian-speaking canton of Ticino (SECO 2018). The "flanking" measures against social and wage dumping, discussed above as one of the important characteristics of Switzerland's way of regulating free movement, target these employment forms and their potential weakening thus disproportionally affects these regions (see also chapters by Mueller and Mazzoleni in this volume).

In terms of labour market competition between immigrants and Swiss citizens, the Swiss State Secretariat for Economic Affairs (SECO) finds that immigrants from the EU/EFTA complement the labour supply of Swiss citizens rather than competing against it for several reasons. As a result, labour market participation rates for Swiss citizens increased between 2010 and 2017 in all regions. The professional profiles of EU/EFTA immigrants show that they are clearly overrepresented among high- and low-qualified employees and that they generally hold jobs corresponding to their education level.

This satisfies the needs of the Swiss economy. Given that, since the 2005 revision of the foreigners law, only highly qualified third-country nationals can obtain work permits in Switzerland, and as most Swiss citizens obtain professional qualifications after secondary school, low-qualified workers must be recruited from EU/EFTA states. With some highly competitive multi-national companies and good universities, the Swiss economy requires more highly qualified workers than are available in the country.

The effects of Schengen and Dublin on immigration policies and numbers

In contrast to the FMPA, the Schengen and Dublin associations did not require substantial changes to Switzerland's immigration policies. Switzerland already had permeable borders before the SAA. In some Swiss border regions, a high degree of control-free movement was achieved well before the abolition of border control was envisaged in Europe. Moreover, Switzerland already had bilateral agreements with neighbouring states ensuring far-reaching police cooperation (Lavenex 2006). The abolition of border controls brought about by Schengen was thus a decision with considerable, but mainly symbolical and political, weight for Switzerland.

Similarly, Switzerland's asylum legislation had provided for responsibility for an asylum seeker by a single state since 1990 (Lavenex 2006: 6). This was one of the results of a gradual formalisation and tightening of asylum rules and procedures in Switzerland in the latter half of the 20th century. Switzerland had a liberal and welcoming asylum practice based only on the Geneva Convention when people from communist countries sought asylum in the 1950s and 1960s. In the 1970s and 1980s, with the arrival of asylum seekers from more distant countries and in increased numbers, asylum became a controversial issue. In 1981,

Switzerland adopted a law on asylum that drastically reduced the number of asylum seekers recognised as refugees (D'Amato 2008).

From the 1980s onwards, Switzerland also started to cooperate with like-minded countries on matters of asylum and migration. Since signing the Dublin convention in the 1990s, Switzerland had aimed to become a member, mainly because assigning responsibility for an asylum seeker to a single state would reduce the number of asylum seekers. Otherwise, as a country in the geographical centre of Europe, Switzerland would have become the country of second chance for asylum seekers rejected by a Dublin state. Therefore, it adjusted its policy early on (Lavenex 2006). The UK, thanks to its geographical separation, is naturally in a different position and never adhered fully to the Schengen and Dublin systems.

The Schengen and Dublin associations influence the number of cross-border movements of tourists with a Schengen visa, and the entry and exit of those seeking asylum. The number of these categories of movers is much lower than the number of workers crossing borders based on the FMPA.

The net migration numbers illustrated in Figure 5.1 were not interpreted in terms of the effects of the entry into force of the SAA and DAA, because the reported numbers only cover persons that have stay permits for periods above 12 months. Persons that enter Switzerland with a Schengen visa are usually only allowed to stay for shorter periods. Persons in the asylum application procedure are counted only once they stay for more than 12 months. The Schengen and Dublin agreements thus have modest effects on the reported numbers.

They are, however, significant for the types of cross-border movements they regulate. Since Switzerland started to publish visa statistics in 2015, over 87% of visas issued by Swiss consulates around the world were Schengen. This means that the majority of entries of third-country nationals concern short stays, because visas for longer stays are still national. Of the Schengen visas, more than half were tourists, while a significant portion were on business or to visit families and friends (SEM 2018).

With regard to association to the Dublin agreement, figures for the number of asylum seekers which Switzerland sends back to other Dublin states and the number it takes back are of interest. Figure 5.4 shows that the number of asylum seekers that another Dublin state agreed to take back (Dublin out approved) is higher than the number to whom asylum was granted with the exemption of 2014 and 2018. Dublin is thus beneficial to Switzerland if one assumes that having responsibility for fewer asylum seekers is an aim to be pursued.

But Figure 5.4 also shows a considerable discrepancy between approved transfers (dotted and dashed lines) and actually transferred persons (solid lines), both for persons Switzerland sent away and those it took back. In recent years, the trend mostly points to a change in the relationship between send-back possibilities and take-back obligations. Since 2016, the number of outgoing Dublin transfers has fallen, and the number of incoming transfers risen. While it is too early to assess whether these figures reverse the trend, they must be interpreted in light of a steep decrease in asylum requests since 2015, and the delay incurred by some Dublin

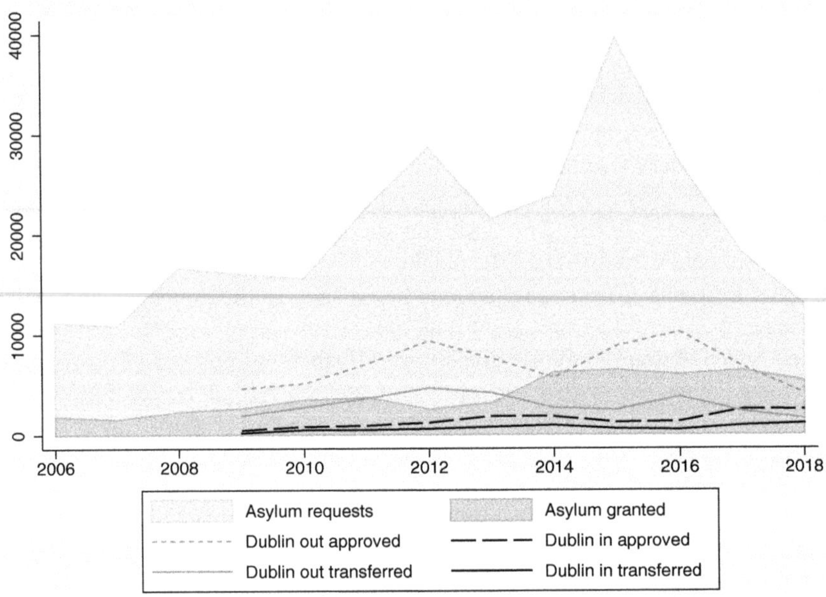

Figure 5.4 Asylum numbers 2006–2018. Source: Federal State Secretariat for Migration; graph by the author.

states in processing asylum cases after the large increase in asylum requests that peaked in 2015 (mainly Germany; see Schäfer 2018).

Current challenges and political conflicts

Statistics show clear and regionally diversified, but overall non-dramatic, effects of immigration on the labour market situation of Swiss citizens, and even suggest that the Swiss labour market not only needs foreign workers but also absorbs EU/EFTA nationals well. Nonetheless, immigration and immigration policies lie at the heart of recent controversies between Switzerland and the European Union. The FMPA faces considerable domestic opposition and the Schengen association is fragile because of its institutional setup.

The domestic opposition to immigration-related agreements

Immigration and the respective Swiss–EU agreements face opposition from the populist right, which aims to restrict immigration for the sake of preserving a nationally defined culture, and because it emphasises solidarity with fellow citizens over solidarity with humans in general. The stance of the populist right is comparable to that of populist right parties in other European countries, including the UK. In contrast, the left has been part of a pro-European coalition, not least thanks to the measures against wage and social dumping accompanying the free movement of persons from the EU. In recent years, with the EU demanding some of these measures be weakened, the FMPA is also under critical scrutiny from the left and potentially broader groups, as the EU requires the extensions of the rights granted to EU citizens (see above on the scope of the FMPA).

The populist right in Switzerland is mainly represented by the SVP and aims to end free movement, re-introduce quotas for immigrants, and occasionally calls for a re-introduction of border controls. The rhetoric usually does not distinguish between Europeans and third-state nationals, though a deliberate anti-Muslim stance to some degree reflects a more negative attitude towards culturally more "distant" persons.

The populist right opposes the FMPA not only because of its anti-immigration stance, but also because of a principled opposition to European integration, including the deepening of Swiss–EU relations through new sectoral agreements or an IFA. The fear is that any kind of closer relationship with the EU would undermine aspects of Switzerland's political system such as federalism, neutrality, and direct democracy, all fundamental symbols of Switzerland's political identity (Christin and Trechsel 2002; Theiler 2004). While it is undisputable that European integration challenges aspects of the Swiss political system, the populist right and probably broader groups overlook that the current arrangement also undermines the democratic legitimacy of some institutions. The main reason is that Switzerland has no decision rights at the EU level but is in many areas *de facto* compelled to abide by EU law (Jenni 2016).

Criticism from the left, namely trade unions and social democrats, concerns increasing competition in the labour market. When the FMPA was to be adopted, free-market and left forces thus agreed control and sanction measures to ensure that firms posting workers from the EU to Switzerland respect local labour regulations. As seen, these "flanking" or "accompanying" measures are intended to protect Swiss wages and ultimately local workers against wage and social dumping.

Switzerland's trade unions firmly oppose any weakening of these flanking measures and they consider the rules provided for in the draft IFA to constitute such a weakening. The IFA would introduce rules for the updating of Swiss–EU market access agreements, including the FMPA. Although the EU granted Switzerland some concessions regarding anti-dumping measures, which go beyond what is allowed in the EU, the left criticises the weakening and fears the increasing influence of the CJEU (Tobler and Beglinger 2020).

The free-market forces are generally in favour of the free movement of persons, but sceptical towards extending social rights. For the time being, some aspects of the Union citizenship directives, which currently regulates important free movement rights in the EU but is not part of the FMPA, could be considered such an extension of social rights. At the time of writing, the draft IFA neither explicitly obliges Switzerland to transpose the citizenship directive, nor explicitly excludes the directive from a future updating of the Swiss–EU version of free movement (Gmür 2018; Tobler and Beglinger 2020).

The role of direct democracy

Immigration and the relationship between Switzerland and the EU have repeatedly been subject of popular votes. Switzerland has an extensive system of direct democracy, whereby most bills adopted by parliament, including federal laws and international agreements, can be challenged in referendums. In addition, Swiss citizens can propose constitutional amendments that must be brought to the polls, an instrument called "popular initiative".

Direct democracy has played an ambiguous role in shaping Switzerland's immigration and European policy. The agreement-based relationship with the European Union has been approved in five popular votes since 1972 (see chapters by Sciarini and Mueller in this volume). More ambitious forms of integration, such as those envisaged by membership of the EEA or EU, as requested by a popular initiative, were rejected in 1992 and 2001, respectively. Since the beginning of the 21st century, an alliance bringing together the government, the business organisations, and the centrist and left parties has been the necessary condition for winning popular votes on closer relations with the EU (Jenni 2020).

The populist right has used popular initiatives to put the issues of immigration on the political agenda since the 1970s. In the 1970s, 1980s, and 1990s, all nine popular initiatives aiming to reduce immigration were rejected at the polls. The first major success of the populist right in a popular vote was the referendum against the EEA agreement in 1992 (see Kreis, this volume). Since 2009, three popular initiatives by the SVP restricting the rights of non-Swiss citizens or aiming at limiting immigration have been adopted, and two anti-immigration initiatives were rejected.

The most recent, the initiative "against mass immigration", led to an unprecedented conflict with the EU. The initiative required the parliament to introduce quotas for immigrants and re-negotiate the FMPA. It was approved by a tiny majority of 50.3% of voters on 9 February 2014. Although the initiators downplayed the relationship in the referendum campaign, the initiative clearly targeted foreigners from the EU and EFTA states, as immigration from all other countries is subject to quotas and limited by a national preference rule (Najy and Schwok 2018). The EU not only refused to re-negotiate the FMPA, but punished Switzerland by refusing to renew its participation in the framework programmes for research, as Horizon 2020, and audio-visual production (MEDIA). As a result, the Swiss parliament adopted a very soft national preference rule for job vacancies and did not implement the initiative literally (Maiani and Boillet 2017). EU and EFTA nationals are still not subject to quotas while Switzerland was eventually re-admitted with full rights to Horizon 2020 and is negotiating participation in "Creative Europe", MEDIA's successor programme.

The Schengen association has come under stress by direct democracy instruments as well. When Switzerland had to transpose the directive on biometric passports, parliamentary approval was challenged by a referendum, which, however, failed (Tobler 2017). The same happened to the new firearms directive (2017/853), which qualifies as Schengen legislation and had to be transposed into Swiss law

(BBC 2019). An SVP popular initiative to end the free movement of persons with the EU was turned down by a large majority in September 2020. Whether or not Switzerland's association will develop as smoothly as in the past depends on the politicisation of new Schengen legislation.

Any comparison between popular votes on EU related issues in Switzerland and referendums in other European countries, including those on EU issues in EU member countries, must consider the very crucial institutional differences. In Switzerland, direct democracy votes are regular events occurring more than once a year and are embedded in the parliamentary decision-making process. This is very different form a "once-in-a-lifetime" vote such as the Brexit referendum in the UK (Heidbreder et al. 2018; see also Church, this volume).

An overview of the political conflict lines

In recent years, with immigration becoming more hotly debated in EU member states as different as Germany and Hungary, and with the UK taking its first steps negotiating with the EU as a non-member state, the Swiss experience became interesting and appealing to some political actors. While one indeed can learn from the Swiss and other third states cases, lessons learnt must be transferred cautiously and with a careful analysis of specific cases.

A first important consideration is that Switzerland's agreements with the EU, including the important FMPA were negotiated in the 1990s, with a smaller and less supranational EU. In recent years, the European Commission's attitude has become more uncompromising. Swiss diplomats experienced this in the negotiations over the IFA, which, after several years spent on preparatory work, lasted officially from 2014 to 2018. In a nutshell, the experienced Swiss negotiators obtained a fair result that retained some of the particularities of the Swiss form of free movement, at least for the time being. These could be compared to the concessions the EU made to David Cameron before the Brexit referendum.

But, in both cases, the concessions granted were not enough to appease domestic opposition to European integration, which in the two countries is closely related to a negative stance against immigration (e.g. Henderson et al. 2017). In Switzerland, the weakening of the flanking measures, and the danger of a later dispute on the citizenship directive fractured the pro-European coalition between centrist parties and the left, which won many popular votes on Europe.

At the time of writing, it is less clear than ever whether or not the Swiss government will sign the draft IFA, in order to forward it to the parliament and then to a popular vote. Not only are an increasing number of politicians advising the government to wait for the outcome of the negotiations between the EU and the UK on their future relationship, but these negotiations themselves were slowed down by the pandemic (Bondy et al. 2020).

In addition, the EU postponed the application of the new regulation of medical devices in order to prioritise the fight against the pandemic over regulatory adjustments (EC 2020b). In the months prior to the pandemic, the EU repeatedly threatened to veto the updating of a related Swiss–EU agreement in line with this new regulation in case Switzerland failed to finally sign the drafted IFA (Jenni 2020). With the postponed application, Switzerland has gained time.

The history of Swiss–EU relations shows that while large and overarching solutions like the EEA agreement, the institutional framework agreement, or a single agreement to regulate post-Brexit UK–EU relations may be very hard to obtain, a step-by-step approach is possible without full confrontation with the EU and brings some gains to both the third state and the EU. At the same time, European integration history teaches that step-by-step approaches were developed by accident and out of necessity, rather than by design. For example, it took two decades after the fateful "no" to the EEA for Switzerland and the EU to start negotiations on an overarching solution in the shape of the IFA. If we can learn anything from this history for the situation the UK finds itself in, it is that the EU will aim for an overarching solution as long as possible and agree to a patchwork of agreements only as a second-best choice. The current agreement proposals by the EU and the UK reflect this (Bondy et al. 2020).

However, this does not mean that the fundamental challenges of EU – third-state relationships – are off the table. One of these challenges is the close relationship between scepticism towards European integration and hostility to immigration. Immigration and its consequences will remain the main, and most controversial, issue in the discussions on a Swiss–EU IFA, also because the FMPA is closely linked to the cornerstone of Switzerland's access to the EU's single market. As described in the first section, the abolition of the FMPA could lead to the abolition of other Swiss–EU market access agreements. Therefore, the immigration-related provisions of an IFA must be weighed against the costs of a probable slow erosion of several market access agreements.

Currently, the British government aims for far-reaching market access, which in some aspects would go beyond what Switzerland enjoys (e.g. free provision of services), but principally excludes any form of free movement of persons (HMG 2020). In the light of Swiss experience, the British wish-list seems optimistic, to put it mildly. Swiss officials and politicians, with the exception of the populist right, agree that a free trade agreement could not in any case uphold the current tight economic relations and important economic gains for the Swiss economy (BR 2015).

The close connection between immigration and economic development is common to both Switzerland and the UK as third states, but also with other European countries with political actors with strong anti-immigration stances. This is a challenge for governments all over Europe, but the specifics of how to tackle this challenge partly depends on the political system. In Switzerland, with its permanent grand coalition government and extensive direct democracy, every successful step in European integration required a large supporting coalition. This coalition was first built in the 1990s when a "historic" compromise between free marketeers and the left paved the way for popular approval of the Bilaterals I package, including the FMPA.

This coalition has suffered considerably, as the draft IFA threatens to weaken the concessions made to the left to defuse potentially damaging consequences of the FMPA. This shows us that one must distinguish cultural from socio-economic reasons for immigration-scepticism. While nationalist-cultural scepticism is hard to appease with policy answers reconcilable with European integration, socio-economic reasons for immigration-scepticism depend on social policy. Here, it is bound to become a general European question how for example the lowest possible hurdles for the provision of services across borders should be weighed against social rights of service providers living in one state and working in another. Switzerland has had a political answer to that. The 2018 EU directive on posted workers in principle weighs the social rights higher than before (Epiney and Hehemann 2019). The question is whether the enforcement possibilities are strong enough.

The reason why this issue has become important in Switzerland earlier than in other European countries is, beside Switzerland having high immigration numbers, the fact that citizens had to express their preferences on European integration early on. The "package" of integration measures thus had to be more balanced than in countries where a majority government could decide on integration steps.

However, the challenge for political actors, and most importantly for the Swiss government, is mirrored across Europe. The challenge is not to repeat commonplaces about immigration and the relationship with the EU, but to explain to the voters the choice they have based on facts about immigration and European integration, including a vision for policies tackling challenging aspects of the free movement of workers, such as wage and social dumping.

In the case of Switzerland, facts must include the relationship of immigration to Switzerland's high-income and increasingly internationalised economy. A successful vision must include an explanation of how regional and sectoral disparities will be dealt with. Survey research showed that a considerable proportion of voters who approved the popular initiative against mass immigration will waver in their support of migration restriction, if this posed a fundamental threat to the Swiss–EU agreements, and if they trust the government (Sciarini et al. 2015; Sciarini 2020). A strategy based on facts as opposed to rhetoric is the only possible remedy against populist stances against European integration.

Conclusion

This chapter started with a description of immigration and the relationship to the EU as one of the biggest challenges for Swiss politics. The analysis of the scope of Switzerland's immigration-related agreements with the EU, covering the free movement of persons as well as the Schengen and the Dublin agreements, showed that Switzerland participates in the respective policies almost to the same degree as EU member states.

Differences are small but substantial with regard to the free movement policy. Switzerland managed to retain limits to free movement rights that in all likelihood would not have been possible had Switzerland been an EU member. Mainly, it maintained comparatively strong control and sanctioning measures against social and wage dumping and does not automatically grant EU citizens permanent residence after five years of legal residency. These policies have been criticised by the EU and will remain a controversial and challenging issue at the domestic level as well as in the relationship with the EU, as they affect social cohesion in Switzerland and Europe-wide solidarity.

Switzerland has become an immigration country after World War II. Immigration has been mainly driven by the booming economy and treated by politicians and society at large as a temporary phenomenon. Accordingly, immigration policies were liberal with regard to entry for migrant workers, but restrictive with regard to social and political rights for immigrants. With the coordination of social security systems and the rights for family members, the FMPA required Switzerland to improve social rights of immigrants from the EU.

The FMPA must not be considered the only driver of policy change, as, over time, the policy of short-term work permits gradually lost its role of a safety valve for the labour market. A majority of non-Swiss workers had obtained permanent residence before the FMPA entered into force. In a certain regard, Switzerland managed to maintain policy preferences despite the FMPA. In particular, it keeps checks on competition in the labour market with its measures against wage dumping and restricts social rights of immigrants with its refusal to lower the hurdle for permanent residence for EU citizens.

This chapter suggests that the assumption that the FMPA led to a steep increase in net migration numbers deserves serious scrutiny. The FMPA clearly affected the countries of origin and the structure of immigration to Switzerland, but the descriptive analysis does not hint at a general increase since the entry into force of the FMPA. While net migration numbers reached unprecedented peaks in the aftermath of the financial and economic crisis in Europe, more recently the numbers have decreased and are now at the level of the early 1990s. The peak in the early 1990s was a result of a steady increase in net immigration throughout the 1980s.

A credible explanation is that with the free movement policy net migration numbers smoothly react to economic cycles. As a comparably wealthy economy, Switzerland attracts immigrants, especially in times of recession and high unemployment in other European countries. But the increase in net migration numbers started almost two decades before the entry into force of the FMPA and is most likely a consequence of the increasing internationalisation of Switzerland's economy.

Considering that the FMPA determines the structure of immigration, but that net migration numbers depend on the economy, the challenge for Swiss politics is to acknowledge that immigration comes with a growing and increasingly internationalised economy. The traditional framing of immigration policies and Swiss–EU relations as identity politics runs counter to such an acknowledgement. Switzerland must incorporate the fact that it is an immigration country into its national identity, by acknowledging that immigration is not only a consequence of, but also a reason if not a condition for, its economic success.

This insight is the most valuable lesson the Swiss case offers for the challenges also present in other European countries: the challenge is that intra-EU migration is part and parcel of the single market as we know it, but plays a salient political role in the perception of many citizens and tends to trigger simplifying and emotional reactions. While not all countries look back on an immigration history as long and as pronounced already before the amplification of free movement of persons by the process of European integration as Switzerland, the relationship between migration and economic disparities is as important to analyse as the relationship between migration and EU principles. This is especially important for the case of the UK, where immigration was one of the most important discussions leading to Brexit, and now is almost absent in the debate over an economically beneficial relationship with the EU after the end of the transition phase.

Regional and sectoral discrepancies and disadvantages do not disappear with a better understanding of causes and consequences of immigration. While, as a whole, Switzerland's economy functions well, the labour market absorbs immigrants and unemployment rates have remained low compared to other European countries, average numbers do not depict the actual situation of all Swiss regions and residents. Immigration, also because of the FMPA, has had stronger and more ambiguous effects on certain regions (Ticino, Geneva) and certain economic sectors (see Mueller, this volume). Opposition to immigration is not only based on identity considerations, but also on the experience of increasing competition on the labour market. The conclusion to be drawn thus holds for the UK too: policies enhancing social cohesion across regions, economic sectors, and occupational groups need to be implemented if opposition to migration is not to derail beneficial economic relations with the EU and beyond.

6 European integration and state structures

What connections?

Paolo Dardanelli

Studies of Swiss politics often begin with an analysis of three features that supposedly define Switzerland's political system: neutrality, direct democracy, and federalism (e.g. Kriesi and Trechsel 2008). If none of them is exclusively Swiss – for they are present to a greater or lesser extent in other systems – taken together they undoubtedly have an importance in Switzerland that is unmatched elsewhere. Given their status as fundamental traits of the system, they have also acquired over time a symbolic dimension that has led them to being considered part of the Swiss national identity. Hence, they have a wider significance beyond their practical effects. It is thus inevitable that in the context of the relations between Switzerland and the European Union, neutrality, direct democracy, and federalism are at the heart of the debate. The perception that Europeanisation – outside or, even more so, inside the UE – poses a threat to Switzerland's federal system has, as we will see, loomed large in the country's debate over Europe. Involvement in European integration is not, of course, just a matter of identity or symbolism. On the contrary, it has a far-reaching impact on the country, hence on its federal system. This chapter aims to: (a) briefly summarise the main features of contemporary Swiss federalism and the challenges it faces; (b) identify the principal aspects of Europeanisation's impact on the federal system; (c) discuss in what ways this impact has been addressed within the current bilateral framework and how it could be addressed in the hypothetical scenario of membership; and (d) draw insights regarding the impact that exit from the EU is likely to have on the UK's system of territorial governance. The chapter argues that the process of "Europeanisation without membership" has exacerbated some of the domestic challenges Swiss federalism currently faces, the process of legislative centralisation in particular. A series of safeguards have been put in place, however, which, though not fully satisfactory, address nonetheless reasonably effectively the challenges integration raises. Chiefly among them is coordination between the cantons and the federal government in foreign policy. Switzerland's membership of the EU would thus not present a major problem for the federal system; it would represent an evolution of the current situation rather a revolution. EU membership had the opposite effect in the UK, a centrifugal one, but in the post-Brexit scenario effective management of the connections between relations with the EU and internal governance will require a policy response similar to that developed in

Switzerland: strengthened communication channels and co-decision fora between levels of government.

Swiss federalism today: Challenges and prospects

Federalism remains a central element of the Swiss political system and continues to receive strong support from the population. Nevertheless, it faces multiple challenges that could profoundly alter its character in the near future. The cantons and their role in the system, in particular, are at stake. In this section I briefly discuss the most pressing challenges.

The legislative autonomy of the cantons

Although Switzerland is often considered a highly decentralised federation, in reality there has been a vast process of centralisation over time that has greatly eroded cantonal autonomy. This centralisation has been particularly marked in the legislative sphere, while in the administrative and fiscal spheres the cantons have managed to maintain much of their original autonomy (Dardanelli and Mueller 2019). Although this process has long been acknowledged as a threat and much effort has been made to try to stem it – such as the intensification of inter-cantonal cooperation – the forces that feed it are far from exhausted.

The field of education is emblematic of these dynamics. This sector, long considered an exclusive preserve of the cantons, is facing increasing interference from the federal government. In the wake of Switzerland's poor performance in the 2001 PISA international study, a mobilisation of industry professionals and political actors, supported by public opinion, led to the adoption of a constitutional amendment in 2006 that established a unified "Swiss Educational Space" (Menzi 2010). Under the new constitutional clause, although the cantons formally retain their legislative powers, the federal government has obtained the right to impose some measure of harmonisation on certain fundamental aspects (Fischer et al. 2010; Giudici 2017). Since education is in many ways the last bastion of the legislative autonomy of the cantons, further interference by the federal government in this sector fuels fears that the legislative role of the cantons may finally fade away, turning them into mere executors of federal legislation. The COVID-19 pandemic has shed a sharp light on these threats, as the federal government's use of emergency powers has severely limited the cantons' room for manoeuvre (e.g. Altherr 2020).

The administrative capacity of the cantons

The cantons are not only under pressure in the legislative sphere, but they also face increasing administrative challenges. Most of them are very small compared to the constituent units of most other federations and in some cases also have irregular borders, with numerous exclaves and enclaves (Bochsler 2017; Kübler 2014). Moreover, cantonal borders no longer match the spatial pattern of economic activities, particularly in metropolitan areas, which often span several cantons (Zurich being the most prominent example) or even, as in the case of Basel and Geneva, the territory of neighbouring states (Kübler 2014). In essence, this is a growing divergence between "functional" territories and administrative territories, with the result that the cantons find it increasingly difficult to fulfil their role of regional administration units. However, the option of uniting multiple cantons into larger "super cantons" – mimicking the process of merging at the municipal level – remains very unpopular and all attempts have so far failed (Kriesi and Trechsel 2008: 47; Kübler 2014). Some have therefore proposed to replace the cantons with functional regions centred on the main urban areas or on the current inter-cantonal conferences (Blöchliger 2005; Bochsler 2017; Kübler 2014). But these proposals are no less controversial and their implementation would have to overcome huge obstacles.

Attachment to the cantons

The failure of all attempts to merge the cantons, even in the face of the challenges mentioned above, seems to indicate that, after all, citizens are still very much attached to their canton. The contrast with the relative ease with which mergers are implemented at the municipal level (Geser 2004: 351-3; BfS 2018c) points in the same direction, i.e. it suggests that there remains an important qualitative difference in the eyes of the citizens between their municipality and their canton. Nevertheless, many are concerned that cantonal identity is declining in favour of linguistic identities, and that this poses a danger to the functioning of the federal system. A number of trends can indeed give rise to concerns in this regard. Inter-cantonal mobility, for example, measured on the basis of the proportion of the population (both Swiss and non-Swiss nationals) born in a canton other than the canton of residence, grew from 7.3% in 1860 to 24% in 1960 and remained at about that level in the following decades (BfS 1982: 30; 2014). Although exact data on this are not available, the majority of those moving from one canton to another are likely to remain within the same language region.

With regard to the media, on the other hand, we observe a process of concentration among newspapers and a parallel process of marginalisation of the press as a whole in favour of television and new media such as the internet and social media which tend to operate at the level of the linguistic region, rather than canton (Bochsler 2017). Public television, in particular, is organised in language channels aimed at the three main language communities. Discussions on Twitter, to take another example, tend to revolve around hashtags that vary from one language to another.[1] The result has been a certain weakening of the cantons and a corresponding strengthening of the language communities as spheres of public debate.

Since language regions do not coincide with cantonal boundaries and do not have their own institutions (Bochsler 2017), these trends can jeopardise the institutional architecture of Swiss federalism and lead to a more pronounced politicisation of the divisions between language communities. Traditionally, the linguistic cleavage has not been particularly pronounced in Switzerland, especially so if we compare it to the religious one (Linder et al. 2008). However, since the 1990s it has gained a more marked profile, as a result of differences between the language communities in terms of openness to the world as well as some tensions regarding teaching of the national languages. Attitudes to the EU and to international cooperation in general have revealed a significant difference between the *Suisse romande* on one side, with more positive orientations, and German-speaking Switzerland and Ticino, on the other side, where hostility often prevails (see chapters by Theiler and Mazzoleni in this volume). Teaching of the national languages has caused controversy following the decision by some German-speaking cantons to prioritise the teaching of English at the expense of French as a second language in primary school, thus potentially creating a deeper divide between the language communities.

Although these trends undoubtedly have a disruptive potential, their impact should not be exaggerated. It is important to bear in mind that citizens continue to be strongly attached to the cantons, that collective identification with the language communities remains generally weak, and that the legitimacy of the institutional system of Swiss federalism, as we have seen, remains high (Kriesi et al. 1996; Dardanelli 2011). A 2001 survey found that 69% of respondents were "very proud" or "rather proud" of federalism and 77% thought it was "very important" or "rather important" for the future of the country while 76% felt "very attached" or "rather attached" to their canton (Kriesi and Trechsel 2008: 46–7).

Federalism-democracy tensions

Although the legitimacy of the system remains high, the way in which Swiss federalism is operating today puts it at odds with democratic principles in several respects. The mechanism of the cantonal majority in mandatory referendums, for example, gives a veto power to a very small proportion of the population, from an average of 20–25% to a theoretical extreme of 9% (Vatter 2018: 44). Combined with the fact that double-majority votes are becoming more frequent and as a result there are also more frequent cases of disagreement between the popular and the cantonal majority, this mechanism is an increasingly problematic anomaly from a democratic point of view (Vatter 2018: 43–7).

The Council of States – the upper house of the federal parliament and, arguably, the most important institution established by the founding fathers to bind the cantons and the federation together – is under pressure. Since members of the upper house started to be directly elected, as opposed to being appointed by the cantonal parliaments, a logic of party representation has prevailed over a logic of cantonal representation. This change has been compounded by the distortions produced by the electoral system, which leads to a considerable over-representation of the centrist parties against the more radical ones. The result is that the Council of States finds it increasingly difficult to play the role of "voice of the cantons" in the federal parliament (Vatter 2018: 33–43).

The growth of inter-cantonal cooperation is seen by many (e.g. Sciarini 2005) as the only practical way in which further centralisation can be contained. Horizontal cooperation, however, is not without its downsides, particularly in terms of transparency of the decision-making process and decision makers' accountability (Bochsler 2017; Kübler 2014). Agreements between cantons are negotiated and concluded by cantonal governments and cantonal parliaments can only approve or reject, but not amend, them (Germann and Klöti 2004: 343–4). In other words, and despite some recent efforts to increase parliamentary scrutiny, horizontal cooperation is widely perceived to be problematic from the perspective of democratic legitimacy as it implies the replacement of democratically decided federal laws with "treaties" between cantonal governments subject to little democratic oversight by cantonal parliaments (Germann and Klöti 2004: 343–4; Rhinow 2006: 76–8). The growth of horizontal cooperation thus presents a dilemma for the Swiss federal system for citizens face a choice between transferring an ever greater range of competences to the federal level, thus increasing centralisation but also keeping it within the federal democratic process, and retaining responsibilities at the cantonal level but paying the price in terms of democratic control. A similar dilemma is posed by inter-municipal cooperation (Kübler 2014).

Last but not least, the increasing migration flows both within the country and across its borders have already greatly diluted the original ethnic and religious homogeneity of the cantons and in all likelihood will continue to do so in the future. The populations of the small rural and Catholic cantons are therefore no longer the only or the most significant minorities in the country. Since many aspects of the Swiss federal system were established with the intention of protecting the interests of these cantons, it follows that the institutional architecture of Swiss federalism is less and less in tune with the social realities of today's Switzerland. Moreover, given that the new minorities are not geographically concentrated as the old ones were, one could go even further and argue that federalism is not an appropriate institutional mechanism to ensure them effective democratic representation. In other words, the rising heterogeneity of the cantonal populations and the concomitant erosion of differences between cantons pit the institutional design of Swiss federalism increasingly at odds with democratic principles.

Fiscal federalism

As mentioned above, Switzerland is still considerably decentralised from a fiscal point of view. The cantons have retained substantial tax-raising autonomy and engage in vigorous fiscal competition with each other (Cappelletti 2017; Dardanelli and Mueller 2019). Even so, the system is not free from tensions. The extent to which cantons can decide the base and rate of direct taxation has been progressively reduced over time. With regard to income tax, in particular, there is a growing trend towards harmonisation (Dafflon 2006). To date, this harmonisation has covered issues such as the definition of the tax base and the criteria for deductions, but pressures for rate harmonisation remain. An important factor that fuels them is the perception by many, particularly on the left of the political spectrum, that tax competition between cantons has reached excessive levels. Some cantons, for example, have gone so far as to introduce regressive rates in an attempt to attract wealthy taxpayers. Although these rates were subsequently struck down by the Federal Court as unconstitutional, in the eyes of many this unbridled competition prevents redistribution within the cantons and undermines the federal cohesion between them. A Socialist Party–sponsored initiative to limit competition, although rejected in a popular vote in November 2010, was a signal of the tensions that linger on.

However, international tax competition coexists with an elaborate equalisation system, whose recent reform has been judged by many to be a significant success (Braun 2009; Cappelletti 2017). In this respect, Switzerland can rightly be seen as an example of a federation that has successfully combined fiscal autonomy for each constituent unit – and the responsibility and accountability vis-à-vis the citizens that comes with it – with high cohesion among them. Nevertheless, the equalisation system is not without tensions and the latter could become more severe in the future as the sums transferred through it are periodically renegotiated and disputes between the cantons that are net contributors and those that are net beneficiaries are never far from the surface (Cappelletti 2017).

Integration without membership

As the other chapters in this book show, although Switzerland has so far remained outside the European Union, it has nonetheless undergone an extensive process of Europeanisation. This process has mainly affected public policies but has also had an impact on the federal system, in particular on intergovernmental relations between the cantons and the federation.

The main aspect of this impact is that in the context of its bilateral agreements with the EU Switzerland has to adapt its legislation to that of the Union in many areas. As these areas often fall entirely or in part under cantonal competences, the decisions taken by the Federal Council in European policy have directly concerned the cantons. Since the cantons were traditionally not involved in the country's foreign policy, a disconnection has emerged between the consequences of the policy for the cantons and the latter's ability to make their voices heard in defining this policy. This has led to significant consequences for how foreign policy, European policy in particular, is being formulated. The new federal constitution adopted in 1999 stipulates in Article 55 that the cantons participate in "foreign policy decisions that touch their essential competences or interests" and for this purpose requires the federation to inform the cantons in a timely manner and to properly involve them in international negotiations. The new constitutional clause was subsequently implemented through the Federal Law on the Participation of the Cantons in the Foreign Policy of the Federation, which came into force in 2000 (see also Thürer and MacLaren 2009: 275–8, 283).

Before the constitutional revision, the cantons had already moved to improve horizontal coordination and their ability to communicate in a coherent manner with the federal authorities. The main instrument was the creation, and subsequent strengthening, of the Conference of the Cantonal Governments (CCG). Although inter-cantonal cooperation has deep roots in Switzerland, for a long time it proceeded along sectoral tracks and lacked a generalist forum such as the CCG (Schnabel and Mueller 2017; Vatter 2018: 73–83). It is no coincidence that the CCG was established in 1993 in the wake of the traumatic referendum on Switzerland's entry into the EEA in December 1992. This body quickly became one of the key players in the federal system, not only as an instrument of inter-cantonal cooperation – its main original mission – but above all as a vehicle to represent cantonal interests as a whole vis-à-vis the federal institutions. The fact that its secretariat was transferred in 2003 from Solothurn to Berne, a short walk from the federal palace, was significant in this regard. The CCG has often taken a stand on European policy issues and facilitated the participation of the cantons in the negotiations.

In addition to negotiations on specific issues, the CCG has sought to develop a collective position of the cantons so as to ensure that they speak with a unified voice to the Federal Council. For this purpose, the CCG created in 1998 a *Europe-Reforms-Cantons* working group. The group's work ended with the adoption (by a majority) in 2004 of a report containing the main principles of a European policy strategy for the cantons (CCG 2004), which is still the most extensive document on the subject. The report pointed out the challenges that European integration presents to Swiss federalism, particularly that of transposing European law into Swiss law and of the fact that the Federal Council often does not consult the cantons adequately, despite the constitutional clause requiring it to do so (CCG 2004: 16, 21). As a result, according to the CCG, Switzerland's integration with the EU has introduced additional centralising pressures that add to the domestic dynamics at work, as seen above (CCG 2004: 16–24). To meet these challenges, the report called for a four-pronged strategy. First, the bilateral approach has clear limits as a long-term strategy, while EEA membership remains sub-optimal, so the cantons advocated maintaining EU membership as a long-term goal. Second, the pursuit of membership as a long-term goal and membership itself must not pose a threat to the country's federal system. Third, in order for this threat not to materialise, domestic reforms must be undertaken. Fourth, but not least, close cooperation between the cantons and the Federal Council is essential if an effective European policy is to be conducted and at the same time the country's federal order safeguarded (CCG 2004: 5–8, 27).

The CCG has since revisited these issues on several occasions but has not deviated much from the line set in 2004. A second position paper, published in 2007, reaffirmed key objectives such as the need to undertake internal reforms in view of possible EU membership, and the importance of maintaining cooperation between the cantons and the federation (CCG 2007). Three years later, the Conference reformulated some aspects of its position, in particular in relation to the possible signing of a framework agreement with the EU. In this regard, the CCG voted in favour of a framework agreement, provided the latter does not require Switzerland to automatically transpose European law, which would be incompatible with maintaining the country's sovereignty, nor grants the CJEU a mandate to supervise compliance with such an agreement (CCG 2010: 2–4). In addition, a framework agreement should only cover new areas of application and not replace the bilateral agreements currently in place (CCG 2010: 4). According to the CGC, it is necessary to go beyond the provisions of Article 55 of the constitution, which regulates external relations in general, and include clauses that explicitly refer to European policy, in order to ensure that the specifics of the latter are taken into account. These clauses should in particular regulate the implementation of European legislation by the cantons and how federal supervision of such implementation should be conducted, so that the cantons are adequately supported in carrying out this task and at the same time their autonomy is safeguarded (CCG 2010: 6). The other crucial aspect of the reforms to be undertaken is the strengthening of cooperation between the federation and the cantons, in the following terms: (a) the cantons should obtain the right to be informed as soon as possible about any development in European policy that concerns them and to this end should also have the right to maintain observers within the federal administration and its delegations in Brussels; (b) their position should be binding on the Federal Council; and (c) a permanent coordination forum should be set up between the cantons and the federal authorities (CCG 2010: 7–8). A subsequent position paper confirmed these demands, stating that cantons-federation coordination should be governed by a convention between the two parties and that the Federal Court should have the power to check that federal legislation respects the constitutional division of powers (CCG 2011: 4–5). An agreement between the cantons and the federation concerning "dialogue on European issues" was finally signed in 2012, which provides for bimonthly meetings between representatives of the federal departments of foreign affairs and the economy, representing the federal administration, and the CCG, on behalf of the cantons (CCG 2012). At the invitation of the Federal Council, the cantons have taken a collective position on the draft IFA. They consider the proposed agreement to be broadly in line with their demands on matters such as the transposition of EU law and the dispute resolution mechanisms but that some aspects, such as the extent to which the new agreement affects the 1972 free trade agreement, regulation of state aid, and the retention of labour market safeguards, require further negotiations. In light of this, they called on the federal government to defend their right to co-decide Switzerland's European policy and to participate in EU decision-making within their areas of competence (CCG 2019).

The cantons are therefore aware that even if Switzerland-EU relations remain on a bilateral track, the country cannot insulate itself from the process of Europeanisation these relations generate and the latter's consequences for the federal system. As we have seen, they are ready to speak out against the Federal Council and the results so far seem to indicate that they have sufficient negotiating strength to make their case heard. We can therefore say that the Swiss federal system has not been compromised for the time being by the process of Europeanisation without membership.

What insights for the UK?

At first sight, the impact of EU membership on the UK's state structure was very different to that experienced by Switzerland, so there is little to be learned from the latter. A closer look at some of the implications of Brexit, however, suggests otherwise.

It is certainly true that EU membership had a decentralising, even a disintegrative, effect on the way the UK state is structured as opposed to the mainly centralising effect experienced by Switzerland. A major factor accounting for this difference is that, of course, the two countries' constitutional order at the outset was very different. While Switzerland was a rather decentralised federal state, the UK was a unitary state with a high concentration of power in the Westminster parliament. The different directions in which the two systems have since travelled is thus to a significant extent accounted for by these markedly different starting points. Switzerland, as seen above, has undergone a process of centralisation, especially in the legislative sphere, which Europeanisation has somewhat deepened. If the main effect in the two countries has been different, there have also been secondary effects going in the opposite direction. In the early phase of integration in Switzerland there were widespread fears that the contrasting attitudes to Europe between the German-speaking and the French-speaking areas (see chapters by Kreis, Sciarini, Mueller, and Theiler in this volume), would drive a wedge between the two communities and threaten the unity of the country. Conversely, in the UK, there are fears that Brexit may lead to a reversal of devolution, particularly where Scotland and Wales are concerned.

In the UK, Europeanisation has been an important factor in leading to devolution to Scotland and Wales, and the restoration of autonomy to Northern Ireland. In understanding the channels through which it has operated, though, we need to distinguish between Scotland (and Wales), on one side, and Northern Ireland, on the other. In Scotland, Europeanisation mainly operated via the "independence in Europe" strategy adopted by the Scottish National Party (SNP) in the late 1980s, whereby the party pursued secession from the UK but continuing membership of the EU as an additional member state. The competitive pressure the SNP, armed with its "independence in Europe" strategy, put on Labour, the hegemonic party in Scotland, was instrumental in leading the latter to establish a devolved Scottish parliament (and a Welsh assembly) in 1999 (Dardanelli 2017: 135–50, 197–207). In Northern Ireland, Europeanisation operated via reconciliation between the unionist (Protestant and British-identifying) and the nationalist (Catholic and Irish-identifying) communities. Although Northern Ireland had a devolved parliament for 50 years, it was disbanded in 1972, i.e. the year before the UK joined what is now the EU, in the wake of mounting sectarian violence. Given that Ireland joined at the same time as the UK, closer integration within the EU offered a golden opportunity to build relationships across the Irish border and foster reconciliation in the North. While the opportunity took time to bear fruit, it did eventually create the conditions that made the Good Friday agreement, thus the restoration of devolved government to Northern Ireland, possible (Hayward and Murphy 2018).

Brexit has radically changed, of course, this context, not least because both Scotland and Northern Ireland voted by large margins to remain in the EU. The effect on the two regions, however, is once again different. In Scotland it has produced a dramatic tension between conflicting forces. On the one hand, the prospect of being dragged out of the EU against its will has renewed calls for independence. On the other hand, an independent and EU-member Scotland would face severe challenges in managing relations with an out-of-the-EU rump UK, which would remain its largest market and most important partner in so many ways. Thus, Scotland's independence faces at the same time renewed urgency in the eyes of many and even more formidable political and economic obstacles than at the time of the 2014 referendum. Support for independence may also be fuelled by a perception that the UK government intends to weaken Scotland's autonomy by taking control of powers repatriated from the EU – such as subsidies to industry – that, according to the Scottish government, should be instead transferred to Scotland (Foster et al. 2020). From this perspective, Brexit would have both a centralising effect, in the short run, and a disintegrative effect in the longer run.

In Northern Ireland it has also generated deep tensions, but of a different kind, achieving the rare feat of angering both communities. The return of a hard border between Northern Ireland and the Republic of Ireland has raised fears that the nationalist community may not remain fully committed to the Good Friday agreement, with radical elements within it even contemplating a return to violence. The unionist side has been angered by the emergence of a de facto economic border between Northern Ireland and Great Britain as a result of the UK's withdrawal agreement with the EU. This has been perceived by many as Westminster's betrayal of Northern Ireland for the sake of securing an acceptable Brexit deal (e.g. Tonge 2020: 14). The combined effect of these tensions is Northern Ireland's further alienation from London, making a united Ireland a realistic prospect for the first time since the partition of the island a century ago.

In both Scotland and Northern Ireland, thus, Brexit and its ramifications pose a severe territorial integrity threat to the UK as well as a less dramatic but not insignificant challenge in terms of territorial governance and intergovernmental relations. With regard to this latter aspect, Brexit had thrown a sharp light on an important aspect of the 1990s devolution settlement: intergovernmental channels between Westminster and the devolved institutions in Scotland, Wales, and Northern Ireland. While formal channels do exist, a great deal of intergovernmental relations is carried out informally through intra-party means (e.g. Gallagher 2012). While these generally work smoothly when the same party is in power both at the centre and in the devolved governments the tensions described above are bound to make things much more fractious. Relations between an SNP Scottish government and a Conservative UK government, for instance, compound left-right, centre-periphery, and Europe-related divergences. The fact that the mainstream British parties do not operate in Northern Ireland, of course, does not facilitate intra-party channels, especially in a context in which the Conservatives and the unionist parties, although ideologically close, do not see eye to eye on European matters. Even in the sphere of formal bodies, the lack of an inter-institutional channel between Westminster and the devolved legislatures (e.g. Fowler 2020) does not help coordination. All this points to the importance of strengthening inter-institutional dialogue and collaboration between executives and legislatures if the tensions in territorial governance are to be effectively diffused. While inter-institutional dialogue by itself would not eliminate the more fundamental threats to the territorial integrity of the UK, it would at least help govern the country effectively in the post-Brexit world while Scotland and Northern Ireland are still part of the (British) union.

It is in this respect that the Swiss experience offers helpful insights for the United Kingdom. As seen above, the cantons highlighted the importance of effective communication channels with the federal government and cantonal involvement in the formulation of Switzerland's European policy in addressing Europeanisation's potentially negative effects on the country's federal system. The willingness on the part of the federal authorities to work with the cantons along these lines has gone a long way in allaying cantons' fears, thus avoiding creating additional "vertical" tensions in the system. In light of the challenges Brexit raises for the unity of the country and its system of territorial governance, the UK government would thus be well advised to heed this lesson from Switzerland's experience.

Conclusions

Federalism continues to be the backbone of the Swiss political system. While the cantons have lost much of their original legislative autonomy and face multiple challenges, they remain a key element of the system and important references for citizens' collective identity. The symbolic importance of federalism, moreover, goes beyond the practical role that the cantons play. The recent reform of the equalisation system also demonstrates its ability to adapt.

This ability has also been highlighted by the challenge posed by relations with the European Union. While remaining outside the EU, Switzerland has undergone a broad process of Europeanisation which has exacerbated the centralising pressures already at work internally. However, the system has reacted positively and has set up institutional and political countermeasures that have enabled it to respond effectively to these pressures. The creation of the CCG, the provisions of Article 55 of the new federal constitution, and the developments that followed were the key elements of this response. The strategy that the cantons have pursued, which is to require co-decision in European policy with the Federal Council in exchange for their help in generating popular support and ensuring the proper implementation of European legislation, has therefore paid off. The willingness of the federal authorities to work with the cantons along these lines has been a necessary ingredient to make cooperation work. While not all problems have been resolved, the cantons and the federal government have found a modus vivendi that minimises possible negative effects on Switzerland's federal system.

At first sight the challenges facing the United Kingdom are very different from Switzerland's. While the main challenge in the latter is how to avoid deepening centralisation that risks hollowing out the country's federal system, Brexit raises challenges primarily of a disintegrative kind. The policy response called for is nonetheless similar, hence Switzerland still holds valuable insights for the UK. The key lesson in this respect is the importance of strengthening inter-institutional channels between Westminster and the devolved governments and legislatures, particularly in Scotland and Northern Ireland. While partisan and other barriers make this not an easy task, Switzerland's experience points to the significant benefits to be reaped from such inter-institutional cooperation.

Note

1 I thank Sean Mueller for suggesting this point to me.

7 Political parties and Europe

An enduring dilemma

Blaise Fontanellaz and Paolo Dardanelli

In the wake of the United Kingdom's withdrawal from the EU, it is helpful to examine Switzerland–EU relations from the perspective of political parties, with an eye to identify some of the key dilemmas the Swiss parties have had to deal with and that the UK parties may encounter in the future. If parties play a major role in shaping public opinion and voting behaviour in all political systems, this is particularly true in Switzerland, where they perform this role not only at election times but also in referendum campaigns, which are crucial arenas in Swiss politics. This chapter focusses on the evolution in the orientation of the four main Swiss parties, all of whom have been represented in the federal government over the last 30 years: the FDP, a party of the liberal centre-right, which like the UK Liberal Democrats is a member of the transnational Alliance of Liberals and Democrats for Europe; the CVP, a member of the European People's Party; the SVP, a right-wing nationalist and populist party which has some similarities with both the UK Conservatives as well as the United Kingdom Independence Party (UKIP) and the Brexit Party;[1] and finally, the SP, a member, like Labour, of the Party of European Socialists. The chapter outlines the arguments put forward by these parties and connects them with government positions and with the referendums and popular initiatives on European integration held in Switzerland since the 1990s. By doing so, the chapter seeks to uncover the factors that have shaped party orientations to European integration over this period (Helbling et al. 2010).[2] It then briefly compares these patterns to the evolution of attitudes to European integration among the UK parties and concludes by identifying the main takeaways emerging from the comparison.

The European Economic Area

Since the beginnings of European integration, Switzerland's European policy has been characterised by the willingness to engage in economic integration but at the same time avoid political integration in order to safeguard some characteristics perceived as being inherent to Swiss democracy: federalism, semi-direct democracy, and neutrality in foreign policy. This aim was shared by all the main Swiss parties until the end of the Cold War. A little earlier, in January 1989, Jacques Delors, then President of the European Commission, proposed that the EEC and

EFTA, of which Switzerland is a member, form an EEA bound together by common institutions and where the four freedoms – of services, people, goods, and capital – would apply. Together with its EFTA partners, Switzerland accepted the EEC's invitation and entered into negotiations to form an EEA.

At the time of the campaign for the EEA referendum scheduled for 6 December 1992 only the SVP was opposed to it, thereby going against the views of the media, churches, trade unions, employers' organisations, the government, the main parties, etc. (see Kreis, this volume). At that time, the party, the smallest of the four parties represented in the federal government, was moving away from its agrarian origins towards a right-wing nationalist and populist ideology, under the leadership of the businessman Christoph Blocher (Mazzoleni 2008). Together with its flanking organisation, the Campaign for an Independent and Neutral Switzerland (AUNS), the SVP embodied the main opposition to the EEA treaty and in the wake of its victory in the referendum, Blocher emerged as the principal defender of "Swiss values".

The other main Swiss parties, by contrast, supported the EEA treaty. The treaty presented a delicate dilemma for the FDP, which was born out of national liberalism and was the embodiment of the "nation" in the second part of the 19th century. Led by economy minister Jean-Pascal Delamuraz, who was in charge of the EEA *dossier*, the FDP reversed its long-held position of non-participation in European political integration and actively campaigned in favour of the treaty, primarily on the ground of securing the economic benefits of preferential access to the EU market. There were minority views within the party at both end of the spectrum, with a Eurosceptic wing opposing the treaty and a pro-integration wing, led by university professors, advocating EU membership. The CVP – originally a party defending Catholic interests and the historical opponent of the FDP – supported the treaty primarily under the influence of the historically leading role Christian Democrats played in European integration. The SP, which originated in the labour movement, quickly emerged as the most pro-European party in Switzerland. Little interested in this issue during the Cold War, it committed itself to the EEA and then, in 1991, to EEC membership. It experienced tensions, however, regarding workers' rights, as discussed below.

On 6 December 1992, after a very intense campaign, 50.3% of voters cast their vote against this treaty. French-speaking Switzerland overwhelmingly supported the treaty, which led to strong tensions at the national level with the German-speaking part of the country, which broadly rejected it (see Kreis, this volume). The referendum's result created a political crisis in Swiss–EU relations, which would not be resolved until the first set of bilateral agreements were concluded in 1999 (see Schwok, this volume).

Membership of the European Union

Proposed by the Federal Government in May 1992, Switzerland's membership of the EEC/EU has been a prominent issue for all the Swiss parties. Given the uncertainties surrounding the outcome of the bilateral negotiations, the majority of the two centrist parties, the Christian Democrats and the Liberals, came out in favour of Swiss membership. For the FDP, it was at its April 1995 congress in Interlaken that its pro-European wing succeeded in changing the party's orientation. Reversing a 40-year-old stance, the congress endorsed membership as the overriding goal of Switzerland's foreign policy. The CVP decided to support membership at a meeting of delegates in Basel in 1998. At the opposite end of the spectrum, the SVP positioned itself, particularly from 1995 onwards, as Switzerland's most anti-EU party. In 1996, Ueli Maurer, a supporter of Christoph Blocher's, took over as party leader and instigated a strong ideological shift, against the opposition of some of its cantonal sections (such as those of Vaud, Berne, and Grisons), which espoused a more moderate position. Under Blocher and his followers, the SVP would attract higher electoral support throughout Switzerland over the course of the 1990s and 2000s.

However, it was the constitutional initiative proposed by the New European Movement of Switzerland (NEBS) that forced the parties to take a stand. This initiative proposed the immediate opening of membership negotiations. The FDP opposed the initiative, mainly out of a concern to support the government's position, as did the SVP, while the SP supported it. The CVP leadership also supported the initiative, but 18 of its cantonal sections were opposed, reflecting widespread tensions within the party. In the end, the initiative was rejected by 76.8% of voters, in a context in which the bilateral agreements between Switzerland and the EU had just been signed. This came as a shock to the pro-Europeans, and effectively buried the issue of membership to the present day.

It is worth mentioning that the SP and the SVP took a position on membership fairly quickly, while the other two wavered, particularly during the 1990s. The centrist parties' positions led to tensions between the leadership and the rank-and-file, which were later resolved once the leadership, in the wake of the evolution of public opinion and the referendum result mentioned above, abandoned their advocacy of membership. The SP thus remained the sole party still committed to membership whereas Blocher's faction consolidated its hegemony within the SVP, thus helping to strengthen the latter's leadership among opponents.

The free movement of persons

Following rejection of the EEA, bilateral negotiations took some time to get off the ground. The agreements did not come into force until 2002 (see Schwok, this volume). Here we are focussing on the agreements concerning the free movement of persons, signed by Switzerland at the request of the EU (see Jenni, this volume). A first referendum against this agreement was launched by the Swiss Democrats, a small far-right party, later supported by the rank-and-file of the AUNS, against its leadership, as well as by some cantonal sections of the SVP, also going against the party leadership. The agreement, rejected only by the cantons of Schwyz and Ticino, was accepted by 67.2% of the votes in 2000. The agreement was supported by the Liberals and the Christian Democrats, as well as by the Socialists, on condition that it be complemented by accompanying measures to protect workers against wage dumping.

A referendum on the extension of the free movement of persons to the ten new EU member states took place on 25 September 2005, following a referendum on the Schengen and Dublin agreements held in June of the same year, in which the SVP and the AUNS had unsuccessfully opposed the end of border checks (see Jenni, this volume). This referendum, launched by the Swiss Democrats, was supported by the assembly of delegates of the SVP, which was nevertheless divided: its federal ministers, including Christoph Blocher (who had been elected to the federal government in 2003), and its pro-business wing, including about a third of its representatives in parliament, supported the agreement, whereas the rest of the party was against. The FDP, the CVP, and the Socialists supported the extension of the agreement while still being concerned about the measures. The extension was approved by 56% of the voters.

A new referendum was held in 2009 on the renewal of the free movement of persons agreement and its extension to Romania and Bulgaria, the two topics being presented to the voters as a single package. This referendum had, once again, been launched by the Swiss Democrats, this time together with the Lega dei Ticinesi, a Ticino-based regional populist party (see Mazzoleni, this volume), and the youth wing of the SVP. The SVP leadership initially called for two separate votes, on the grounds that it was prepared to support a renewal but opposed its extension. It threatened to oppose both if presented as a single package but refrained from launching a referendum challenge. It later came out against it under pressure from its rank-and-file and in the face of objections from its pro-business wing. The FDP and the CVP confirmed their support for the free movement of persons. The campaign focused mainly on the question of cross-border workers, particularly in the border cantons of Geneva and Ticino, where regional populist parties – such as the Mouvement des Citoyens, or Geneva Citizens' Movement, in the former and the Lega dei Ticinesi in the latter – fronted it and often employed sensationalist tactics.

The 2009 referendum challenge, however, failed and in its wake the SVP announced the launch of a new constitutional initiative aiming to re-establish quotas for immigration and a national preference on the Swiss labour market, in defiance of the bilateral agreements, which was put to the vote on 9 February 2014. This new referendum campaign opened with a poster from Switzerland's leading employers' organisation, Economiesuisse, while the SVP conducted a restrained campaign emphasising left-leaning themes such as the threat of wage undercutting, rent increases, and environmental damage. The government remained on the sidelines of the campaign, largely confining itself to relativising the salience of immigration and pointing out its importance for the economy, with the other governmental parties by and large following suit.

On the referendum day, to the surprise of many, 50.3% of the electorate voted in favour of the initiative. This was the first time since 2000 that a majority of voters opposed the principle of the free movement of persons between Switzerland and the European Union. A national survey showed that the SVP initiative received the highest support among the lowest-paid voters (see Sciarini, this volume). There was also a cleavage between cities, on the one hand, and the small towns and the countryside, on the other, which matches the findings of the French geographer Christophe Guilluy: “It is striking that the Swiss electoral geography also intersects the cleavage between the large cities, which are in favour of openness and immigration, and a ‘peripheral Switzerland’ opposed to migration flows. This is a de facto European model” (Guilluy 2014: 94–95). This cleavage also resonates with voting patterns in the Brexit referendum, where non-metropolitan areas heavily favoured Leave (Guilluy 2016).

The consequence of the vote on 9 February 2014 was a protracted diplomatic crisis between Switzerland and the European Union, during which the risk that the EU would denounce all the bilateral agreements negotiated in the first round (on the basis of the famous “guillotine clause” which binds them together; see Schwok in this volume) became dangerously real. In 2016, however, the Swiss Parliament finally adopted an accommodating implementation of the new constitutional articles emerging from the initiative providing only for a soft preference for Swiss workers (employers must recruit local workforce if the unemployment rate in a given sector exceeds a certain average). According to the Swiss authorities, this solution did not contravene the agreement on the free establishment of persons, but it also pushed the SVP into launching yet another popular initiative in the hope of restricting immigration and, and once again, challenging the free movement of persons agreement.

An institutional framework agreement (IFA)?

The Swiss–EU bilateral agreements were designed to be static. It was therefore necessary to find a mechanism to enable Switzerland to transpose EU law more dynamically, in particular to guarantee its companies’ access to the EU market. This was the reason behind the negotiations of an IFA between the two partners. The negotiations were particularly lengthy (2013–2018). At the end of the negotiations, the Swiss government did not find itself in a position to sign the agreement and decided to buy time by submitting it for consultation with a range of stakeholders (see Schwok, this volume). One of the main stumbling blocks was the proposed dispute settlement mechanism. The solution adopted was that of a joint arbitration tribunal, which would rule on disagreements in light of the case law of the CJEU. Disagreements on interpretation of EU law would be referred to the CJEU, which would give a binding ruling. If Switzerland did not follow this ruling, the EU would then be entitled to take so-called compensation measures that it deemed necessary. For the SVP, this would imply an unacceptable subjugation of Switzerland to EU law and the jurisdiction of the CJEU. The parties of the left, for their part, disagree with Protocol 1 on posted workers, which is perceived to weaken the measures (known as “accompanying measures”) introduced to avoid wage dumping at the expense of Swiss workers (Fontanellaz and Saint-Ouen 2020; see also chapters by Schwok and Jenni, this volume). Given such opposition from the left and the trade unions, as well as from the SVP, the agreement is unlikely to be ratified by parliament in its current form. Moreover, these controversial aspects make it equally unlikely that the agreement would be approved by the people in a referendum, even if parliament ratified it (Fontanellaz and Saint-Ouen 2019).

A synoptic and longitudinal view

It may be useful, at this point, to provide a summary view of the evolution of the arguments put forward by each party considered in this chapter. The data were collected from arguments identified in articles published in party newspapers and magazines from 1989 to 2014. Using consistent coding categories grounded in framing analysis, we can identify the main arguments and compare them across party and over time. This will allow us to understand the factors shaping each party's position on the European Economic Area, EU membership, and the bilateral agreements.

The FDP's arguments

As Figure 7.1 shows, the FDP clearly emphasised economic arguments over the course of the period covered. The party framed Europe as a necessary market for Swiss companies and a beneficial source of competition for them and their employees. Calls for protectionist measures to defend the Swiss economy were absent. This appears to reflect the party's conversion to neo-liberalism, which began at the 1979 federal election. This conversion led to the disappearance of

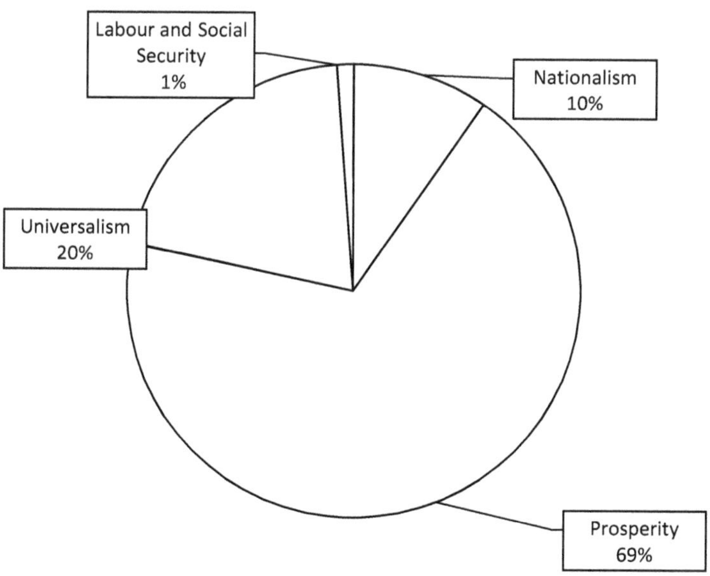

Figure 7.1 FDP (1989–2014).

its "social" and more economically centrist wing at the federal level. Moreover, these economic arguments reflect the FDP's close links to companies active on the global or European market, i.e. multinationals, rather than to the craftsmen or farmers, who were more inclined to support the SVP. The party was also facing competition from the SP for the representation of the "internationalised" elite. Hence, it called for European solidarity in the name of a universalism stemming from progressive thinking, in the philosophical sense of the term, which saw the European Union as the culmination of a historical process, or from solidarity with the other European countries and, although more rarely, with immigrants, as in the case of the extension of the freedom of movement in 2005.

Finally, the nationalist argument of the FDP was especially prominent between 1989 and 2001. It then disappeared, especially so far as the bilateral agreements are concerned, including in relation to votes on border checks such as the Schengen referendum. European integration thus presented a challenge for the party, which accounts for its hesitations and change of position over time, of which its, somewhat rushed, endorsement of EU membership in 1995 is a clear example. Its abandonment of the nationalist argument signals a breakdown of the party's original national-liberal character in favour of a free-market ethos. As Cassidy and Loser (2015) have noted, the FDP has lost "its" country by forsaking, at least partially, the values linked to the idea of a Swiss *Sonderfall*, or special case. This shift has to be understood in the context of competition with the SVP for "ownership" of the nationalist discourse.

The CVP's arguments

As Figure 7.2 illustrates, the economic theme was as dominant among the arguments put forward by the CVP as it was for its liberal cousin. At the same time, universalism occupied an important place in the Christian Democrats' discourse. This often articulated solidarity with the EU member states, which can be explained by the CVP's roots in the strongly pro-European Christian Democratic party family, from which leading "Fathers of Europe" such as Konrad Adenauer, Alcide de Gasperi, Robert Schuman, and Paul van Zeeland sprung. To this day, the CVP maintains close links with its ideological fellows in the other European countries.

The CVP deployed a nationalist argument, mainly present in relation to the EEA and to EU membership but not in relation to Schengen. In this regard, the CVP thus seemed to have followed the same path as the FDP. The Christian Democrats voiced "social" concerns, i.e. labour and social security arguments, to a greater extent than the Liberals. This is likely to be due to the CVP's former nature as a "catch-all party" and the enduring influence of its Christian-social wing. It should be noted that the CVP was pro-European in the post-war period, subsequently toned down its enthusiasm, and later resurrected a pro-European stance.

The SP's arguments

The Socialist Party defended EEA and EU membership against a background of economic difficulties in Switzerland and a widespread presence of

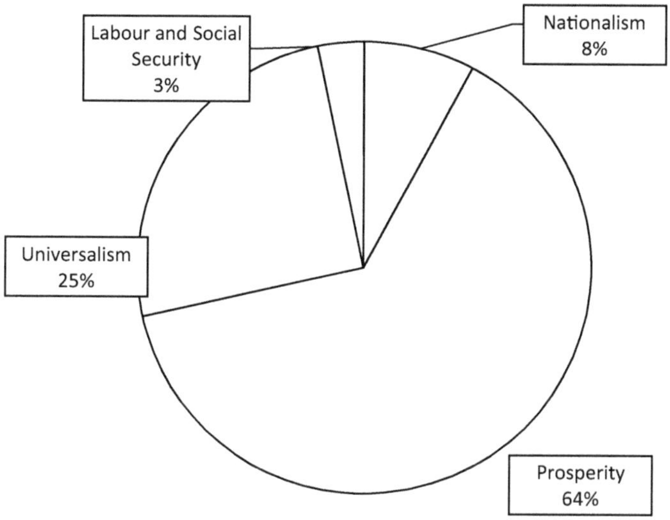

Figure 7.2 CVP (1989–2014).

social-democratic governments in the EU member states. Despite coming rapidly to a position and seemingly presenting it with a united voice and with the help of a range of arguments, internal tensions can be detected. It is striking, for instance, to find as many negative as positive arguments on issues relating to work and social security, which are captured in Figure 7.3. In our view, this reflects a tension between internationalism and worker protection. In other words, the party was torn between two possible courses of action: should we favour the protection of national workers by excluding European workers, or should we favour opening up with risks of competition or dumping on the labour market for Swiss or resident workers? This tension is only reconciled when the universalist argument is deployed. In this case, the emphasis is on solidarity with migrant workers and the countries of the European Union, which in the end proves to be qualitatively dominant if one takes into account the tensions in the, quantitatively more prominent, labour and social security theme. Does this emphasis on universalism reflect a new orientation more in favour of the middle classes than the working classes? There is no firm answer, even though the results of Line Rennwald's (2015) survey of the relationship between the working classes and the socialist parties seem to point in this direction. Indeed, she notes that: "In Switzerland, the socialist party seems to have chosen to attract new segments of the electorate by integrating the ecological, feminist and societal demands of the new left into the heart of its programme". This element implies that: "In Switzerland the predominance of the socialist party's cultural agenda has transformed the workers' vote" (Rennwald 2015: 242). Also of note is the importance of the economic prosperity argument, within which the party

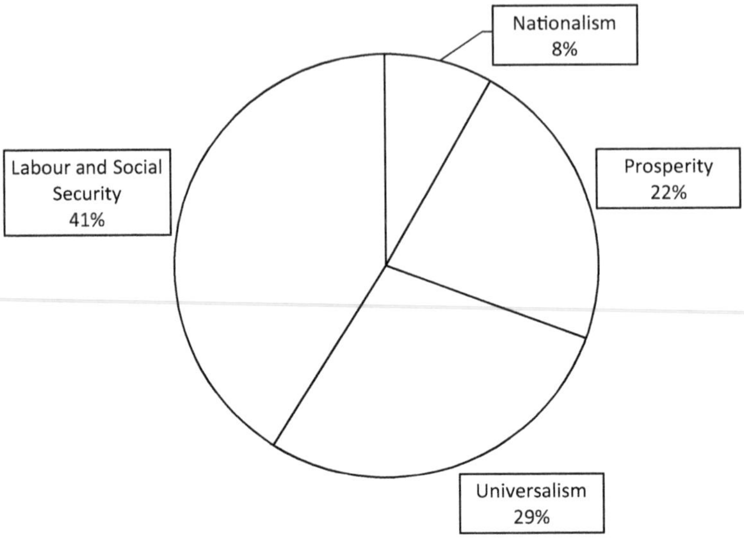

Figure 7.3 SP (1989–2014).

voiced fears that unemployment may soar were Switzerland to be cut off from the EU's market. The nationalist argument, although little used, centred on fears of negative repercussions for semi-direct democracy in case of too great a rapprochement with the European Union.

The SVP's arguments

Figure 7.4 illustrates the positions of the fourth governing party on Europe. The SVP played the nationalist card every time. European integration in its different dimensions was portrayed as a threat to the independence and sovereignty of the country, but also to the fundamental characteristics of Switzerland as a nation – such as federalism, neutrality and direct democracy – particularly as regards the question of joining a supranational organisation such as the EU or removing border checks as required by Schengen. As prominently, the SVP deployed economic prosperity arguments, emphasising the negative consequences of integration and often calling for protectionist measures. Switzerland's economic integration with the EU was seen as negative because it would lead to a rise in unemployment and would be detrimental to Swiss companies. This protectionist stance appears to stem from the party's closeness to small business owners, who are more traditionally oriented towards the domestic market, as well as to farmers. In this sense, the protectionist and conservative tendencies within the Swiss Association of Crafts and Trades (which represents SMEs) and the Swiss Farmers' Union favour the SVP's stance rather than the FDP's. These concerns for the interests of small

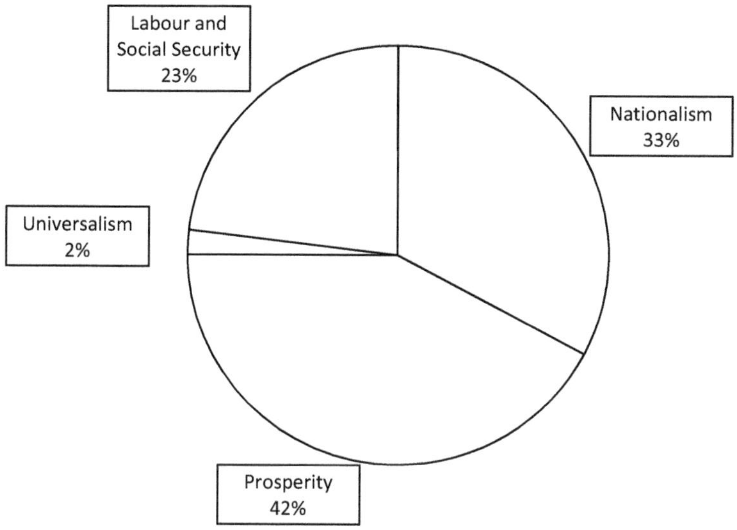

Figure 7.4 SVP (1989–2014).

business owners and farmers went hand in hand with attacks against the perceived "winners of globalisation" such as the export-oriented sector and bankers.

The SVP also voiced left-wing arguments on social protection, and did so exponentially from 2000 onwards. This reflects an attempt to appeal to the "losers of globalisation", i.e. primarily blue-collar workers, by denouncing the expected downward pressure on wages brought about by wage dumping and foreigners' supposed abuse of the social security system. The SVP's ideology on European integration, centred around the protection of national culture, institutions, and economy, fits the wider characterisation of the party as national-populist referred to above. The SVP in fact meets all the criteria of populism generally agreed upon in the scholarly literature such as appealing to the "will of the people", being led by a charismatic leader, and displaying an anti-elite and anti-immigration discourse, nationalism, and aggressive political marketing (e.g. Reynié 2013).

Its roots in Swiss democratic conservatism and its ability to bring together both Protestant and Catholic conservatives, thus bridging the historically deepest cleavage in Swiss politics, have contributed to its success. It has also somehow managed the tension between an ideological commitment to free markets and an actual discourse advocating protectionism, as seen above. It is above all by its courting of the "losers of globalisation" (Kriesi et al. 2012) that the party wins votes, attracting a greater share of the working-class vote than the Socialist Party. It does so by stressing that the high rate of immigration brought about by a highly globalised and Europeanised Switzerland inevitably leads to more intense competition on the labour market. However, as Simon Bornschier (2015) has pointed out, this struggle is not limited to European integration, but is part of the emergence of a cultural divide between the new left and the populist right on societal or cultural issues such as authority, public order, and universalism. This can be seen as a real-world "silent counter-revolution", as theorised by Piero Ignazi (1992), which rejects the societal revolution symbolised by May 1968 and finds refuge in the kind of national conservatism espoused by the SVP. According to Bornschier's (2015) longitudinal research, this wider societal cleavage is even more pronounced than that over European integration per se.

A brief look at the UK

These findings on the Swiss parties' attitudes to European integration find clear echoes in the United Kingdom. Here too, parties have changed their positions radically over time and have experienced, indeed are still very much experiencing, the kind of internal tensions and competitive challenges the Swiss parties had to deal with. In the early days of European integration, both Attlee's Labour government in office from 1945 to 1951 and the Conservative Party governing for the remainder of the 1950s under prime ministers Churchill, Eden, and Macmillan refused to join the the European Coal and Steel Community (ECSC) and the EEC. As recalled in Kreis's chapter in this volume, the UK sought instead to lead an alliance of "reluctant European" countries in the pursuit of an alternative form of international co-operation, embracing free trade but rejecting supranationalism, to which Switzerland was equally warmly disposed. This led to the two countries, together with five others, founding EFTA in 1960.

As early as the following year, however, that same Conservative Party, still led by Harold Macmillan, changed its tack and applied to join the EEC, only to see its application vetoed by France's president Charles de Gaulle. Despite that setback, and a renewed one when a second application was again vetoed by France in 1967, the Conservative Party remained broadly in favour of European integration in the subsequent years whereas Labour was generally hostile to it. Both parties approached it primarily from an economic perspective, the former welcoming the business opportunities offered by wider markets and freer trade and the latter fearing negative consequences for the working classes and government's ability to regulate the economy (e.g. Morris 1996; George and Haythorne 1996).

The different positions of the two parties came to a direct clash in the first half of the 1970s. The Conservative government of Prime Minister Edward Heath took the United Kingdom into the EEC in 1973. Two years later, however, the Labour Party, who had come to power in 1974, called a referendum to decide whether the country should remain an EEC member or withdraw. While the Conservatives, including a young Margaret Thatcher, campaigned in a largely unified manner in favour of a Yes, Labour was deeply divided, with a few leaders in favour of integration and a largely hostile wider membership (Butler 1996). With 67% of the electorate endorsing continued membership, the Conservatives came out on the winning side, reassured that their pro-EEC stance found favour in the electorate.

Although the Conservatives were the more pro-European of the two main UK parties, they were still rather tepid in their endorsement of integration compared to, for instance, Germany's Christian Democrats. A particular bone of contention was the UK's net contribution to the EEC budget. When the Conservative Party returned to power under Prime Minister Thatcher in 1979, it set out to change the terms of the UK's contribution, on the battle cry of wanting "our money back" (Thatcher 1979). The successful resolution of the budgetary dispute in 1984 and the launch of the single market programme the following year deepened the Conservative Party's support for integration. While the Labour Party had reservations about the potentially unbridled competition unleashed by the single market programme, the UK's general attitude to the EEC in those years were among the most positive in the entire post–World War II period.

It would not take long, however, for things to change. The far-reaching plans for institutional reforms and monetary union, which culminated in the 1992 Maastricht Treaty, posed a challenge to both the Conservatives and Labour in that they appeared to erode the sovereignty of the UK to which the two parties were equally attached. It was, however, the ambition to develop a "Social Europe" that more than anything else pushed the parties towards a reversal of their long-standing positions. The prospect of an EU "super-state" engaging in Europe-wide social regulation was anathema to the Conservatives. Thatcher famously warned: "We have not successfully rolled back the frontiers of the state in Britain, only to see them re-imposed at a European level" (Thatcher 1988). In a mirror fashion, though, a "Social Europe" made the EU genuinely appealing to the Labour Party (e.g. Rosamond 1993). From then on, the Conservative Party has become increasingly anti-EU while Labour has displayed more positive, by UK standards, attitudes.

Higher immigration flows since 2004 and the eurozone crisis of 2009–2012 contributed to the politicisation of European integration in the UK. These themes were seized upon by UKIP, which, particularly after its success in the 2014 European Parliament election, posed an increasingly significant challenge to the Conservative Party. Matters came to a head with the Conservative government's decision, under Prime Minister David Cameron, to call a referendum on EU membership. While most of the leadership of the two main parties campaigned in favour of Remain, prominent figures from both joined the opposite side or remained on the sidelines. The divisions among the electorate, however, were even more significant: while a majority of Conservative supporters voted Leave, whereas a majority among Labour supporters voted Remain, 39% among the former and 35% among the latter voted in the opposite direction (Moore 2016). This disconnection between party leaders and followers ultimately pushed the two parties to increasingly identify themselves with either side of the Leave/Remain divide, at the price of turning their backs on their traditional social constituencies. This was prominently on display in the 2019 election, which saw the Conservatives courting the vote of lower-class Brexit supporters and achieving significant inroads in traditional "red" areas, whereas Labour was at pains to retain the vote of the middle class and metropolitan Remain electorate (Curtice 2020).

Conclusions

The chapter has sought to outline the positions taken by the main Swiss political parties on European integration and to uncover the key drivers of these positions before comparing them with those of the UK parties, with the aim of identifying similarities and differences between the two sets of cases. We have seen that the positioning of the FDP and the CVP broadly in favour of Europe is primarily grounded in their expectation that it would deliver greater economic prosperity, as well as, though to a lesser extent, to universalist reasons. The SP supports closer links with the EU primarily for universalist reasons and secondarily to defend labour interests. European integration, though, poses a significant challenge for the party, as reflected in its decision not to support the proposed IFA. As for the SVP, it opposes European integration on the grounds that the latter calls into question the national characteristics of Switzerland and would lead to unfair competition for workers and companies. Party alignment on the IFA, which brings together the social-democratic left and the national-populist right marks a significant departure from recent Swiss political history and signals that the anti-EU camp has broadened.

When set against the trajectory of party positions on Europe in the UK, the Swiss patterns outlined above suggest two main points. The first is that the UK parties, like their Swiss counterparts, had to navigate the tensions between "national" interests, such as the protection of sovereignty, and "constituency" interests such as the benefits of economic integration for business versus the possible costs for workers in the case of liberal-conservative parties and vice-versa for their social-democratic opponents. How parties dealt with these tensions changed significantly between parties and over time, due, not least, to the different configuration of the party system and other national characteristics. The second is that European integration has played a central role in the reconfiguration of political cleavages, whereby the traditional capital–labour cleavage has been to a significant extent superseded by a new cleavage pitting the "winners" of globalisation against its "losers". This reconfiguration has had a major impact on political parties. Social-democratic parties such as Labour and the SP have had to "square the circle" of retaining the support of working-class "losers of globalisation" while at the same time attracting the votes of the intellectual middle class who count among the "winners of globalisation" and have generally been more successful at the latter than the former task. On the opposite side of the spectrum, liberal-conservative parties such as the Conservatives and FDP have to face an increasingly serious challenge from national-populist such as UKIP/Brexit Party and the SVP, and the tension between commitment to free trade and the lure of protectionism. The divergent trajectories of the Conservatives and the FDP illustrate the dilemma liberal-conservatives face: either retrench on a platform of free-market and cosmopolitan liberalism in the case of the FDP or seek to embrace national-populism in a "soft" form in the case of the Conservatives, helped by barriers the electoral system placed in the way of more radical challengers. Conversely, in Switzerland, where such barriers do not exist, the SVP has demonstrated the electoral potential of a national-populist strategy built on a de facto repudiation of free markets in favour of protectionism. The Swiss experience appears to indicate that these tensions and challenges are likely to endure; hence the UK parties will continue to grapple with them in the future. This may have significant consequences for post-Brexit UK–EU relations notably under a future Labour government.

Notes

1 The youth organisation of the SVP is a member of the European Conservatives and Reformists grouping, which was founded by the Tories.
2 The chapter draws on a wider study of Swiss political parties and European integration (Fontanellaz 2019).

8 Explaining support for European integration in direct democracy votes

Pascal Sciarini

The European literature on voting behaviour in direct democracy votes flourished during the 1990s and 2000s, as a result of the growing number of referendums on European integration held in several countries (e.g. Christin and Hug 2002; Franklin et al. 1994; Hobolt 2009; Hug and Sciarini 2000; Mendez et al. 2014). More recently, the 2016 Brexit referendum has sparked the interest of many researchers, and a number of studies help to shed light on which voters cast their ballot for Leave or for Remain, and why (e.g. Hobolt 2016; Vasilopoulou 2016; Curtice 2017; Clarke et al. 2017).

While in most European countries direct democracy processes are rare events, in Switzerland they have been an integral part of government for a long time (Kobach 1994). Direct democracy is a centrepiece of the Swiss political system and part and parcel of Swiss national identity (Kriesi 1999, 2005; Sciarini et al. 2001). As the country with the most extensive experience in direct legislation, Switzerland is often referred to as a "laboratory" (Kriesi and Trechsel 2008; Linder 2010; Sciarini and Tresch 2014). Moreover, while Switzerland is a distinctive case in terms of the development and use of direct democracy, it stands especially apart with respect to the co-decision rights granted to citizens in foreign policy, which has no equivalent worldwide. One can thus learn a lot about the individual determinants of support for European integration from the Swiss case.

This chapter analyses the voting behaviour of Swiss citizens in direct democracy votes relating to Switzerland–EU relations, one of the most crucial and most sensitive issues in contemporary Swiss politics. In the first section, I briefly discuss the structural and institutional context in which direct democracy votes on European integration took place. In the second section, I start with a brief review of the relevant literature and then show the results of two analyses. First, I conduct a meta-analysis of so-called VOX reports, i.e. of reports from opinion polls carried out after the nine democratic votes relating to Switzerland's European policy between 1992 and 2014.[1] I then proceed with my own analysis of VOX survey data. Specifically, I pool the data from the nine separate surveys and I run multiple regression analyses. This twofold strategy helps to identify the factors that have most strongly and most systematically influenced voters' decision for or against European integration. The conclusion summarises the main results and relates them to the findings of recent studies on the Brexit referendum.

The context

Europeanisation and direct democracy

For a long time, Switzerland's foreign policy was not subject to direct democracy. In Switzerland (Marquis and Sciarini 1999; Sciarini 1994), as elsewhere (Lippmann [1922] 1965, Almond 1950, Morgenthau 1956), the dominant view was that foreign policy should be protected from citizens' influence, because citizens were said to be particularly ignorant in this area. However, two amendments to the Swiss Constitution in 1977 and 2003 substantially extended the scope and number of international treaties subject to direct democracy. Structural changes, namely the globalisation of the economy and the internationalisation of politics, further reinforce the consequences of these constitutional reforms. In the era of globalisation, domestic politics and international politics have become increasingly entangled. Political issues that used to be domestic in nature are strongly influenced by economic, political, or technological changes taking place on the international level.

As a result of the multiplication of bilateral or multilateral agreements, i.e. of so-called "direct internationalization" (Fischer 2005, 2007; Sciarini et al. 2002, 2004; Sciarini and Nicolet 2005), the proportion of legislation of international origins out of the total legislative output has considerably increased in Switzerland over time (Linder et al. 2009, Linder 2014). Since the mid-1990s, legislation of international origin has been more voluminous (in terms of pages or articles) than legislation of domestic origin. The two series of bilateral agreements and related implementation laws strongly contributed to this trend (see Schwok, this volume).

The latter point above reminds us that in the European context internationalisation mainly means Europeanisation. Although Switzerland is not a member of the EU it is strongly influenced by the European integration process. After rejection of the EEA in a referendum on 6 December 1992, Switzerland negotiated bilateral agreements with the EU (see Kreis and Schwok, this volume). The two series of negotiations resulted in a number of agreements in various fields (Dupont and Sciarini 2007; Afonso and Maggetti 2007; Schwok 2006) and enabled Switzerland to reach a "customised quasi-membership" in the EU (Kriesi and Trechsel 2008).[2]

The great importance of Europeanisation transpires from Sciarini et al.'s (2015) study of the 11 most important decision-making processes of the 2001–2006 period (see also Sciarini 2014; Fischer and Sciarini 2014). Among those 11 processes, three pertain to "direct Europeanisation": the extension of the agreement on the free movement of persons, the association to Schengen–Dublin agreements, and the bilateral agreement on the taxation of savings (see also Jenni, this volume).[3]

In sum, the extension of direct democracy in the field of foreign policy, together with the internationalisation/Europeanisation processes, have dramatically increased citizens' influence on Switzerland's foreign policy in general, and on its European policy in particular. No wonder then that, ironically, there have been more direct democracy votes on EU-related issues in Switzerland than in any EU member state.

"Permissive consensus" versus "constraining dissensus"

During the first few decades of the EEC, the deepening of the integration process was to some extent premised on the de-politicisation of EU-related issues. The resulting "permissive consensus" among the public allowed elites to take important steps towards European integration (Lindberg and Scheingold 1970; Inglehart 1971). This "permissive consensus" reached its limits with the Maastricht treaty (Gabel and Palmer 1995; Franklin et al. 1994) and then turned into a "constraining dissensus" (Hooghe and Marks 2009).

In Switzerland, by contrast, the requirement to submit EU membership to a compulsory referendum and the option of challenging bilateral agreements with the EU through optional referendums, have prevented the emergence of a "permissive consensus" over European integration (Afonso et al. 2014). Instead, from the outset the institution of direct democracy has contributed to the politicisation of EU matters and stimulated the emergence of a "constraining dissensus".[4]

Already in 1973, Swiss citizens were asked to ratify a free trade agreement on industrial goods with the EEC (see Kreis, this volume).[5] Although the camp opposing the treaty was very small (it consisted of only two small nationalist parties), that opposition prefigured the value conflict on the dimension of "openness-closure" or "integration-independence" between "winners" and "losers" of globalisation that would become central in Swiss politics by the end of the 1980s (see below).

During the 1990s and 2000s, the Federal Council and the Parliament were able to cope with the constraints of direct democracy. After rejection of the EEA – by a narrow majority of the people (50.3%) but an overwhelming majority of the cantons (16 of 23 cantonal votes) – the Federal Council enjoyed consistent popular support for its strategy of cautious, sectoral integration with the EU through bilateral agreements (see also Schwok, this volume). The list of successful direct democracy votes is indeed impressive – seven votes in a row between 1997 and 2009: rejection of the popular initiative "Let the people decide" calling for a withdrawal of the membership application in 1997 (74% of No votes); support for the first set of bilateral agreements in 2000 (67% of Yes votes); rejection of the popular initiative "Yes to Europe" asking for a reactivation of the membership application in 2001 (77% of No votes); support for the agreement on Switzerland's participation in Schengen–Dublin in 2005 (55% of Yes votes); support for the extension of the agreement on the free movement of persons (AFMP) to the ten new EU member states in 2005 (56% of Yes votes); support to the federal law on cooperation with the new EU members in east-central Europe (Switzerland's contribution to the EU's cohesion Fund) in 2006 (53% of Yes votes); renewal of the agreement on the free movement of persons and its extension to Romania and Bulgaria in 2009 (60% of Yes votes).[6]

The successful series came to an abrupt end with the acceptance of the popular initiative “Against Mass Immigration” sponsored by the Swiss People’s Party on 9 February 2014. On that occasion, a narrow majority of the Swiss people (50.3%) but a large majority of the cantons (14.5 of 23) said Yes to the initiative. The initiative “Against Mass Immigration” contradicted the bilateral agreement with the EU on the free movement of persons, since it aimed to reintroduce control over immigration through quotas on foreign workers and a preference for national workers in the labour market (see chapters by Schwok and Jenni, this volume). It also demanded that the Swiss government renegotiate international commitments within three years, to put them in line with the initiative’s requirements.

As a result of the so-called “guillotine clause” included in the first set of bilateral agreements concluded in 1998 (see Schwok, this volume), the termination of the agreement on the free movement of persons would invalidate the other six agreements.[7] After the European Commission rejected Switzerland’s repeated requests to renegotiate freedom of movement, the Swiss Parliament took the lead and opted for a (very) light implementation of the popular initiative. In autumn 2016, it passed a law that under certain conditions requires Swiss employers to inform job agencies about vacancies before hiring a non-Swiss, but does not limit the free movement of EU workers to Switzerland (see Jenni, this volume).

The determinants of voting behaviour in direct democracy votes on European integration

Brief literature review

In the scholarly literature, there are mainly two types of studies on Swiss citizens’ voting behaviour on European integration matters. A first set of studies, based on aggregate data or on individual survey data, focused on specific direct democratic votes, for example that on the EEA in 1992 (Kriesi et al. 1993; Vatter 1994; Anson and Cadot 2004; Sciarini and Listhaug 1997). A second set of studies relate to Switzerland’s foreign policy more generally and thus include, in addition to direct democratic votes on European policy, votes on foreign and security policy and/or on immigration and asylum policy (Sciarini 1999, 2000; Marquis and Sciarini 1999; Sciarini and Marquis 2000; Sciarini and Tresch 2009, 2011). Existing studies show that citizens’ political predispositions (as measured by partisanship, left–right ideology, or political values) strongly influence their voting choices. First, citizens often vote in line with the voting recommendation of their preferred party, and according to a line-up of partisan positions that is specific to foreign policy. On issues relating to domestic policy the usual dividing line is between the Left (Socialists and Greens) and the Right (Liberals, Christian Democrats and Swiss People’s Party). On foreign policy issues, by contrast, left-wing parties often ally with moderate right parties (Liberal and Christian Democrats) against right-wing parties (Swiss People’s Party and smaller nationalist parties) (see Fontanellaz, this volume). In line with this, in direct democracy votes on foreign policy citizens’ vote choice correlate closely with their self-location on the left–right scale.

Furthermore, foreign policy votes typically give rise to a value conflict on the "openness-closure" or "integration-independence" dimension (Brunner and Sciarini 2002; Bornschier and Helbling 2005). The conflict about the desired level of openness of the country towards the outside world was first identified in 1980s direct democracy votes on immigration or the army (Sardi and Widmer 1993). The "openness-closedness" conflict then became salient in foreign policy votes in the 1990s (Christin et al. 2002) such as the 1992 referendum on the EEA (Kriesi et al. 1993; Vatter 1994; Sciarini and Listhaug 1997). Its importance further increased in the 2000s, in particular in votes on Switzerland's European policy (Feddersen 2011). The "integration-independence" conflict opposes the "winners" and "losers" of the globalisation process (Kriesi et al. 2008), i.e. the people who see that process as an opportunity, and those that feel left behind.

Another strand of research has analysed the relative weight of cultural considerations and utilitarian factors in opinion formation on foreign and European policy. As a rule of thumb, it can be said that political scientists deem cultural and identity-related factors as crucial (Kriesi et al. 1993; Vatter 1994; Sciarini and Listhaug 1997), whereas economists emphasise the importance of utilitarian factors (e.g. Brunetti et al. 1999, 2000). Analysing the 1992 EEA referendum and the 2000 referendum on the first set of bilateral agreements with the EU on the basis of municipal-level data, Anson et Cadot (2004) reach a more balanced conclusion: they find that both types of factors matter and are, additionally, linked to each other. However, based on hierarchical models combining project-related and individual factors, Sciarini and Tresch's (2009) analysis of 25 votes in foreign, European, and immigration policy shows that cultural considerations are both more influential and less dependent on the context than utilitarian considerations: cultural factors nearly always matter, irrespective of the "framing" of the referendum campaign, whereas utilitarian considerations play a role mainly when economic issues dominate the campaign.

A meta-analysis of VOX survey reports

Table 8.1 summarises the results of the VOX surveys covering the nine direct democracy votes on European policy mentioned above (see also the list in the appendix to this chapter). It shows whether the bivariate relationship between each socio-demographic or political factor and the vote decision was statistically significant and, if so, what was the difference in votes (Δ) between the two (extreme) categories of the factor in question. The last column ("total") reports the number of cases in which that factor had a significant influence.

We first see that men's vote never differed significantly from that of women. Similarly, age hardly played a role. By contrast, support for European integration varied systematically as a function of the level of education. As Table 8.1 shows, all direct democracy votes under consideration were characterised by considerable differences in voting behaviour between people with the lowest and with the highest level of education. Those differences vary between 22 and 46 percentage

Table 8.1 Summary of bivariate relations from VOX survey reports for the nine direct democracy votes on European policy

	EEA agreement (1992)	*Pop. Init. "Let the People Decide" (1997)*	*First set of bilateral agreements (2000)*	*Pop. Init. "Yes to Europe" (2001)*	*Schengen–Dublin agreement (2005)*	*Extension of the FMPA (2005)*	*Cooperation with Eastern Europe (2006)*	*Extension/ renewal of FMPA (2009)*	*Pop. Init. "Stop Mass Immigration" (2014)*	*Total*
Sex	n.s.	n.s.	n.s.	n.s.	n.s.	n.s.	n.s.	n.s.	n.s.	0/9
Age	n.s.	n.s.	***	n.s.	n.s.	n.s.	n.s.	n.s.	**	2/9
Language (Δ with French speakers)	*** (TI 37, SA 33)	n.s. (TI 17, SA 4)	*** (TI 34, SA 12)	*** (TI 19, SA 15)	*** (TI 25, SA 19)	n.s. (TI 25, SA 6)	n.s. (TI 21, SA 5)	ns (TI 32, SA 7)	** (TI 26, SA 10)	5/9
Rural–urban (Δ)	*** (25)	n.s.	*** (33)	*** (24)	*** (32)	** (19)	n.s.	* (8)	** (13)	7/9
Education (Δ between extreme categories)	*** (33)	** (29)	*** (45)	*** (22)	*** (37)	*** (35)	*** (30)	*** (44)	*** (46)	9/9
Income (Δ between extreme categories)	n.a.	* (12)	*** (32)	n.s.	*** (30)	* (23)	* (24)	*** (22)	*** (30)	7/8
Interest in politics	** (17)	n.s.	*** (14)	n.s.	*** (23)	*** (25)	** (27)	*** (27)	** (22)	7/9
Trust in government (Δ between yes and no)	*** (43)	*** (19)	*** (53)	n.s.	*** (45)	*** (23)	*** (39)	*** (57)	*** (55)	8/9
Left–right (Δ between extreme cat.)	*** (30)	* (15)	*** (55)	*** (55)	*** (64)	*** (69)	*** (53)	*** (56)	*** (73)	9/9

(*Continued*)

Table 8.1 Continued

	EEA agreement (1992)	*Pop. Init. "Let the People Decide" (1997)*	*First set of bilateral agreements (2000)*	*Pop. Init. "Yes to Europe" (2001)*	*Schengen–Dublin agreement (2005)*	*Extension of the FMPA (2005)*	*Cooperation with Eastern Europe (2006)*	*Extension/ renewal of FMPA (2009)*	*Pop. Init. "Stop Mass Immigration" (2014)*	*Total*
Party proximity (Δ SP–SVP)	*** (37)	*** (34)	*** (69)	*** (52)	*** (78)	*** (76)	*** (76)	*** (74)	*** (79)	9/9
Political values: Openness	n.a.	*** (20)	*** (78)	*** (37)	*** (70)	*** (70)	*** (60)	*** (58)	*** (53)	8/8
Political values: Foreigners	n.a.	*** (13)	*** (48)	*** (31)	*** (54)	*** (47)	*** (45)	*** (53)	*** (54)	8/8
N	*870*	*479*	*644*	*712*	*718*	*522*	*589*	*676*	*1065*	

Sources: VOX survey reports (numbers in grey show results that were not mentioned in the VOX report and that I calculated myself).
Notes: ***Significant on the 0.001 level; **Significant on the 0.01 level; *Significant on the 0.05 level; n.s. Not significant; n.a. Non-available.

points across votes. Results regarding household income tell a similar story, yet the effects are slightly weaker and less systematic than those of education.

Next, regional differences in votes were often at work in matters of European policy, be it between linguistic regions/communities or between cities and the countryside. On the one hand, the linguistic cleavage was very salient on the EEA vote, which was strongly supported by French-speaking Swiss but rejected by the German-speaking and Italian-speaking Swiss (more than 30 percentage points difference). However, subsequent votes showed a narrowing of preferences between the German-speaking and the French-speaking communities, even if the latter has remained more supportive of European integration than the former (see also chapters by Mueller and Theiler, this volume). Yet Ticino, the Italian-speaking canton, stood apart since it increasingly opposed European policy and repeatedly appeared as the canton with the highest rejection rate (between 17 and 37 percentage points more of No-vote among Italian speakers than among French speakers) (see also Mazzoleni, this volume).

The weakening of the linguistic cleavage between French speakers and German speakers went hand in hand with a deepening of the urban-rural cleavage. In seven votes out of nine, people living in the countryside have been less supportive of European integration than people living in cities (between 8 and 13 percentage points difference). Moreover, residence location is measured rather crudely in surveys. Therefore, its influence on the vote is presumably underestimated in Table 8.1. It features more prominently in studies based on aggregate data – at the municipality or district level (Linder et al. 2008; Seitz 2014; see also Mueller, this volume). The cosmopolitan and multicultural orientation of city-dwellers opposes the more conservative and inward-looking values of people living in the countryside. Note that the evolution of preferences by linguistic community and that by residence over the last 25 years are arguably linked. That is, the decrease in support for European integration among French speakers living in the countryside and the increase in support among German speakers living in cities contributed to the narrowing of preferences between the two linguistic communities (Engeli and Tresch 2005).

Turning to political factors, one first notes that citizens' vote decision depends on their level of interest in politics: in seven of the nine votes, the higher the interest in politics, the higher support for European integration (the difference in support between people who feel "uninterested" and those who feel "highly interested" varies between 10 and 32 percentage points). Trust in government displays even stronger and even more stable effects: in all votes but one, trust in government correlates significantly with the vote decision; the only exception (the vote on the popular initiative "Yes to Europe" asking for a reactivation of the membership demand) is easy to explain, since it is the only case where the Federal Council recommended to vote against international openness, i.e. to reject the initiative.[8]

Political predispositions, as measured by left–right ideology and partisanship, also appear as consistent determinants. Both factors strongly correlate with the vote choice in all direct democracy vote under consideration. On the one hand, support for European integration decreases markedly as one moves from the left to the right of the political spectrum: in one case (the initiative "Let the People Decide"), the difference in support between citizens who self-locate on the left pole and those who self-locate on the right pole amounts to 15 percentage points only. But in the other cases, the difference varies between 30 and 73 percentage points. On the other hand, there is a strong correlation between partisanship and voters' decision. In all cases but one, the direct democratic vote pitted citizens who feel close to the Swiss People's Party – and accordingly opposed European integration – against followers of the Socialist, Liberal or Christian Democratic parties, who supported integration. This result confirms that in European policy as in foreign policy more generally, the "standard" configuration of partisan conflict is a centre-left coalition against the far right. The "Yes to Europe" initiative again constitutes the exception to the rule. Yet the conflict between followers of Left parties and followers of (both moderate and far) Right parties that dominated in that specific case was in accordance with the vote recommendations of the party elite: the Liberal Party allied with the Swiss People's Party and opposed the initiative, whereas the Socialist Party recommended a Yes vote.[9]

Finally, the last two rows of Table 8.1 confirm that support (or opposition) to European integration is determined by underlying, entrenched political values about Switzerland's international openness, on the one hand, and attitudes towards foreigners, on the other. All available surveys show a strong correlation between the related value scales and the vote choice. The more a person favours international openness, the higher the likelihood that s/he voted for European integration. The difference in support for integration between people locating on the two extremes of the "openness-closure" scale varies between 20 and 70 percentage points across votes. Similarly, people who wish to offer the same chances to the Swiss and foreigners support European integration much more than people who wish to give priority to the Swiss over foreigners (13–54 percentage points difference across votes).

Although informative, the bivariate analyses presented in Table 8.1 suffer from a major weakness: they do not take into account the possible links existing between explanatory factors. For example, as self-location on the left–right scale and partisanship closely correlate, a bivariate analysis does not tell us if what matters more for the vote choice is being a follower of the Socialist Party or having a leftist ideology (or both). To assess the specific influence of a given factor on the vote decision, while controlling for all other included factors, a multiple regression is required.

Table 8.2 shows the result of such a regression analysis, based on a pooled dataset of all nine surveys at our disposal.[10] The analysis includes all variables discussed above, with the exception of income, for which there are too many missing data. Model 1 focuses on socio-demographic factors, model 2 adds political attitudes, and model 3 the two value scales. Table 8.3 helps to grasp the magnitude of the effects. It shows the predicted probabilities to vote in favour of European integration: the first column shows the probabilities calculated from the first model of Table 8.2, and the second column the probabilities calculated from the third, full model of Table 8.2.

Table 8.2 Determinants of the vote decision in direct democracy votes on European policy (non-standardised regression coefficients, standard deviations in parentheses)

	Model 1	*Model 2*	*Model 3*
Sex	0.22***	0.13	0.14
	(0.06)	(0.08)	(0.10)
Age	0.00	0.00	0.00
	(0.00)	(0.00)	(0.00)
Language (reference category: German)			
French	0.61***	0.48***	0.11
	(0.07)	(0.11)	(0.14)
Italian	−1.01***	−1.19***	−1.32***
	(0.13)	(0.17)	(0.19)
City (v countryside)	0.33***	0.17*	0.01
	(0.06)	(0.08)	(0.10)
Education (reference category: apprenticeship)			
Low	−0.40***	−0.32*	−0.30
	(0.10)	(0.16)	(0.20)
Medium	0.73***	0.51***	0.45***
	(0.07)	(0.10)	(0.12)
High	1.26***	0.64***	0.39**
	(0.09)	(0.12)	(0.14)
Interest in politics (reference category: rather interested)			
Not interested		−0.32**	−0.21
		(0.11)	(0.14)
Very interested		0.04	−0.05
		(0.09)	(0.11)
Trust in government (v distrust)		1.45***	1.41***
		(0.11)	(0.09)
Left–right scale		−0.23***	−0.19***
		(0.03)	(0.03)
Party proximity (reference category: Liberal Party)			
Socialist Party		0.43*	0.26
		(0.17)	(0.21)
Christian Democratic Party		0.23	0.16
		(0.16)	(0.20)
Swiss People's Party		−2.00***	−1.93***
		(0.18)	(0.21)
Other party		−0.23	−0.16
		(0.16)	(0.20)
No party		−0.31*	−0.42*
		(0.15)	(0.18)
Pol. value: Openness (v closure)			0.14***
			(0.03)
Pol. value: Equal chances to foreigners (v priority to Swiss)			0.54***
			(0.04)
Constant	−1.14***	0.52	−2.64***
	(0.17)	(0.32)	(0.43)
N	6,319	4,680	3,873
Pseudo R^2	0.14	0.36	0.46

*** $p < 0.001$; ** $p < 0.01$; * $p < 0.05$

Table 8.3 Predicted probabilities of support for European integration

	Δ Predicted probabilities (in percentage points)	
	From model 1	*From model 3*
Sex (Δ men–women)	5	n.s.
Age (Δ 18 years–85 years)	n.s.	n.s.
Language (Δ with French speakers)	Italian speakers: 35 German speakers: 13	Italian speakers: 18 German speakers: 1
City (Δ with countryside)	8	n.s.
Education (Δ between extreme categories)	35	11
Interest in politics (Δ between extreme categories)		n.s
Trust in government (Δ between yes and no)		20
Left–right scale (Δ between extreme categories)		38
Party proximity (Δ Socialist Party–Swiss People's Party)		38
Political values: Openness (between extreme categories)		51
Political values: Foreigners (between extreme categories)		20

Note: n.s. Not significant.

While bivariate analyses did not show any difference in vote between men and women, the first column of Table 8.2 suggests that women are more supportive of European integration than men. However, the difference is small and disappears in subsequent models. The same holds for the difference between citizens living in cities and in the countryside, and for the difference between French speakers and German speakers. Those differences decrease in model 2, including political factors, and completely disappear in the full model.

Thus, while according to models 1 and 2 the vote of French speakers significantly differs from that of German speakers, this is no longer so in model 3. Substantively, this means that French speakers hold political values that are more favourable to international openness and to equal chances for foreigners than German speakers. This in turn, accounts for their stronger support to European integration (see also chapters by Mueller and Theiler, this volume).

By contrast, Italian speakers' opposition to European integration does not weaken in models 2 and 3, which underlines the peculiarity of this opposition (Mazzoleni et al. 2007; see also Mazzoleni, this volume). As Table 8.3 shows, even when controlling for all socio-demographic, political, and value-related factors, the probability to support integration is 18 percentage points lower among Italian speakers than among French or German speakers.

The influence of education on vote choice also remains significant in all models in Table 8.2. According to Table 8.3, the difference in the probability of supporting European integration between the least and most educated people amounts to 35 percentage points in the simplest model and remains sizeable (11 percentage points) when controlling for political attitudes and values.

This result confirms that education has a considerable influence on opinion formation in European policy, as in foreign policy more generally (Sciarini 2000).

The "globalisation cleavage" (Kriesi et al. 2008) between "winners" and "losers" offers a plausible explanation for this result (Giugni and Sciarini 2009): people with low education see European integration as a threat (for their job and/or for the country's traditions and culture), whereas highly educated people believe they possess enough cognitive skills to take advantage of international openness, which they see as an opportunity.

In the multiple regression setting, interest in politics no longer has any effect. By contrast, trust in government, self-location on the left–right scale, party proximity, and political values all contribute to the explanation of individual votes on issues relating to European integration. According to Table 8.3, whether one trusts the Federal Council or not results in a difference in support for European integration of about 20 percentage points. Furthermore, Tables 8.2 and 8.3 show that the remaining four factors have a distinct – and considerable – influence on the vote choice: support for European integration increases by 38 percentage points between the left and right poles of the left–right scale, by 51 percentage points between the "closure" and "openness" poles, and by 20 percentage points between the "priority to the Swiss" and "equal chances for foreigners" poles; finally, support for European integration is 38 percentage points higher among followers of the Socialist Party than among those of the Swiss People's Party. These results confirm that direct democracy votes on European policy are characterised by a complex mix of ideological conflict between the left and the far right, and value/identity conflicts regarding the desired level of openness of the country, which only partly overlap.

Conclusion

Swiss citizens' voting behaviour on EU-related issues show similar characteristics across ballots. Socio-demographic factors and – even more so – political attitudes and values have a strong and systematic influence on voters' support to European integration. Among socio-demographic factors, both the meta-analysis of VOX surveys and my own analysis of the pooled dataset highlight the strong influence of citizens' level of education and the peculiarity of preferences of Italian-speaking persons. Residence location, i.e. the distinction between cities and countryside, also plays a role, and this role is certainly underestimated in survey data. In line with the "winner-loser" divide, well-educated people and voters living in urban areas tend to support European integration, whereas low-educated people, people living in the countryside and Italian speakers tend to oppose. More generally, the strong impact of socio-demographic factors backs the view that the "social stratification of the vote" reaches a high in European policy, as in foreign policy more broadly (Papadopoulos 1996).

The impact of political orientations, as measured by ideology (left–right self-location), party proximity and political values, is – unsurprisingly – even stronger than that of socio-demographic factors. Direct democracy votes on European policy give systematically rise to a sharp conflict between the left and the moderate right, on the one hand, and the radical right, on the other. In addition, these votes also translate into a conflict between supporters of openness (towards the outside world and towards foreigners) and supporters of isolation. This value conflict materialises the conflict between winners and losers of globalisation.

While comparing the determinants of voters' decision in Swiss direct democracy votes on European integration and on the 2016 Brexit referendum is beyond the scope of this chapter, a cursory comparison shows some striking similarities, but also some differences (Clarke et al. 2017, Curtice 2017, Hobolt 2016, Vasilopoulou 2016). Starting with similarities, as in our Swiss (broader) study, voting for Leave or for Remain was strongly influenced by education – and to a lesser extent – income. Studies on the Brexit vote also highlight the overriding importance of political attitudes. More specifically, citizens holding a strong national identity, a right-wing ideology, concerned about immigration, or distrustful towards the government were more likely to cast their ballot for Leave. Differences between the Swiss and the British context are scarcer. First, while age does not play a role according to my results, it is commonly accepted that Leave support was higher among older voters. Second, partisanship had mixed effects on the Brexit vote, with a majority of Conservative supporters voting for Leave, against the Conservative-led government advocating Remain.

Yet the main take-home message of this – tentative – comparison probably regards the importance of the winner-loser divide in both the Brexit referendum and in direct democracy votes on European integration in Switzerland. In both contexts, the better educated and wealthier citizens support open borders, immigration and international cooperation, whereas low-skilled and less well-off people feel threatened, and oppose it. These results further suggest that citizens' attitudes towards European integration are driven by some deep-seated factors impervious to short-term government action.

Notes

1 Since 1981, the VOX surveys interviewed a representative sample of Swiss citizens in the three weeks after a given direct democracy vote, based on a similar questionnaire. The resulting, cumulative database called Voxit now covers more than 300 direct democracy votes. It is available at https://forsbase.unil.ch/datasets/dataset-public-detail/13832/1281/.

2 In addition to this direct form of influence, there is an indirect form of internationalisation or Europeanisation, which is not covered by the present chapter but is nevertheless highly important. Indirect internationalisation takes place notably when a state decides to adapt unilaterally to international or supranational rules, without having participated in their development (Fischer 2005, 2007; Sciarini and Nicolet 2005; Sciarini et al. 2002, 2004). In the last few decades, Switzerland has unilaterally incorporated several European directives and regulations into domestic law (for a summary, see e.g. Linder 2011, 2013). According to Jenni (2014, 2016), a third of legislative changes operated in Switzerland between 1990 and 2010 resulted in regulations that were at least partly compatible with EU rules, in three-fourths of cases through unilateral adaptation and in one-fourth as a result of the bilateral agreements concluded with the UE.

3 Moreover, two additional processes (the revision of the foreigners law and the revision of the telecommunication law) were "indirectly Europeanised" (see note 2).

4 According to Germann (1994), Swiss diplomacy faces a number of constraints that have no equivalent worldwide. In addition to ratification of international treaties being subject to a, mandatory or optional, referendum, the Swiss people also have a say on the resulting implementation laws.

5 Note that Swiss MPs swiftly adopted the free trade agreement but spent more time discussing whether one should submit its ratification to a referendum (Sciarini 1991). The ratification referendum was not constitutionally required, but the parliament decided to hold one, owing to the economic and political importance of the agreement. That referendum set a precedent and stimulated the 1977 constitutional amendment mentioned above (see also Kreis, this volume).

6 To this list, one could add support to the introduction of biometric passports and travel documents as part of the Schengen regulations in 2009 (50.1% of Yes). However, this ballot measure was only weakly connected to European policy and has thus not been included in the analysis. Furthermore, an in-depth study of the decision-making process regarding two agreements (that on the extension of the free movement of persons with the EU and that on Schengen–Dublin) shows that the successful outcome was notably due to the ability of decision-makers to form an oversized coalition in support for their plans (Fischer 2015). This ability, in turn, owes much to the pro-active and inclusive strategy of executive state actors (Fischer and Sciarini 2013).

7 Given the EEA experience, the EU wanted to protect itself against a possible new popular rejection that would hurt the overall balance of concessions. Already during the bilateral negotiations the EU insisted on the "parallelism of the talks", i.e. that any agreement on a given topic was dependent on the acceptance of an agreement on the other issue areas (Dupont and Sciarini 2001, 2007). The "guillotine clause" followed the same logic. If one agreement was rejected by the Swiss, then the whole package would fall.

8 Although at that time the Federal Council still considered EU membership as its long-term objective, it wanted to implement the first set of bilateral treaties and thus considered the initiative "Yes to Europe" as premature. Therefore, while the Federal Council shared the goal of the initiative, it advocated what it called a "reasonable No" to the initiative.

9 Note that this vote divided the leadership and the rank-and-file of the CVP: to many observers' surprise, the party recommended a Yes vote to the initiative, but its followers voted strongly against it (only 16% of Yes-vote according to the VOX survey, see Hirter and Linder 2001).

10 In two cases, the vote decision was recoded so that a No vote meant support for European integration. This regards the initiative asking for a withdrawal of the membership application in 1997 and the initiative "Against Mass Immigration" in 2014.

Appendix

Appendix: List of VOX analyses used in this chapter

Delgrande, M. and W. Linder. 1997. *Analyse des votations fédérales du 8 juin 1997*. Berne: Université de Berne/Institut de recherche GfS, Analyse VOX No 61.

Engeli, I. and A. Tresch. 2005. *Analyse VOX des votations fédérales du 5 juin 2005*. Genève/Berne: Université de Genève/gfs.bern.

Hirter, H. and W. Linder. 2000. *Analyse des votations fédérales du 21 mai 2000*. Berne: Université de Berne/Institut de recherche GfS, Analyse VOX No 70.

Hirter, H. and W. Linder. 2001. *Analyse des votations fédérales du 4 mars 2001*. Berne: Université de Berne/Institut de recherche GfS, Analyse VOX No 73.

Hirter, H. and W. Linder. 2006. *Analyse des votations fédérales du 24 novembre 2006*. Berne: Université de Berne/gfs.bern.

Hirter, H. and W. Linder. 2009. *Analyse des votations fédérales du 8 février 2009*. Berne: Université de Berne/gfs.bern.

Kopp, L. and T. Milic. 2005. *Analyse des votations fédérales du 25 septembre 2005*. Zurich/Berne: Université de Zurich/gfs.Berne.

Kriesi, H., C. Longchamp, F. Passy and P. Sciarini. 1993. *Analyse de la votation fédérale du 6 décembre 1992 (EEE)*. Genève/Berne: Université de Genève/Institut de recherche GfS, Analyse VOX No 47.

Sciarini, P., A. Nai and A. Tresch. 2014. *Analyse de la votation fédérale du 9 février 2014*. Genève/Berne: Université de Genève/gfs.bern.

9 Rooting for Europe

Territorial patterns in voting behaviour

Sean Mueller

Few countries have held as many referendums on Europe – meaning the EU or other forms of Europe-wide cooperation – as Switzerland. In just under 30 years between 1992 and 2018, Swiss citizens were called to the polls no fewer than 11 times, and these votes were always binding on the government. By comparison, the UK as a whole has experienced a total of three referendums in its entire history, of which two have been on Europe (in 1975 and 2016) and one on the electoral system (in 2011).[1] Clearly, then, there is an intimate connection between Europe and direct democracy in Switzerland – one that is sometimes harmonious, sometimes arduous.

At the same time, Switzerland is not currently a member of the EU, nor has it ever voted directly on whether to join or not. Instead the country is linked to the EU via a few general and several policy-specific agreements (see Schwok, this volume). The Swiss case is thus not only illustrative of what happens when supranationalism meets direct democracy. It is also instructive of paths between full EU membership and mere third country status. Indeed, in some policy areas – notably Schengen/Dublin – Switzerland is more "in" the EU than some member states, including the UK before Brexit, which had also never joined the eurozone (e.g. Schimmelfennig 2017).

We can draw several further parallels between Switzerland and the UK. First, just like the Brexit decision of June 2016 was a watershed for UK politics, the 1992 referendum on Switzerland's accession to the EEA was the beginning of a new era in Swiss politics (see Kreis, this volume). Intra-party turmoil, three prime ministers in as many years, court cases pitting government against parliament and two early elections find their Helvetic equivalent in several subsequent and highly contested EU referendums, accentuated polarisation and an overturning of the traditional party hierarchy on the right. Notably the SVP, which in 1991 had obtained just 12% of the nationwide vote, almost tripled its support by 2007 (UFS 2020). It subsequently took almost ten years for Plan C to come into effect (the EEA had been Plan B and EU membership had been Plan A).

Second, both Brexit and the 1992 vote on the EEA – and Swiss referendums on Europe more generally – left behind *territorially* divided countries (Curtice 2017: 16; Goodwin and Heath 2016: 331). While Scotland and Northern Ireland (and Gibraltar) supported Remain with vote shares between 56% and 62%, Wales and England (excluding London) supported Leave with vote shares of 53% and 55%, respectively.[2] Similar divides appeared in the wake of the 1992 vote in Switzerland: French-speaking municipalities supported the EEA with 72%, on average, but German-, Italian-, and Romansh-speaking municipalities recorded only between 28% and 36% votes in favour (own calculations based on UFS 2020). Both Brexit and the EEA referendum also mobilised a large number of voters, resulting in turnout figures of 72% and 79%, respectively (ibid.). Europe is not only divisive but also salient.

Third and finally, both EU referendums also revealed stark *vertical* differences, that is between the people and the political elite, or between voters and MPs. In Switzerland, although both chambers of parliament had clearly recommended joining the EEA, the National Council with 68% and the Council of States with 91% in favour, and although three of the four government parties – Liberals, Socialists, and Christian Democrats – as well as business associations and trade unions all supported that position, 50.3% of voters and 16 out of 26 cantons rejected it (see Kreis, this volume). That was clearly not what the establishment had expected or hoped. The British situation seems similarly puzzling at first sight: both the governing and the main opposition party, the Conservatives and Labour, respectively, were mainly in favour of staying, as were the SNP and the Liberal Democrats (Curtice 2017: 25ff.). However, in the end "voters who backed opposition parties were more likely than government supporters to back the government's position" (ibid. 33). Moreover, as many as 17.4 million citizens ended up supporting the policy long advocated by UKIP, which in May 2015 had garnered fewer than four million votes and only obtained a single seat (although UKIP was not the lead organisation in the Leave campaign).

The purpose of this chapter, then, is to use the opportunity afforded by Swiss data – 11 referendums between 1992 and 2018 on separate but related European questions, with detailed results available at the level of all circa 2,000 municipalities – and distil some key insights for the post-Brexit UK, in particular, and the relationship between supranationalism and direct democracy, more generally.

Swiss referendums on Europe, 1992–2018

Table 9.1 lists all of the 11 referendums held in Switzerland on Europe between 1992 and 2018. Shown are the final results of each of these votes at the national level, both regarding turnout (number of votes cast as a share of all eligible voters) and approval (number of Yes votes as a share of all valid votes).

Most famously, the 1992 vote concerned Switzerland's proposed membership of the EEA. It marked the start of the SVP's sovereigntist campaign – at that time together with radical left and green parties (Trechsel 2007: 42; Fontanellaz and Dardanelli, this volume), although for completely different reasons. The no camp was strongly supported by the AUNS (*Aktion für eine unabhängige und neutrale Schweiz*, i.e. "Action for an Independent and Neutral Switzerland"), founded a few years before to fight Swiss UN membership because it was seen as infringing upon Swiss sovereignty (ibid.). The result of the 1992 vote highlighted the so

Table 9.1 Swiss referendums on Europe, 1992–2018

Year	*Type*	*Title/Content*	*Electorate*	*Turnout (%)*	*Yes (%)*
1992	MR	Accession to the EEA	4,546,571	78.7	49.7
1997	PI	"EU accession negotiations"	4,614,662	35.4	25.9*
2000	OR	Bilateral Treaties I	4,664,482	48.3	67.2
2001	PI	"Yes to Europe"	4,688,461	55.8	23.2
2005	OR	Schengen–Dublin	4,836,712	56.6	54.6
2005	OR	Extension of free movement of persons	4,852,272	54.3	56
2006	OR	Development payments for east-central Europe ("cohesion billion")	4,902,608	45	53.4
2009	OR	Continuation and extension free movement of persons to Romania and Bulgaria	4,999,664	51.4	59.6
2014	PI	"Against mass immigration"	5,211,681	56.6	50.3*
2014	PI	"ECOPOP"	5,247,512	50	25.9*
2018	PI	"Swiss law instead of foreign judges (initiative for self-determination)"	5,420,789	48.4	33.7*

Note: Shaded = accepted; MR = mandatory referendum; PI = popular initiative; OR = optional referendum. *Yes = anti-EU, for all others: Yes = pro-EU. Source: Own compilation based on DFAE (2018b) and UFS (2018a).

called *Röschtigraben*, i.e. the divide in political preferences between the *Romandie* and German-speaking Switzerland (Linder et al. 2010: 500). The EEA road having failed, the five optional referendums of 2000 and 2005–2009 approved discrete steps in the so called "bilateral" (meaning policy-specific and tailor-made) *rapprochement* between the EU and Switzerland (Schwok, this volume).

The popular initiative rejected in 1997 was an attempt by the radical right (including the regionalist-populist Lega dei Ticinesi, but not the SVP) to stop the ongoing EU accession negotiations and continue only once the explicit approval by the people and the cantons had been given (Linder et al. 2010: 552ff.).[3] In turn, the initiative rejected in 2001 had been launched by the pro-EU camp to speed up negotiations through defining full EU membership as a constitutional goal (Linder et al. 2010: 601ff.; Trechsel 2007: 45). The two popular initiatives voted in 2014 concerned Swiss–EU relations only indirectly, namely via demanding an explicit cap on immigration also from EU member states ("against mass immigration") and attempting to limit the annual population growth caused by immigration ("ECOPOP") (Linder and Mueller 2017: 461). While the latter was rejected, the former was accepted by a narrow popular majority of 50.3% and 14.5 (out of 23) cantons. However, the new constitutional article 121a was implemented by parliament in a way that preserved the free movement of persons – against great protest by the SVP in parliament but without having to pass an optional referendum. The SVP initiative of 2018, finally, called for the Swiss constitution to have precedence over international law and jurisprudence in all instances (except jus cogens), requiring the country to renegotiate conflicting international treaties or, if necessary, withdraw from them (e.g. Mueller and Heidelberger 2020). Furthermore, had the initiative been accepted, the Federal Court would only have been permitted to consider international agreements that had passed the optional referendum test, which is, for example, not the case for the European Convention on Human Rights (ECHR).

Except for the four votes of 1997, 2014, and 2018, when voting "yes" meant opposing the EU or the ECHR, supporting voters can thus be said to be pro-Europe. Figure 9.1 shows how strongly the results of the 11 referendums at the municipality level correlate with each other (for 1997, 2014, and 2018, the share of "no" votes was used so that positive values indicate pro-Europe): the lowest correlation coefficient is 0.51, while several coefficients reach 0.9 or more. Most rank between 0.6 and 0.9, indicating a fairly strong and remarkably stable temporal similarity in the underlying voting behaviour (see also Linder and Mueller 2017: 456), although of course different people will have voted in these various instances. For the sake of comparison, also the results from the 1972 vote on the free trade agreement with the EEC are added. Coefficients with this referendum are however much lower, though still positive and substantial, reaching between 0.3 and 0.5 with the other 11.

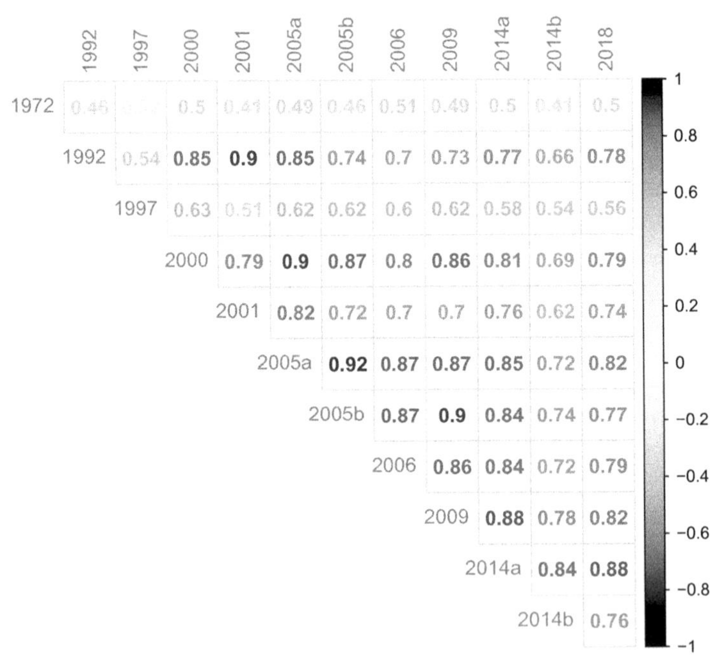

Figure 9.1 Correlation coefficients for 12 EU-related referendums, 1972–2018.

With the exception of the proposed membership in the EEA in 1992, the people (and the cantons, if need be) have thus always supported the Swiss government's EU policy. This seems somewhat ironic: whereas the 1992 vote was mandatory as it entailed constitutional changes, all other votes were optional, that is they occurred only because of post-parliamentary challenges by domestic political actors. But although the Swiss government generally fares better in mandatory than optional referendums (75% v 57% success rate, Linder and Mueller 2017: 303–5), the only major defeat of a government proposal happened precisely in such a mandatory vote.

Next to mandatory and optional referendums, also the third main direct democratic instrument available in Switzerland has affected EU policy. No fewer than six popular initiatives were launched over the past 20 years that directly or indirectly dealt with Switzerland's existing or future relations with the EU.[4] Of these, four were rejected, the latest in 2018, and thus remained without consequences; the one accepted in 2014 was implemented by parliament in a way that did not violate the agreement on the free movement of persons; and the May 2020 vote on the latest SVP initiative has been postponed because of COVID-19 (BR 2020). Initiatives are instruments by which constitutional amendments are proposed from outside the representative institutions. Although they have an even lower success rate than optional referendums, namely just over 10% (22 accepted of 216 voted between 1893 and March 2020; BK 2020b), in EU matters one out of five voted so far has been accepted. Again, then, the "normal" predictions on direct democratic success or failure do not seem to apply.

In sum, not only do we have 11 popular votes spread over almost three decades, from 1992 until 2018, but also different types: one mandatory referendum, five optional referendums and five popular initiatives. All 11 are instances where the Swiss electorate was called upon to bindingly decide the country's European policy. They thus offer us a formidable opportunity to study the territorial distribution of Eurosceptic and Europhile voters in Switzerland. Which areas are most in favour of Europe, which ones are most opposed? Territory matters not just for people's collective identity and a country's cohesion. Given that Switzerland is also otherwise rather diverse, with four regionally entrenched official languages, two historically important and again territorially rooted Christian denominations (Catholics and Protestants) and cross-cutting differences in topography, urbanisation, and economic structure, several interesting hypotheses can be developed and tested empirically.

The main question studied here, therefore, is *whether and why there are differences in the territorial distribution of Europhile voters*. Has it to with the dominant language, with which comes a different set of cultural values (Kriesi et al. 1996; Mueller and Dardanelli 2014), a separate media landscape (Erk 2008), and different challenges and opportunities linked to EU integration (Mazzoleni 2017a)? Or is a pro-EU stance driven by *socio-economic structure*, linked in turn to urbanisation, population density, border location and immigration perceived as enriching or threatening (Senti 2012)?

The next section develops three main hypotheses on the territorial distribution of pro-Europe votes in Switzerland. "Europeanism" captures support for

Switzerland's specific form of European integration, be it through accession to the EEA, embracing bilateral agreements, or the rejection of immigration caps and accepting to be bound by international law such as the ECHR. Swiss Europeanism is thus functionally equivalent to the UK's 2016 Remain option.

Explaining Swiss Europeanism

Who among the Swiss is or should be most in favour of the EU, as such, and of Switzerland's very specific legal, political, cultural, and economic integration into it, in particular? Plunging into the depths of the various dimensions, motivations, and actors of Swiss Europeanism is beyond the scope of this chapter. Nevertheless, we can deduce some general hypotheses from the wider literature on Swiss politics, especially when it comes to the territoriality of voting behaviour. The two main sets of factors that are usually found to influence the propensity to embrace supranational integration are of a cultural and economic nature (e.g. Safi 2010: 107; Sciarini, this volume).

With regard to *culture*, there is the opinion that the lesser the people feel their culture to be under threat, the more international openness and continental integration are seen as an enrichment rather than a danger. Nationalism can be understood in an inclusive or an exclusive way, with opposite consequences regarding newcomers, foreigners, and outsiders in general (e.g. Hooghe and Marks 2018). Applied to Switzerland, we can hypothesise that threats to their cultural status are perceived in a particularly acute manner by members of the linguistic majority, i.e. (Swiss-)German speakers. With some 72% of the Swiss population and corresponding shares in parliament, government and the judiciary (Linder and Mueller 2017: 50), it is they who have the most to lose domestically. Also, although forming the linguistic majority, Swiss-Germans in fact lack a specific political structure that would protect their dialect(s) (Theiler, this volume).

In turn, members of cultural minorities – French, Italian, and Romansh speakers – could be expected to embrace Europe: EU integration signifies closer cooperation with linguistically similar neighbouring countries, France and Italy, that might assist them in counteracting Swiss-German dominance (Trechsel 2007: 42; also Mazzoleni 2017a). Romansh speakers, too, can be argued to be in favour of EU integration since it offers them a similar check on majority dominance as in the case of the other two language groups. They also lack a linguistic kin state and are a minority even within their canton, whereas most members of the other two language groups are in a majority position within their canton.[5] Applied to the logic of territoriality, the first hypothesis thus reads:

H1: French-, Italian-, and Romansh-speaking areas are more in favour of Europe than German-speaking areas.

Turning to the *economy*, Europe opens the door to further job opportunities, investments, markets, and trade more generally – but only for those who are already well-off and/or educated enough to make the most of the chances on offer. Territorially speaking, such is the case for the inhabitants of large and prosperous cities, such as Zurich, Switzerland's financial hub; Basel, the location of major chemical companies; and Geneva, seat of several international governmental and non-governmental organisations. Cities are also the most likely place to encounter cosmopolitan persons with universalist values (e.g. Safi 2010: 113; also Bornschier 2010: 127; Kriesi et al. 2005). Relatedly, Kriesi (1998) has shown that value change is slower in the Swiss countryside, whereas Kübler (2014: 317) delineates the neat mapping of progressive, liberal and conservative ideologies onto urban, suburban and rural areas, respectively. To these political ideologies can be added religious legacies. Although Catholicism has traditionally been associated with the rural hinterland – particularly Central Switzerland, Fribourg, and Valais, losers of the 1847 civil war – and Protestantism with urban liberalism, the main distinction has come to be that between the religious and the secular (Rapp et al. 2014). Secularism, measured through the share of residents professing no religion, thus constitutes an alternative measure of urban cosmopolitanism, so that the second hypothesis comes in two versions:

H2a: Urban areas (with a high population density) are more in favour of the EU than rural areas (with a low population density); and

H2b: Areas with a large share of atheist residents are more in favour of the EU than areas with either many Catholic or many Protestant residents.

A final aspect concerning territoriality and Europeanism relates to borderlands. In principle, one could expect the inhabitants of borderlands – i.e. areas situated along a country's international border – to be in favour of both Europe as such and the EU more particularly. Harmonisation of legal standards and economic integration encourage trade, with cross-border cooperation potentially offsetting the neglect experienced (or at least felt) in many peripheries vis-à-vis their state capital (e.g. Mazzoleni 2017a). However, whether a borderland thrives with the fall of international borders surrounding it or is in turn exposed and overrun depends on the area's particular economic situation. In other words:

H3: Economically prosperous borderlands will embrace Europe, whereas stagnating or declining borderlands will oppose it.

To control for potentially distorting influences in the subsequent analyses, I shall employ population size and area, among structural factors; and the share of the Swiss People's Party (SVP) at the National Council elections of 2015, since in Switzerland the EU debate has been framed and fought almost exclusively by that party over the past few decades (e.g. Kriesi et al. 2005). Couched in anti-universalist, anti-multiculturalist, traditionalist, sovereigntist, and communitarian terms, the SVP has consistently argued against EU integration, globalisation, supranationalism, and immigration (Bornschier 2010: 123ff. and 132; also Fontanellaz and Dardanelli, this volume). Since the SVP is particularly strong in German-speaking, rural, and Protestant areas, care has been taken to avoid multicollinearity problems.

To construct the dependent variable, Swiss Europeanism, I simply average the share of "Yes"-votes in seven and of "No"-votes in four of the 11 referendums listed in Table 9.1. All data are aggregated at the level of the municipalities existing as of January 2020, numbering 2,205, as several municipalities have been "merged away" in the period observed here.[6] Figure 9.2 shows the distribution of Europeanist votes calculated in this way for each of the 26 Swiss cantons. With a minimum of 17.6%, a maximum of 80.6% and a mean value of 53.1%, the emerging picture is thus broad and varied indeed. There is a clear east–west and urban–rural distinction, as hypothesised: French-speaking Geneva, Jura, Neuchâtel, and Vaud clearly lie above the 60% mark, as does Basel City and the cities of cantons Aargau, Berne, Solothurn, and Zurich. However, we can also observe a markedly lower level of Europeanism in the Italian-speaking canton of Ticino, with some communes scoring below 20%, which contradicts H1. Bern is the most diverse canton, almost stretching along the full spectrum. Fifteen cantons have their mean below the 50% line, 11 above.

The subsequent analyses will try to further refine that assessment by means of OLS regressions. As independent variables, I mainly use data from 2000 on the share of German, Italian, French, and Romansch speakers and the extent of religious affiliations (Catholics, Protestants, and atheists) in each municipality. Since this information is drawn from an actual census (the last one conducted in Switzerland) and not merely based on triangulation among registry, survey, and other data (UFS 2011: 2), I regard the information from 2000 as more reliable than later data. It also falls neatly into the middle of the entire period studied here.

Next to information on language and religion, the dataset also includes information on the number of inhabitants (population), area size, and population density; age distribution (0–19, 20–64 and 65+ years old) and the share of non-Swiss residents (aliens); marriage, divorce, birth and death ratios (all as of 2016); the number of persons employed and the number of businesses operating in the three main economic sectors (as of 2015); empty flats in 2017 and new flats per 1,000 inhabitants as of 2015; the share of people receiving social benefits (social ratio, again as of 2016); and the vote shares of all major political parties in the 2015 National Council elections.

Analysing Swiss Europeanism at the municipal level

Let us first look at some of the basic characteristics of Swiss municipalities – population and area size, share of residents aged 19 or below, birth rate and share of non-Swiss residents – and their connection to Europeanism as defined above, next to our key independent variables: language, religion, and population density. Table 9.2 shows the results of three basic models: the first including structural, the second cultural, and the third both types of factors. Looking at model 1, population size, youth, and the share of non-Swiss residents are all positively connected to Europeanism, whereas area size is negatively connected. In model 2, all three variables are highly significant, whereas turning to model 3, only population size, youth, and non-Swiss residents remain significant when confronted with these

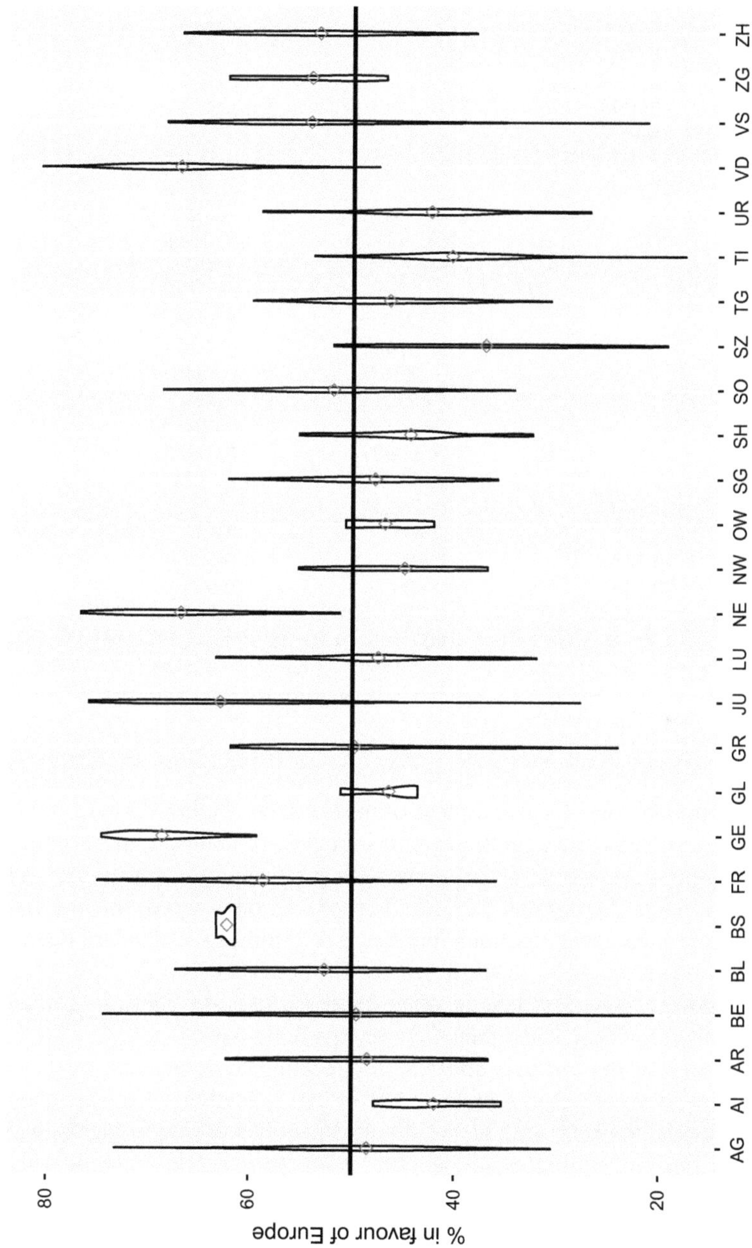

Figure 9.2 Europeanism across the Swiss cantons, 1992–2018.

Table 9.2 Structural and cultural predictors of Swiss Europeanism

	(1)	(2)	(3)
Population size	0.0001***		0.00003**
	(0.00002)		(0.00001)
Area	−0.032***		−0.008
	(0.007)		(0.005)
% young	0.710***		−0.175***
	(0.064)		(0.048)
Birth rate	−0.008		-0.033
	(0.053)		(0.036)
% aliens	0.286***		0.068***
	(0.023)		(0.018)
French		12.752***	13.002***
		(0.343)	(0.364)
Italian		−9.302***	−10.150***
		(0.626)	(0.652)
Romansh		8.222***	8.344***
		(1.574)	(1.613)
% atheist		0.581***	0.554***
		(0.030)	(0.031)
Density		0.002***	0.001***
		(0.0002)	(0.0002)
Constant	33.910***	43.793***	47.221***
	(1.486)	(0.292)	(1.112)
Observations	2,185	2,185	2,185
R^2	0.148	0.601	0.607
Adjusted R^2	0.146	0.600	0.605
Residual Std. Error	9.924 (df = 2179)	6.789 (df = 2179)	6.747 (df = 2174)
F Statistic	75.916*** (df = 5; 2179)	657.465*** (df = 5; 2179)	336.194*** (df = 10; 2174)

Note: *$p < 0.1$; **$p < 0.05$; ***$p < 0.01$.

very strong cultural factors. To give a sense of these effects, Figure 9.3 (a) graphically displays the standardised coefficients of model 3. In addition, these standardised coefficients are arranged by their strength, from the most positive to the most negative impact. The number 1.21 for "French", in other words, means that Europeanism in French-speaking municipalities is 1.21 times the standard deviation in the dependent variable. In other words, Europeanism is $1.21 \times 10.74 = 13$ percentage points higher. Italian-speaking municipalities, by contrast, are ten percentage points less Europeanist than German-speaking ones.

The second step of the analysis consists in checking the robustness of these results by adding the vote shares of the SVP in 2015 (National Council elections) and economic controls, such as the share of people working in the service industry and of those receiving social benefits. With the exception of Romansh, population, and youth, all factors shown in the upper part (a) of Figure 9.3 remain significant also in the lower part (b), even if the variable "% aliens" has changed

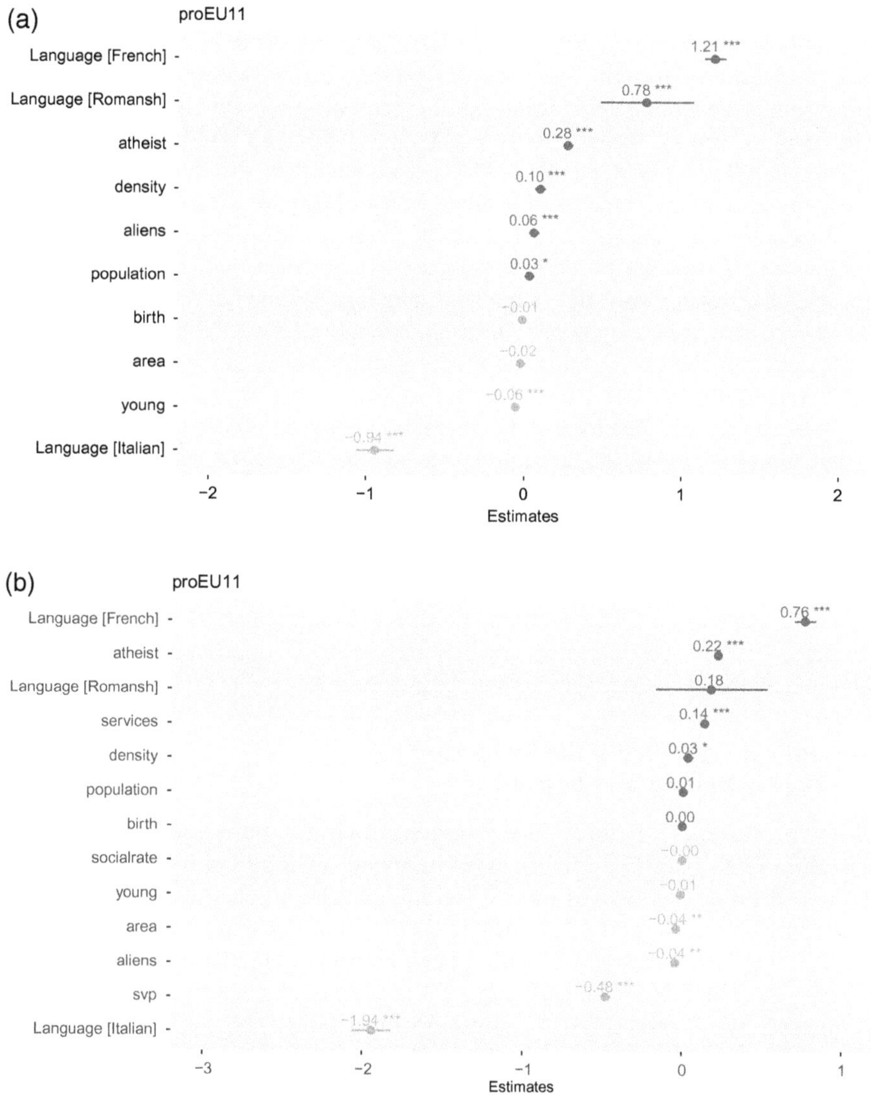

Figure 9.3 Structural-cultural (a) versus political-economic variables (b).

direction and is now negatively correlated with Europeanism. Needless to say, the strength of the SVP in any given municipality is also strongly correlated with Europeanism. Across the board, however, linguistic variables – French on top, Italian at the bottom – continue to exert the strongest influence on Europeanism. Atheism, our – admittedly rather peculiar – measure of local cosmopolitanism, comes honourable second, in line with H2b.

In a third step, we are interested in the importance of borders. Borders matter in several ways, yet the single-most-important aspect for Swiss politics concerns cross-border workers: *Grenzgänger*, in German; *frontaliers*, in French; and *frontalieri*, in Italian. The term describes persons working in Switzerland yet living in and commuting from neighbouring (i.e. EU) countries, notably Italy, France, and Germany, on a daily basis. Between 2002 and 2018, their total number doubled from 160,000 to 320,000 (UFS 2018b). Throughout that period, some 60% of all cross-border commuters worked in Geneva, Basel City, or Ticino.

Accounting for the special situation of municipalities located in these three cantons via a separate borderland dummy, we are even better able to predict Europeanism using only five variables: language (French and Italian speakers versus German speakers), border location, strength of the SVP in 2015, atheism, and population density. Adding the border dummy increases the model fit to $R^2 = 0.775$ (N = 2,175).

In the fourth step, we look at the interaction between border location and economic situation, measured through the social rate. Figure 9.4 shows that outside border areas, the social rate does *not* have a significant effect on Europeanism. *Within* border areas, that is in the cantons of Geneva, Basel City, and Ticino, which are most affected by cross-border workers, the social rate has a negative effect on Europeanism. In other words: in borderland municipalities where many residents depend on social welfare, Europe is less popular. H3 is thus equally verified – relative economic deprivation and territorial exposure to cross-border commuters matter jointly for dampening Europeanism.

Broader insights from the Swiss case for Brexit-Britain and beyond

What to make of all this? The preceding analyses have provided five key insights. First, overall attitudes in Switzerland towards Europe seem to have remained rather stable over time. Even the correlation coefficient between the free trade referendum of 1972 and the SVP's "self-determination" initiative of 2018 – the Swiss version of "taking back control" (Mueller and Heidelberger 2020) – is a high 0.5, although some 50 years have lapsed and surely most of the people who voted in 2018 did not do so in 1972. The correlation between the all-important EEA vote of 1992 and the Europe-related referendum of 2018 is even a high 0.78, as shown in Figure 9.5 for illustration purposes. The difference is of course that the 1992 treaty was rejected, leading to years of insecurity and isolation, whereas the 2018 initiative was equally rejected, but in this case amounting to confirming the status quo and continuing Switzerland's peculiar integration path – for now.

A second insight, therefore, is that nothing is pre-ordained. While a (slim) majority did indeed reject closer economic cooperation with the EU in 1992, the resulting alternative – Switzerland's "bilateral way" – has repeatedly found broad popular support. In fact, as noted above, the Swiss way of cooperating with the EU

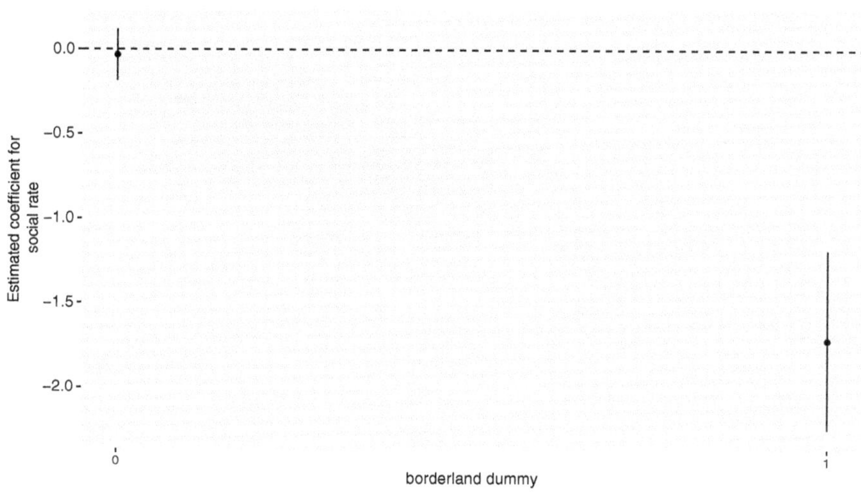

Figure 9.4 Effect of the social rate by borderland dummy (1=borderlands).

has led to even deeper integration in some areas than is or was the case for some member states, including the UK. And even when the tide seemed to have turned again, in that the SVP initiative "against mass immigration" was accepted in 2014 by yet another slim majority, immediately afterwards even clearer anti-European proposals were defeated again. Parliament also found a method to implement the 2014 initiative without restricting the free movement of persons and, in so doing, without jeopardising the whole "bilateral way".

A third insight when comparing these 11 (or 12, if we include 1972) different referendums is that territoriality and communities matter. French-speaking areas in particular have consistently voted more pro-EU than German-speaking areas (64% versus 49% overall), and this even after controlling for urban location, economic situation and partisan factors such as SVP support. However, the same is not true for the second largest minority, the Italian-speaking community, which has turned into the most Eurosceptic part of Switzerland (40%) (see Mazzoleni, this volume). Strikingly similar differences in support for Europe can be observed in the case of Brexit, with Scotland (62% Remain) and the West Midlands (41% Remain) marking the regional endpoints.

Fourth, then, in both the UK and Switzerland territory is intimately connected to political values and economic structure. Both the *Romandie* – French-speaking Switzerland – and Scotland are more social-democratic than the rest of their respective countries; both regions are also unafraid to lose a position of dominance since they are both minorities. Ticino, Switzerland's only Italian-speaking

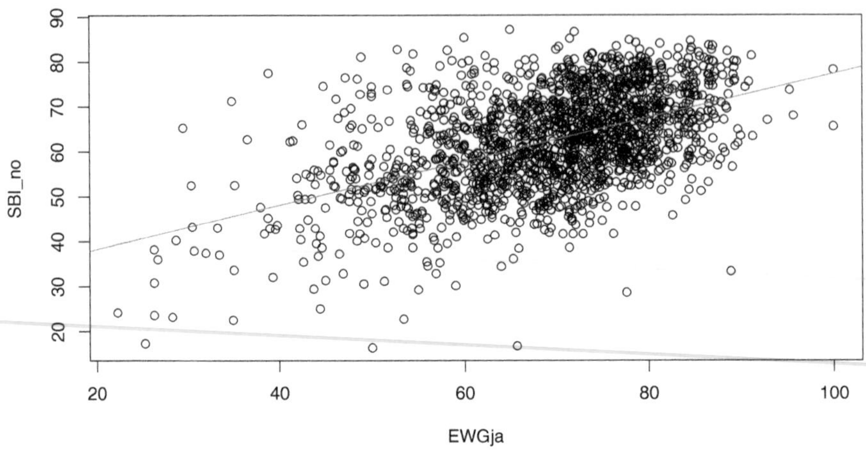

Figure 9.5 Referendums of 1992 versus 2018, local-level results.

canton, is equally in a minority position, but the difference to the *Romandie* is that its economy is much more fragile: highly reliant on services, notably banking; correspondingly hard hit by the fiscal and economic crisis; yet still very attractive to Italian cross-border workers given (a) lower salaries in Italy and (b) the ease with which the commute across the border can be undertaken both physically and mentally. Hence, if for the *Romandie* European integration offers an opportunity to counter German-speaking economic, cultural and political dominance, for Ticino Europe is much more perceived as a threat (see Mazzoleni, this volume). Border location and relative economic deprivation interact to make Europe seem more threatening for Ticino voters.

Fifth and finally, what to say about direct democracy and supranationalism more generally? On the one hand, when "ordinary" voters are asked to decide complex questions with a simple yes or no, or with a choice between "remain" and "leave", we often end up with surprising results. Party ties may function as heuristic cues, or they may not; voters might vote on the question at hand, or they might think of other issues instead; and a rift between elected MPs and electing citizens may open up that takes time to heal. On the other hand, giving voters a chance to have a direct say on public policy might often seem the only way to arrive at a decision at all. If the representative process is blocked because of intra-party fissures, the electorate functions as a neutral arbiter. At the same time, nothing can silence the supposed "defenders of the people" better than the people itself. The irony, of course, is that "taking back control" and giving it to the UK parliament was supported above all by those distrusting that very same parliament (Curtice 2017: 33). The Swiss case, too, is not without paradoxes: notably the 2014 initiative by the SVP "against mass immigration" was supported mainly in those areas where there was little to no immigration but rather emigration, especially by the young and well educated, into the big Swiss cities. And when Switzerland subsequently refused to extend the free movement of persons to Croatia, the EU's retaliation measures in the education, research and culture sectors primarily hit those in favour of Europe.

Conclusion

This chapter has focused on the territorial distribution of Europhiles and Eurosceptics in Switzerland. Through an analysis of local government-level results of 11 key referendums over almost 30 years (1992–2018), it was shown that culture, economic situation, and border location all matter for understanding voting patterns. Thus, French-speaking, densely populated, and proportionally more atheist areas are most enthusiastic about Switzerland's EU integration, whereas German- and Italian-speaking, rural, and borderland municipalities are most sceptical. The Romansch-speaking parts of Switzerland are also in favour of closer ties with Europe.

Hence, to speak of a simple east–west divide when it comes to answering the question "Who's in favour of the EU?" in Switzerland is only partially correct. Instead, what we see is a west–centre–east divide, with the Eurosceptic Centre perforated by urban pockets of Europeanism, notably Bern, Zurich, Winterthur, and St Gallen – but not Lugano or Bellinzona in Ticino. Here, the fact of being a borderland has trumped the urban location, which can be explained by a more fragile economic situation when compared to the rest of Switzerland and a particularly successful regionalist-populist party, the Lega dei Ticinesi (e.g. Mazzoleni 2017a; Mazzoleni, this volume).

More generally, looking at the Swiss experience with direct democratic choices has taught us this: the people sometimes root for Europe, sometimes against it–but where they have put down their own roots matters, too.

Notes

1 See https://www.parliament.uk/get-involved/elections/referendums-held-in-the-uk/ [26.3.2020].

2 Own calculations based on data from the UK Electoral Commission, at https://www.electoralcommission.org.uk/who-we-are-and-what-we-do/elections-and-referendums/past-elections-and-referendums/eu-referendum/results-and-turnout-eu-referendum (26 March 2020).

3 Somewhat clumsily, the official request for full EU membership was sent off by the Swiss government in the midst of the EEA campaign, in May 1992. It was withdrawn only in 2016. See https://www.nzz.ch/schweiz/aktuelle-themen/nach-26-jahren-schweiz-zieht-eu-beitrittsgesuch-zurueck-ld.89101 (10 October 2018).

4 Through popular initiatives, actors can change the Federal Constitution. For this to happen, they need to collect 100,000 signatures within 18 months and gain a double majority in the ensuing referendum, i.e. a majority of people (simple popular majority) and of cantons (cantonal majority).

5 The only exception are French speakers in the Canton of Berne and Italian speakers in the Canton of Grisons, both cantonal and national minorities.
6 Six municipalities in fact do not have their own polling station, bringing the total number of observations per referendum down to 2,199.

10 The cultural roots of Euroscepticism in German-speaking Switzerland and England

Tobias Theiler

Switzerland and the United Kingdom are both Eurosceptic. In the UK, voters opted to leave the European Union in the 2016 Brexit referendum after several decades during which EU membership had met with a mixture of lukewarm acceptance and outright hostility among large sections of the British public. Switzerland, for its part, never joined the EU and is unlikely to do so in the foreseeable future. If membership were put to the Swiss people in a referendum around 85% would currently oppose it.[1]

In addition to their high overall levels of Euroscepticism Switzerland and the UK share yet another characteristic: in both countries their respective majority groups – Switzerland's German speakers and the English in the UK – are more hostile to the EU than the two main minority communities, Swiss Francophones[2] and Scots. In Switzerland, these internal divisions have reproduced themselves throughout a cascade of popular votes, ranging from the ill-fated referendum on EEA membership in 1992 (which was approved by 72% of voters in the predominantly Francophone cantons and 44% in the mainly German-speaking cantons) to a myriad of subsequent referendums on various aspects of Switzerland's relationship with the EU (see chapters by Sciarini and Mueller, this volume).[3] Likewise, 53.4% of the electorate in England voted to leave the EU in 2016 while only 38% of Scottish voters did so (Henderson et al. 2017), after several decades during which attitudes towards the EU in the two societies had increasingly drifted apart.

These figures raise two important questions. First, why are Switzerland and the UK relatively Eurosceptic at the aggregate level? Second, why are their internal majority groups more opposed to EU membership than their main minority counterparts? The first question appears less puzzling than the second as both countries' reluctance to embrace the European integration process fits into a well-established pattern. Countries with relatively successful economies and stable democratic legacies are generally less keen to participate in a supranational project that entails a partial transfer of powers from (sub)national to supranational institutions alongside some economic redistribution and inward migration (Theiler 2004). In addition to Switzerland and the UK, this reluctance also defines other wealthy and historically stable democracies including Norway and Iceland (which never joined the EU) and Sweden and Denmark. By contrast, the internal discrepancies in EU-related attitudes in Switzerland and the UK seem harder to explain. Why do French-speaking Swiss and Scottish voters perceive the EU more favourably than their respective majority counterparts even though they share the same successful historical legacies and economic prosperity?

This chapter focuses on Switzerland to illustrate how such internal divisions can be conditioned by cultural factors. It further argues that a similar culture-centred approach helps explain comparable differences between Scotland and England. In a nutshell, German-speaking Switzerland's internal political fragmentation (into different cantons) and linguistic fragmentation (into different Swiss German dialects) coupled with its lack of institutional backing and complex relationship with its northern neighbour helped generate a sense of cultural vulnerability among the Swiss German population and a desire to limit political exposure to the outside world. These factors continue to shape attitudes towards European integration but they are slowly becoming less significant. The gradual "defragmentation" of the Swiss German idiom accompanied by its growing use at the expense of standard German has pushed Swiss German further along the dialect-to-language continuum while helping to culturally disentangle German-speaking Switzerland from its northern neighbour and render its cultural boundary more secure. Partially as a reflection of this, German-speaking Switzerland's stance towards European integration has softened. This is further aided by the Swiss government's pragmatic policy of consensus-building around a strategy of flexible economic semi-integration with the European bloc and by a widespread desire among German speakers not to further alienate the Francophone minority over Switzerland's relationship with the EU.

The final part of the chapter applies a similar perspective to the UK. Differences between England and Scotland over EU membership are historical rather than linguistic in origin, yet England and German-speaking Switzerland share a similar predicament. Within the UK's complex political edifice, England represents a culturally distinct majority society in a plural state. Its cultural 'content' is contested and it lacks devolved institutions. Such fragility on the inside made parts of the English electorate prefer a measure of political closure towards the outside. Even so, the current reassertion of English national identity across English public life may gradually render Englishness less contested, more inclusive and more secure, somewhat analogous to the gradual solidification of a distinctly Swiss German social and cultural identity. Were this to happen, English, attitudes towards the EU could soften over time. Moreover, the Swiss example suggests that a desire to foster internal unity can further help heal rifts over European integration and generate consensus around a pragmatic rapprochement with the EU.

The "inverted causality" of Euroscepticism in Switzerland

As suggested, explanations for Swiss voters' reluctance to embrace the European integration process often focus on a mix of economic and political factors. Wealthy, stable, and democratic with a successful political history, Switzerland has several attributes that make societies throughout Europe more reluctant to integrate with a bloc that is somewhat redistributive, generates immigration for its wealthier members and entails some transfer of powers from (sub)national to supranational institutions. Some observers also focus on factors more specific to Switzerland, highlighting fears among Swiss voters that closer ties with the EU could damage Switzerland's traditions of neutrality and direct democracy. Neutrality in particular is valued by the Swiss electorate not just for its presumed practical usefulness (e.g. in keeping Switzerland out of foreign disputes) but also as a cornerstone of Switzerland's defining political ethos. Social scientists have termed this neutrality's "identity function" (Szvircsev Tresch et al. 2019: 117).

In accounting for high levels of Euroscepticism among the Swiss electorate at large such explanations appear broadly plausible. Economic concerns and anxieties related to immigration and neutrality figure prominently in the rhetoric of Eurosceptic politicians (see Fontanellaz, this volume). Yet by themselves such concerns cannot account for the difference in EU-related attitudes between German and French speakers. After all, both language communities value Switzerland's defining political principles, above all neutrality, in broadly equal measure (Najy and Schwok 2018; Szvircsev Tresch et al. 2019) and they share similar demographic and socioeconomic characteristics: from (very high) average incomes and immigration levels to (very low) unemployment rates. In light of this, why do more German than French speakers perceive the EU as a threat?

A useful analytical starting point is the concept of "inverted causality" between perceptions and beliefs. A belief that "X harms Y" can cause someone to oppose X, but that belief may itself be sparked by negative perceptions of X that emerged prior to and independently of the belief that X harms Y. For example, a study in the United States shows that people in urban areas with a high percentage of African American residents overestimate the rate of crime in their neighbourhood. Rather than the experience of crime fuelling racial prejudice against African Americans, racial prejudice drives inflated perceptions of crime – the relationship between the two is in effect inverted (Quillian and Pager 2001). Similarly, since Switzerland's French and German speakers share similar socioeconomic circumstances and political attachments, more widespread fears among German speakers that closer relations with the EU could inflict political and economic harm are likely to emanate from negative perceptions of the EU that for their part cannot be reduced to political and economic considerations. Explaining such negative perceptions instead must focus on factors that *do* divide German and French-speaking Swiss – above all language and its social, cultural, and psychological correlates.

Linguistic explanations

The linguistic situation of Switzerland's German-speaking population differs from that of its Francophone counterpart and is quite unlike that of any other society in Europe. Few analysts outside Switzerland appreciate its full complexity and fewer still have related it to attitudes towards European integration. As argued in the following paragraphs, the most important factor is the intricate coexistence of two Germanic idioms.

All German-speaking Swiss use both the Swiss German and the standard – or high – German idiom. Swiss German is the language of everyday communication, used across all social backgrounds and age groups in most social interactions. Standard German, by contrast, has traditionally dominated more formal and public situations such as news bulletins on radio and television, school teaching, speeches by German-speaking federal parliamentarians and religious sermons. Moreover, since Swiss German lacks a standardised written idiom, almost all writing is in standard German. Accordingly, Swiss Germans refer to standard German as *Schriftdeutsch*, or written German. Standard German, in short, is a language that most German-speaking Swiss write often, hear occasionally, and speak rarely.[4]

Unlike in some other diglossic settings, Swiss German and standard German are not outer ends on a linguistic continuum and there are no intermediary registers. Instead, the two are distinguished in a binary fashion. Switching between standard German and Swiss German thus means, in effect, changing from one language to another (Hägi and Scharloth 2005). At the same time, reflecting the historical absence of linguistic homogenisation drives, the Swiss German idiom remains internally fragmented with strong differences in vocabulary, pronunciation, grammar, and syntax between different cantons, areas, and localities.

The Swiss German idiom carries positive connotations for Swiss Germans and helps anchor a distinct social identity. As early as the second year of primary school, children in the German-speaking part of Switzerland develop positive affect towards the Swiss German idiom and negative evaluations of standard German and the two idioms become bound up with their ingroup and outgroup perceptions as they perceive Swiss German as "their" language and standard German as "someone else's" language (Häcki Buhofer and Studer 1993; Sieber and Sitta 1994). Adult surveys reveal similar attitudes: 76% of respondents believe that Swiss German rather than standard German is the language of German-speaking Switzerland while around two-thirds think that Swiss German should be the default language for all spoken communication (Hägi and Scharloth 2005). The growing use of a (non-standardised and highly informal) written version of Swiss German in private electronic communication and on social media reflects the same differentials in how Switzerland's German speakers perceive the two idioms (Ueberwasser 2013). Swiss German signifies intimacy, community, spontaneity, and authenticity whereas standard German to some extent carries opposite connotations.

In combination, these factors place Switzerland's German speakers in a peculiar position vis-à-vis their northern neighbour. The Swiss German idiom is sufficiently distinct from standard German for a social and cultural boundary to have crystallised and become internalised. Being a German-speaking Swiss entails not being German, not to belong to the same cultural category as Germans and to use a different language in almost all spheres of everyday life. Yet because Swiss German remains internally fragmented, because the two idioms are to some extent in competition with each other and, crucially, because Swiss Germans need to "borrow" standard German as their formal written language, the cultural boundary between German-speaking Switzerland and Germany is neither secure nor unproblematic and Switzerland's German speakers remain linguistically entangled with their northern neighbour. Language separates the two societies as much as it binds them together.

From that perspective, the cultural situation in German-speaking Switzerland differs from that of the French-speaking minority. As standard French speakers, many Francophone Swiss reconcile a sense of full and unambiguous membership in the wider Francophone cultural and linguistic space with an equally firm sense of political separateness. Their German-speaking counterparts, by contrast, are *to some extent* part of the wider transnational German-speaking cultural realm yet they cannot fully belong to it; they must locate themselves inside and outside at the same time.

What is more, Switzerland's German speakers must walk this cultural tightrope without institutional backing since German-speaking Switzerland lacks bespoke institutions that could aggregate and articulate an overarching Swiss German interest in relation to Switzerland's federal government, its other language groups and the outside world. The closest lower-level political units are Switzerland's cantons. Most are officially unilingual and under Switzerland's federal system they hold most powers in areas related to language and culture (including education). Yet Switzerland's German-speaking cantons are too heterogeneous and politically fragmented to form a German-speaking political bloc. For its part, Switzerland's federal government must remain culturally and linguistically neutral so as not to privilege one language group over others. It, too, therefore cannot represent German-speaking Switzerland as a linguistic region. As a consequence, Switzerland's German speakers find themselves in a peculiar kind of double bind: just as the overarching Swiss state lacks a unified culture to reinforce its political boundaries, its German-speaking majority cannot lend institutional support and expression to its cultural boundaries because it has no institutions. It inhabits a state that lacks a unifying overarching culture and a distinct culture that lacks overarching institutions.

How does German-speaking Switzerland's cultural predicament influence attitudes towards its northern neighbour and the wider outside world? As is common in situations where "objective" cultural boundaries are fragile and thus attract subjective reinforcement (Cohen 2013), surveys suggest that many German-speaking Swiss believe that they are culturally more different from Germans than from many other groups (e.g. Italians). Similarly, they have long rated German immigrants less favourably than those from most other West European countries (Helbling 2011). Such perceptions started to form long before a substantial increase in German immigration[5] fuelled warnings by some right-wing populist politicians that German-speaking Switzerland faced creeping "Germanisation" (Helbling 2011). Even so, unlike some of their counterparts in east-central and southern Europe (Theiler 2012) most Swiss–EU opponents do not play the "German card" overtly and doing so could easily backfire. Interpersonal relations between German immigrants and their hosts are largely unproblematic and many German-speaking Swiss are frequent visitors to their northern neighbour and avid consumers of German mass media and cultural imports. Most importantly, in Switzerland no overarching political issue is ever fought on overtly cultural grounds since there is no single Swiss culture in a "thick" – e.g. linguistic – sense. Invoking outright cultural arguments could appear as an attempt by one language group to hijack the Swiss state for its particular cultural ends and thus as a betrayal of Switzerland's multicultural ethos.

Yet while debates over Europe are rarely framed in explicitly cultural terms (German-focussed or otherwise), such concerns nonetheless reverberate subtly throughout much of the anti-EU and anti-immigration rhetoric in German-speaking Switzerland. They are embodied in recurrent themes of smallness, encirclement, vulnerability, "over-foreignisation" (*Überfremdung*), and identity loss. During the 1992 EEA referendum campaign, for example, many "no" posters invoked just such themes (see Kreis, this volume). Adopting a graphical retro-style reminiscent of "morale-boosting" posters during World War II, some depicted Switzerland as a tiny red-and-white island amidst a dark European landmass from which other national boundaries had faded. Others featured a crossbow-brandishing Wilhelm Tell as a symbol of Swiss independence, calling on voters to honour his legacy by once again resisting surrender to foreigners. The message was clear: then as now, preserving Switzerland and Swiss identity demands caution and suspicion when dealing with the outside world. It was not an explicitly anti-German message (though that connotation was subtly present) so much as a more general warning against unbridled foreign exposure. During the 2014 campaign on the "mass immigration" initiative (which sought to curb immigration, including from EU countries) the "yes" side played on similar themes. Its most iconic poster depicted Switzerland in the habitual red-and-white livery, this time facing a battalion of dark-clad shadowy figures marching in from the north. The subtext echoed unease vis-à-vis Switzerland's northern neighbour, especially against the backdrop of strong immigration from Germany over the preceding decade (Helbling 2011). It wove such anxieties into a broader narrative of threat and warnings against unchecked openness and exposure to the outside world.

As was argued, such warnings resonate more strongly among many German-speaking Swiss than among their Francophone counterparts because their cultural position is different. It is defined by being separate from a larger (and historically often feared) kin-state while also being culturally tied to it. This has resulted in insecure cultural boundaries of which many German-speaking Swiss are highly protective precisely because they are insecure. Add to this that as a linguistic region German-speaking Switzerland has no political expression and no institutional backing. As a cultural region it confronts the world alone for a cultural region is all it is.

None of this means that most of Switzerland's German speakers perceive European integration as a direct cultural threat. Rather, its complex cultural and political position has conditioned a generally defensive and often inward-looking and isolationist posture in Swiss German society. Switzerland's internal political and cultural equilibrium gives its German-speaking population a niche that reduces its vulnerability. It resents moves that could upset this equilibrium and force it out of its niche. Its unease towards the European integration process is one manifestation of this.

Prospects

How may Swiss German attitudes towards European integration develop in the future? If language has helped shape these attitudes in the past it will likely continue to matter, drawing attention to two interrelated processes that presently characterise the evolution of the Swiss German idiom. First, the balance between Swiss German and standard German is shifting in favour of Swiss German as it continues to encroach into areas traditionally reserved for standard German. Examples include the use of Swiss German in some news bulletins on (especially private) radio and television stations, in some school teaching and on social media where Swiss German has started to make inroads as a (non-standardised) written idiom (Haas 2000; Ueberwasser 2013). Second, while Swiss German remains relatively fragmented, its growing use in the mass media coupled with greater interaction, communication and mobility across Swiss German cantons and regions is slowly reducing differences in syntax, grammar, vocabulary, and pronunciation (Siebenhaar and Wyler 1997; Christen 1998; Haas 2000; Wunderli 2001). If one follows most linguists in distinguishing between a dialect and a language by the range of functional contexts in which they are being used and by their degree of internal standardisation (Laponce 1987), Swiss German has moved further towards the language end of the dialect-to-language continuum. In sociolinguistic terms, the relationship between standard German and Swiss German is moving away from diglossia (a standardised "high" language coexisting with one or more related dialects) towards "asymmetrical bilingualism" with standard German's role increasingly limited to that of a functionally circumscribed second language (Werlen 1998; Hägi and Scharloth 2005). As Swiss German becomes even more widely used and more clearly disentangled from standard German, the boundary between the two idioms will coincide ever more closely with the separation between (formal) writing and speech.

Granted, language does not inevitably shape social identity and political preferences, be it towards European integration or other issues. Even so, if one accepts the logic outlined in this chapter, a Swiss German public which is becoming culturally less fragmented and whose cultural boundary is becoming more sharply delineated, more disentangled from its northern neighbour and more secure might over time become less concerned with protecting and reinforcing that boundary and more confident in accepting greater exposure to the outside world, the EU included.

At the same time, the potential for linguistic and political change in German-speaking Switzerland is limited. Linguistically, the transformation of the Swiss German idiom into a "full" language will remain incomplete as its speakers will continue to write in standard German. Judged by this criterion alone (among several others), German-speaking Switzerland will not in cultural terms become a "normal" European nation, at least not for a long time to come. In addition, German-speaking Switzerland's lack of political institutions is likely to continue indefinitely. The creation of linguistically defined political meta-regions in Switzerland (superimposed on or even replacing the existing cantons) could end German-speaking Switzerland's political "nakedness", matching the gradual emergence of an internally "defragmented" and externally more demarcated Swiss German linguistic space. Yet such a dramatic political reconfiguration seems unlikely even in the very long term and it would risk upsetting the many delicate balances that define Switzerland's decentralised federal system (Métral 2001; see also Dardanelli, this volume).

What, finally, of Switzerland's evolving relationship with the EU? After the defeat of the EEA referendum, Switzerland and the EU negotiated a complex set of sector-specific bilateral agreements (see Schwok, this volume). These integrate Switzerland with most parts of the European single market (including its freedom of movement provisions) but keep it out of the EU's political framework and minimise its subjection to EU law.[6] The bilateral route represents a classic Swiss political compromise. Coinciding with a general decline in the EU's perceived attractiveness to Swiss voters (sparked in part by the Eurozone financial crisis), it eased internal divisions over the issue. Only around 19% of Francophones (versus 14% of German speakers) now "agree" or "rather agree" that Switzerland should seek full EU membership. By contrast, strong majorities in both regions wish to expand economic cooperation with the EU based on the current bilateral relationship.[7] Meanwhile, several right-wing populist movements which built their fortunes on the back of their opposition to EEA membership in the early 1990s have broadened their agenda. They now focus on issues such as the alleged threat Muslim residents pose to "Swiss values" and the expulsion of immigrants with criminal convictions. Such themes, too, bear on Switzerland's relationship with outsiders and they, too, are emotive and divisive. The controversies they generate have partially upstaged Swiss–EU relations at the centre of debates over how Switzerland should interact with the outside world.

As linguistic and political change among its German speakers is partial and uncertain, Switzerland's future relationship with the EU remains unclear. Some signs point to a gradual softening and to a convergence between the language groups on closer economic integration with the Union while staying outside its political framework. Such a softening of attitudes has been encouraged by economic self-interest, by a desire among German speakers not to further alienate Francophones over the issue, by the Swiss government's strategy of consensus-building around an intensification of economic relations with the European bloc, and by German-speaking Switzerland's gradual evolution into a culturally more secure society. Yet this softening of attitudes towards intensified economic integration with the EU is happening slowly and without yet having reached a point of no return. Even if its linguistic regions continue to become less divided over the issue, Switzerland's enthusiasm for the European project will remain muted at best.

Cultural dimensions of English Euroscepticism: Analogies with the Swiss experience

In Switzerland, culture (above all in the form of language) helps shape identity and identity helps inform attitudes towards European integration and drives the (albeit diminishing) divergence between German and French speakers over Switzerland's relationship with the EU. This final section applies a similar approach to the UK, aiming to help explain the divergence in attitudes towards European integration between England and Scotland as highlighted by the Brexit referendum result.

As in Switzerland, it is at first glance tempting to attribute the difference in EU-related preferences between England and Scotland to contrasting instrumental expectations regarding the EU. Surveys have long shown that voters in England associate the EU with greater economic losses and fewer benefits than their Scottish counterparts (Clarke et al. 2017). Yet there are two indications that contrasting economic appraisals of the EU are fuelled by diverging general perceptions of the bloc rather than vice versa, suggesting the same "inverted causality" that also exists in Switzerland. First, economic conditions in England are not so radically different from those in Scotland as to provide a plausible material explanation for highly divergent economic appraisals of the EU. Second, in both Scotland and England instrumental evaluations of the EU co-vary with the *strength* of the respective national identities. English respondents whose English identity is strong and salient to them are "more likely – at a statistically significant level – to emphasise the benefits rather than the costs of leaving the EU" (Henderson et al. 2017: 635) whereas Scottish identity strength correlates positively with expectations of economic gain from EU membership. Against this backdrop, different instrumental evaluations of the EU in England and Scotland do not appear to explain differences in general support for EU membership so much as they reflect them. This begs the question of what causes these differences in attachment to the EU in the first place.

Many analysts point to contrasting historical experiences. Pre-Union Scotland's alliance with continental powers (especially France) implanted perceptions of affinity with Europe into Scottish national identity while England's sustained rivalry with parts of the continent nourished a belief in "English exceptionalism" and separateness. Over many centuries, "the people of the continent, especially the French, became an important 'other' for the English in forming the idea of who they were and who they were not" (Ichijo 2003: 34). In this rendering, the "rediscovery" and revival of English and Scottish nationalism over the past four decades revitalised these contrasting narratives and pushed the two societies further apart. In England, it reduced support for EU membership as "'Europe' [...] developed as Englishness's 'other'" (Henderson et al. 2016: 198), with some commentators arguing that English nationalism and opposition to EU membership became mutually reinforcing (Wellings 2012). By contrast, the rise of Scottish nationalism as a modern political movement steered Scottish society in the opposite direction, epitomised by the Scottish National Party's "independent Scotland in Europe" slogan (Dardanelli, this volume).

The historical origins of Euroscepticism in England thus differ from its linguistic roots in German-speaking Switzerland. Even so, in important respects the two societies share a similar predicament. As argued, German-speaking Switzerland represents an internally fragmented (albeit partially homogenising) linguistic region. Its fragmentation, its need to define itself apart from an overarching Swiss state identity which it numerically dominates and its lack of institutional backing helped produce insecure boundaries and preferences for a degree of political closure. England's boundary, too, is culturally fragile. It attracts competing definitions of what Englishness "means" (or should mean) and how to distinguish it from Britain and Britishness which England numerically and culturally dominates yet in which it cannot simply submerge itself. Since the 1980s, increasing allusions to Englishness, English national identity and English nationalism in public debates and symbolic displays (e.g. in the form of the now-ubiquitous Cross of St George at football tournaments and other public events, see Wellings 2012: 22) have invoked diffuse feelings of community and "patriotically apprehended specialness of place" (English 2011: 5). At the same time, English identity has become increasingly politicised and associated with the conservative and Eurosceptic side of the political spectrum. Reflecting its difficulties in disentangling itself from British identity, however, English nationalism frequently "speaks the language of Britishness" (Wellings 2012: 26) and indeed the language of the UK. This is epitomised by the pro-Brexit UK Independence Party which, despite its name, was an overwhelmingly English movement in both membership and orientation. Finally, like German-speaking Switzerland, England is politically disempowered as it remains the only UK "country" without devolved institutions. Analysts disagree how deeply England's devolution-less status is resented among the English electorate, whether it has promoted or curbed the politicisation of English identity and how strongly it shapes attitudes regarding the EU and other issues (Bond et al. 2010). Clearly, though, the devolution of powers to the UK's other nations in the late 1990s accentuated England's political "nakedness", turning it into a focus for public debate precisely because it made it an anomaly. It left England as the only UK nation without a democratic polity and without institutions of its own, unable to aggregate and express English interests and aspirations.

If England's position thus partially mirrors that of Switzerland's German speakers and if the two regions are similarly Eurosceptic, does this mean that they face similar trajectories from the former to the latter? As with all cultural and identity-centred explanations there is no hard corroboration. Even so, insofar as one accepts that German-speaking Switzerland's complex cultural situation and structural position within the Swiss state has reinforced its reluctance to embrace European integration, it is not far-fetched to draw parallels. England is culturally distinct from other nations in the UK, from Britain and from Europe yet without clearly defined cultural boundaries and without political institutions able to articulate its interests as a distinct society and nation. To the extent that insecurity on the inside encourages protectiveness towards the outside, England's insecure cultural and political position within the British state has likely reinforced its reluctance towards the European project. By contrast, contemporary Scottish nationalism as a political movement has engendered increasingly positive attitudes towards European integration. Largely unencumbered by the cultural insecurities and – post devolution – by the institutional "nakedness" that characterises their English counterparts, it allowed Scottish nationalists to draw on ingrained historical representations when depicting Scotland's relationship with Europe as unproblematic and symbiotic.

What can the Swiss experience tell us about how England's – and the UK's – relationship with the European bloc might evolve? Two observations seem potentially relevant. First, as was noted, in German-speaking Switzerland the gradual transition of the Swiss German idiom into a "fuller" language has strengthened its cultural boundary from the inside and encouraged greater openness towards the outside. Most German-speaking Swiss remain firmly opposed to EU membership but they now support much closer economic ties with the EU than before. Applied to England, the Swiss German experience allows for no firm predictions. What it *does* suggest is that even if England continues to evolve into a more salient category of social identification for its inhabitants (which itself is not certain) this will not *inevitably* deepen English animosity towards the European project still further. To better understand this point, it is important to distinguish between the depth and dissemination of national sentiments on the one hand and the "content" of these sentiments on the other hand. In its current incarnation English national identity is aligned with Euroscepticism (Wellings 2012). Even so, as Benedict Anderson ([1983] 2006) famously argues, nationalism's "content" is neither predetermined nor fixed. It rather represents a blank canvas onto which nationalists may project various political values and agendas. Two developments in particular could help decouple English nationalism from its traditional Eurosceptic anchor. First, the more it draws in parts of the political spectrum beyond its traditional conservative core, the more inclusive and "modernised" English identity will likely become, for instance by shedding its remaining ethnic and racial connotations. That in turn could help steer English-identifying parts of the electorate towards greater openness with respect to the EU and other (often interrelated) issues such as immigration. Generational turnover might further reinforce such an opening as age correlates strongly with EU-scepticism (Curtice 2017). Finally, such a development could be reinforced if England went further than German-speaking Switzerland and obtained devolved political institutions. Only a minority of English nationalists have so far embraced demands for an English parliament though, this too, might change if the movement became more broadly based (Aughey 2010: 512; Brown 2017). The impact of devolution itself on English attitudes towards European integration would of course depend in part on which political forces and ideologies came to dominate a devolved English political system. At a structural level, though, it would end England's current status as a nation without political backing and thereby remove a source of fragility that has likely compounded its scepticism towards the European project.

A second factor that could soften England's aversion to European integration is the danger it poses to Britain's internal unity. In Switzerland, a widespread desire in German-speaking regions not to further alienate the Francophone minority helped the federal government build consensus around forming closer economic ties with the EU. Switzerland's expanding bilateral relationship with the bloc reflects compromise not just externally between Switzerland and the EU but also internally between Switzerland's language communities. In the UK, rifts over Europe threaten national unity much more severely than in Switzerland (Dardanelli, this volume). A quest to secure Scotland's "return to Europe" could clinch a potential future referendum in favour of Scottish independence. During the 2016 Brexit referendum campaign the internal unity theme was overshadowed by other debates yet this does not mean that the English public has become indifferent. This includes relatively conservative voters who are both Eurosceptic *and* concerned about Britain's political survival. The outcome of this remains unclear but in the medium term it brings into view the possibility of a post-Brexit Swiss-style bespoke arrangement that would integrate the UK economically with the European bloc while leaving it outside most of its political structures. The UK government and the EU have both rejected a Swiss-style option so far (Church, this volume). But by reconciling political "exceptionalism" and autonomy with far-reaching economic integration and by mediating between competing demands by English and Scottish electorates, such an arrangement would reflect the kind of pragmatism that in different ways has shaped Swiss and British (and in some measure also the EU's) political traditions.

Conclusion

German-speaking Switzerland and England are majority communities in culturally plural states. Their boundaries are culturally fragile and their "content" fragmented in German-speaking Switzerland and vague and contested in England. Both societies lack institutional backing and articulation. This has left them vulnerable and reluctant to embrace the European integration process. The less insecure they become, the more their reluctance is likely to ease. In German-speaking Switzerland this process is cautiously under way whereas in England it has barely just begun.

One concluding observation: boundaries are not just defined from within but also from without – by what lies on the other side of the boundary. German-speaking Switzerland and England's future relationship with the EU therefore will also be a function of how the Union acts and presents itself. If the EU meticulously avoided interfering in sensitive areas such as culture, education and language, avoided overreaching in response to economic and other crises, and retained a high degree of "constructive ambiguity" and flexibility in policy implementation it would appear less threatening, especially to societies whose own identity is fragile. The future of Euroscepticism in German-speaking Switzerland, in England and beyond will therefore depend not only on how these societies develop internally but also on how the EU evolves.

Notes

1 This is based on the percentage of survey respondents (around 15%) who "agree" or "rather agree" that Switzerland should seek full EU membership (Szvircsev Tresch et al. 2019: 310).

2 This chapter focuses on Switzerland's two main linguistic groups, German and French speakers (comprising around 63% and 23% of the population, respectively). Italian speakers are the third largest community. Of those Italian speakers who belong to the non-immigrant population (rather than to the large Italian diaspora), most inhabit the southern canton of Ticino. There, rejection of closer integration with the EU is broadly as strong as in German-speaking Switzerland, often fuelled by concerns that cross-border workers from neighbouring Italy drive down local wages (see Mazzoleni, this volume). As for the tiny Romansh-speaking population (Switzerland's fourth official language group), clear data are hard to come by since it is scattered across the trilingual eastern canton of Grisons.

3 For detailed data and canton-by-canton breakdowns of referendum results, see BK (2020a).

4 For overviews, see Siebenhaar and Wyler (1997) and Haas (2000). On the complex coexistence of Swiss German, standard German, and French in Switzerland, see Knüsel (1994), Schläpfer (1994), and Wunderli (2001).

5 Immigration from Germany soared after Switzerland had abolished immigration restrictions for most EU citizens in the early 2000s as a result of the bilateral agreements with the European Union (see Jenni, this volume). Of the 2.1 million immigrants living in Switzerland in 2017 around 305,000 were German, which makes them the second largest group of foreigners just behind the Italian diaspora (317,000 members). In several German-speaking Swiss cities, Germans now constitute the largest immigrant group (BfS 2020).

6 In many areas, Switzerland instead continues its declared policy of "autonomously implementing" EU standards (*autonomer Nachvollzug*), thereby (however fictitiously) squaring the circle between safeguarding formal autonomy and partaking in a single market with evolving uniform rules and standards, see Goetschel (2007).

7 More Francophones than German speakers (32.6% versus 43.5%) want Switzerland to move politically closer to the EU without joining, see Szvircsev Tresch et al. (2019: 310 [for data on support for EU membership], 311 [for data on support for closer political relations with the EU], 312 [for data on support for closer economic integration with the EU]).

11 Regionalism and Euroscepticism

The case of Ticino

Oscar Mazzoleni

As discussed in other chapters in this volume, voting patterns on European integration in Switzerland show the relevance of linguistic and urban–rural cleavages. Regionalist mobilisation plays also a crucial role. Although regionalism is not generally expected to emerge in a strong federal system such as Switzerland's, the Canton of Ticino seems to contradict this view. While opposition to EU integration is relatively widespread across the Swiss Confederation, Ticino appears to be a special case. As Tobias Theiler and Sean Mueller show in this book, German-speaking Switzerland is more sceptical of the EU than the French-speaking region, but Euroscepticism is even more pronounced in the Italian-speaking Canton of Ticino. Since the EEA vote in 1992, but especially since the mid-2000s, the proportion of those voting against Switzerland's integration with the EU has always been higher than in the other Swiss cantons. Where does such a strong Euroscepticism come from? How did it change over time? And to what extent is it fuelled by regionalist protest?

This chapter is organised as follows: first, it addresses the relation between regionalism and Euroscepticism. In a second step, it focuses on voting behaviour in federal referendums and initiatives on EU issues in Ticino since the 1970s, before highlighting how regionalist mobilisation frames EU issues and examining the crucial role played by a regionalist party founded in 1991. In the conclusion, the chapter stresses how the case of Ticino illustrates connections that can also be observed in other European regions, e.g. the ways in which Scotland and Northern Ireland are confronting the Brexit dilemma.

Euroscepticism and regionalism

Euroscepticism is a phenomenon increasingly studied within the EU and in countries closely connected to it such as Norway or Switzerland. Scepticism towards the EU is seen as a multi-dimensional phenomenon, involving socio-economic, political-institutional, and cultural aspects (e.g. Szczerbiak and Taggart 2008; Hooghe and Marks 2007; De Vries 2018). Studies on Euroscepticism have not only focused on the relations between national states and the EU. They have also taken into account how certain regions, defined linguistically and culturally but also sometimes institutionally – particularly those characterised by strong regionalist mobilisations – have developed their own specific relationship with European integration (Hepburn 2010; Keating and Hooghe 2006; Dardanelli 2017), where it is not only elite-mass linkages that are at stake, but also people's attachment to their nation and their perceptions of people from other cultures (Steenbergen et al. 2007; Diez Medrano 2003; Hooghe and Marks 2009).

European integration has often been seen by those seeking or defending regional autonomy as a way of weakening the centralism of the nation-state. During the 1980s and 1990s, the regionalist mobilisation of minorities within nation-states on the European continent often identified European integration as an opportunity to facilitate their recognition and self-determination (Gould and Messina 2014). The decline in the sovereignty of nation-states and the development of the single market have emerged as an opportunity to overcome past marginality and discrimination. This has been the case, for instance, of the Catalans in Spain, the Flemings in Belgium, and the Scots and the Welsh in Britain. Until the mid-2000s, the large majority of regionalist movements and parties in Western Europe were far from being openly Eurosceptic (De Winter and Gomèz-Reino 2002; Hepburn 2010; Dardanelli 2017). More recently, however, specific forms of national and regional trade-offs and the EU-mandated austerity have contributed to an emerging Euroscepticism, or, at least, a more critical attitude towards European integration, by actors voicing regionalist claims (Elias 2008; Jolly 2015).

In Switzerland, many analyses have underlined the impact of "nationwide" factors on voting behaviour on EU matters. As Pascal Sciarini's chapter illustrates, voting patterns on the EU and on foreign policy in general show how party identification, levels of education, left–right ideological orientation, and contrasting values regarding Switzerland's future (supranational openness versus national independence), along with the issue of trust in government, almost always have a significant impact. The relevance of territorial issues is also crucial, although this does not imply the same tendencies everywhere, as the chapter by Mueller shows.

Ticino's turn to Euroscepticism

Contrary to the view that may impute Ticino's Euroscepticism to long-term factors, this political orientation was marginal in the canton before the 1990s. Until then, voting behaviour in Ticino was closer to that of French-speaking Switzerland. In the 1920s, Ticino's vote, along with that of the French-speaking cantons and some German-speaking cantons, was a determining factor in Switzerland's entry into the League of Nations (Knüsel 1994: 309). When, in the December 1972 referendum, the electorate approved a free-trade agreement with the European Community (see Kreis, this volume) with 72.4% of votes in favour, Ticino showed even stronger support (with 76% in favour). Since these agreements with the EEC, and subsequently in relation to the International Development Association in 1976, the initiative calling for the introduction of a mandatory referendum for international treaties in 1977, and the first vote on UN membership in 1986, Ticino was clearly among the cantons most inclined to "open up". In the 1986 UN membership vote while 24% voted in favour nationwide, 34.5% did so in Ticino, the highest percentage after Jura and Basel City. On that occasion, all of Ticino's mainstream parties supported the Federal Council's proposal. The campaign led by these parties was relatively cohesive, but not very well fought. Calls for rejection only came from left-wing opposition parties. Again, Ticino confirmed its alignment alongside the other "Latin" cantons as the most open in terms of foreign policy. Consequently, given its previous orientation, the shift that occurred in 1992 was very unexpected: the majority of voters in Ticino opposed Switzerland's accession to the EEA, with a share much higher than the national average (61.5% compared with 50.4%) and in stark contrast with the French-speaking cantons, which tended to be rather EEA-friendly.

The subsequent history of federal votes on foreign policy, especially votes on the EU, reflects a consolidation of the shift that occurred in 1992. The adoption of the bilateral approach enabled in many ways the federal authorities and the main national parties to find agreements with the EU that were able to win the support of a majority of voters and a large majority of the cantons. This did not happen in Ticino, however, where the rejection of any proposal put to a popular vote – the first bilateral agreements, the Schengen and Dublin agreements, and the extension of the free movement of persons – was always clear-cut. Moreover, the gap with the national average widened further since 1992, showing ever stronger majorities voting against European integration. In the six federal votes on European issues that took place between 2005 and 2014, the gap between Ticino and the Swiss average was always well over 12 percentage points. In the vote on the first set of bilateral agreements in 2000, the gap between the national result and that of Ticino was more than double what it had been in the 1992 vote. While the bilateral agreements were approved at the national level with 67.2% voting in favour, including 61.4% approval in the German-speaking region and 76% in the French-speaking region, the level of approval in Ticino only reached 43%. Thus, from the vote on the first bilateral agreements onwards, Ticino's orientation has increasingly set it apart from all the other cantons.

Demand-side evidence

In trying to understand the reasons for this trend, there are some socio-economic factors that seem to have a greater impact in Ticino than in other parts of Switzerland. First of all, there is a question of education and economic resources. Levels of access to higher education and of per capita income in this canton are below the national average. Moreover, other socio-economic and cultural indicators can play a role in Eurosceptic attitudes at a regional or local level, as was recently demonstrated by an in-depth analysis of the Brexit vote (e.g. Lee et al. 2018). Ticino citizens with very low educational attainment face difficulties in finding a job in the French- and German-speaking areas of the country due to the lack of second-language skills. It should also be taken into account that in German-speaking Switzerland it is necessary to speak, or at least to be able to understand, the Swiss-German dialect in addition to standard German (see Theiler, this volume), and this is an obstacle for a large majority of residents of

Ticino. At the same time, in Italy, including in the Northern regions, the severe economic crisis has been hindering access to the labour market for Swiss workers over the course of the past decade. Whilst studies on the voting behaviour of the Swiss in referendums and initiatives on European issues tend to underline the importance of cultural and, in particular, language peculiarities, linguistic realities should be considered in their cultural and identity connotations (Widmer 2004; see also Theiler, this volume).

These aspects are closely linked to centre–periphery concerns among voters. The referendum of 25 September 2005, regarding the extension of the agreement on the free movement of persons to ten new EU member states, was accepted by 56% of voters across the country but only 36% in Ticino. Through multivariate models, an analysis of voting behaviour based on a representative sample showed that, all other things being equal, the most relevant explanatory factor was the degree of confidence in the European Union, followed by an attitudinal measure of territorial representation (Mazzoleni et al. 2007). According to this analysis, rejection or support for this referendum depended very strongly on whether or not Ticino was seen as being a periphery in relation to Berne and to Italy, or a region capable of addressing on its own the economic challenges it faces. Rather than the fear of the so-called "Polish worker", which was one of the main issues discussed in German- and the French-speaking regions, what worried opponents of the expansion of free movement was Ticino's peculiar situation of being squeezed between the growing pressure from the Italian region of Lombardy, especially that from cross-border workers, and difficult relations with Berne. The same patterns emerged from a second opinion poll, also carried out on a representative sample of Ticino citizens, concerning the initiative "Against Mass Immigration", which went to the vote on 9 February 2014 (Pilotti and Mazzoleni 2014: 68–69; Mazzoleni and Pilotti 2015). Once again, feelings of peripherality, vis-à-vis both Berne and Italy, were among the most powerful determinants of the vote. Besides factors highlighted in nationwide surveys across Switzerland – such as support for far-right parties, the perception of one's own personal economic situation, interest in politics, attitudes to Swiss neutrality, and opinions on immigration – perceiving Ticino as an economically vulnerable territory was also a crucial explanatory factor.

Socio-economic crisis and political mobilisation

From a sociological point of view, how are we to explain this trend in Ticino's voting behaviour, that is, the conflation of Euroscepticism and regionalist claims? Three premises are relevant. First of all, each canton enjoys high autonomy, as well as institutional equality with the other cantons, under Switzerland's federal system (see Dardanelli, this volume). Among other aspects, autonomy in the field of education allows Ticino to protect the Italian language within the cantonal territory. Institutional equality, however, does not imply equal levels of prosperity across cantons. Second, it is important to bear in mind that Ticino is Switzerland's only Italian-speaking canton (given that the canton of Grisons is only partially

Italian-speaking). Ticino is also the only canton completely situated to the south of the Alps and the only one whose borders are largely with Italy. Third, it is worth noting that the politicisation of Ticino's peculiar situation within Switzerland emerged at a specific historical juncture, and largely as a result of the role played by emerging political actors who started to express a regionalist and nationalist claim at the beginning of the 1990s.

The shift at the beginning of the 1990s and the subsequent Eurosceptic trend are explained by a twofold component: on the one hand, a rising socio-economic malaise and, on the other, political entrepreneurs' ability to direct this malaise against mainstream parties and European integration. After World War II, the party system and cantonal government were able to a great extent to neutralise the effects of Ticino's position as an economic periphery (Mazzoleni 2017a: 37ff.). Having experienced a period of unprecedented growth from the 1950s to the 1970s, the canton's economy came to be dominated by the tertiary sector, after having been based for centuries on subsistence agriculture. The prosperity achieved by the canton was the result of home-grown investments, positive flows from inter-cantonal financial equalisation, strong growth in the real estate sector, and proximity to Italy, a source of cheap labour and capital flight since the 1950s. In this context of prosperity, European integration was not a political issue within cantonal politics. Against this background, the two-year period of 1991–1992 marked a crucial juncture in Ticino's history, when several challenges emerged and became intertwined. The collapse of the Berlin Wall weakened the classical ideological opposition between left and right. A sudden economic crisis, brought about by a bursting of the real estate bubble, produced galloping inflation (just over 6% in 1991), and unemployment rates unprecedented in the post-war period (from 0.2-0.4% in the 1980s to 4.1% by the end of 1991). This was the most severe socio-economic crisis since World War II and came just a few months before the EEA referendum of December 1992. Suddenly, prosperity started to be perceived as fragile, and memories of the distant past, when Ticino was poor, came back (Toppi 1998).

For the mainstream parties, it was not easy to deal with the feelings of uncertainty and frustration that spread among their electoral constituencies. One of the features of the cantonal party system up to the 1980s was its very high stability, grounded in strong voter loyalty. In 1987, however, the first fissures in the relations between citizens and the traditional parties emerged, with the electoral erosion of the dominant party, the Liberals, the loss of a government seat for the second cantonal force, the Christian Democratic party, and tensions between the canton's two socialist parties. The difficulties for the mainstream parties worsened with the rise of the Lega dei Ticinesi (Albertazzi 2006). While the mainstream parties represented in the cantonal government supported the EEA agreement, the opposition was fronted by two actors: the SVP, at the time still a small party with agrarian roots that had won just 1.59% in the cantonal election of 1991, and above all, the Lega dei Ticinesi, a start-up political movement that contested the 1991 cantonal election and scored a great success, winning 12.5% of the vote. This was a real surprise in the light of Ticino's electoral history and of the fact that never before had a regionalist party been founded in southern Switzerland. Before the arrival of the Lega, all parties in Ticino had belonged to the same party families as their counterparts in the German- and French-speaking regions.

The Lega dei Ticinesi: Between protest and consensus

Ticino's party system has experienced profound change since the 1990s. Step by step, the Lega has become a major player in the canton's political life. This is a prominent exception in the Swiss political landscape, as no other regionalist party has emerged and consolidated itself anywhere else in the country. Since 2011, the Lega has been the main party represented in the cantonal government and the second largest in the cantonal parliament. It has thus been in a position to deeply influence policymaking and shape a new regionalist consensus within Ticino's political system (Mazzoleni 2017b).

The building of a regionalist consensus has been made possible by the Lega's increasingly dominant position in the cantonal institutions, allowing it to develop a coalitional strategy with the mainstream parties but also to frame regional identity as something fragile and under siege from the centre as well as from external challenges. In Rokkan's (1999) definition of the centre–periphery cleavage, there is also an identity component that distinguishes the periphery from the centre, and which contributes to shaping, or giving "coherence", to this sense of peripherality. In Ticino's case, there are two components that reinforce each other. The first is its geographic, linguistic, and socio-economic peripherality. The second is an extensive media network with strong cantonal connotations – currently consisting of three daily newspapers, several periodicals, and one public and one private radio and television channels) – which contributes to the reproduction of a distinct Ticinese identity. It is not by chance that identification with the canton is stronger in Ticino than in the other cantons (Kriesi et al. 1996: 54–56).

The foundation of the Lega may be seen as an expression of the difficulty that mainstream parties faced in addressing the social malaise, while the Lega, has been able, as a political entrepreneur, to impose an interpretation and a narrative of the crisis, that conflates regionalist claims – moulded around the notion of a peripheral canton discriminated by Berne, – and opposition to the opening of national borders (De Lauretis and Giussani 1992). This is a stark peculiarity within the family of regionalist parties: the Lega combined a regionalist and a nationalist (nationwide) claim anticipating some trajectories that can also be observed elsewhere, for instance as regards Italy's (formerly Northern) League. For the Lega, the defence of national borders, that is national independence, is the condition for defending regional interests within a federal system (Mazzoleni and Ruzza 2018). The 1992 campaign on the EEA witnessed the first intense mobilisation of the Lega, which had been founded just a year before. In the history of the Canton of Ticino, it was unprecedented for a grievance movement against Berne, born out of a protest against the traditional parties, to be able to influence the cantonal political agenda to such an extent.

Against Berne and Italy

The critical juncture of the early 1990s opened up a new trend that would characterise the following decades in multiple ways. Ticino has had to face the decline of national protectionism, the rise of neo-liberal policies, and more competitive conditions in the labour market since the 1990s, plus growing economic deregulation under the free circulation of persons and capital. These trends have conspired against any attempts to fix the economic fragilities and reabsorb the social malaise and political protest (Rossi 2015; Mazzoleni 2015). Accordingly, party alignment in referendum campaigns on EU issues in Ticino since the 1990s have tended to reproduce the configuration first seen in 1992. Centre-right mainstream parties such as the Liberals and the Christian Democrats, which were down to 2010 the largest parties in the cantonal parliament, officially supported the federal government's European policy. Their voters, however, did not have clear-cut orientations with regard to EU issues, for instance on the CH-EU enlargement agreement of 2005 (Mazzoleni et al. 2007), which was reflected in intra-party division during the referendum campaign. A study of campaign messages (newspaper articles and letters, advertisements, etc.) for the referendums and initiatives held before 2005 revealed that the Liberals and the Christian Democrats were the two least cohesive parties in the campaign. Moreover, these parties, along with the (pro-EU) Socialist Party, reduced campaign mobilisation in favour of EU integration in the second part of the 1990s (Pilotti and Mazzoleni 2014). Indeed, one of the most important trends in the 1990s and 2000s was the difficulty faced by the mainstream parties in trying to influence popular opinion in federal referendums and initiatives. An analysis of the federal votes between 1993 and 2013 reveals that in 28 cases out of 30, the majority of Ticino's voters diverged from the majority of voters nationwide, going against the advice given by the Liberal Party and the Christian Democratic Party, and instead agreeing with the Lega's recommendations (Stanga 2013: 27). The vote of 9 February 2014 on the initiative "Against Mass Immigration" is a further example. While all of Ticino's mainstream parties recommended rejecting the initiative, the Lega and the SVP supported it. The result was that a large majority (68.2%) of Ticino's voters supported it, compared to 50.3% nationally. Thus, federal referendums and initiatives on European integration became a protest channel through which regionalist demands were expressed against the national government and parliament.

The target of Ticino's new regionalism is not only, as it may be expected, the national "centre", but also neighbouring Italy, because of the challenges it poses in terms of economic competition. The issue of cross-border workers from Italy has become increasingly salient politically from the second half of the 2000s onwards, especially so after the great recession of 2007–2008, when a dispute emerged between the Swiss, Ticino, and Italian authorities regarding relations between the two countries, particularly in relation to cross-border issues (Mazzoleni 2017a: 161ff.). Thus, Ticino's economic problems and the Swiss-EU bilateral agreements have become increasingly linked to each other, given Italy's status as the closest EU country and the growth in cross-border workers (numbering 65,000 in

2019 against a cantonal population of around 350,000). The main argument put forward by the Lega, which has strongly shaped Ticino's political agenda, is that the cross-border Italian workers benefiting from the free circulation of persons (see Jenni, this volume) exacerbate competition in the cantonal labour market and threaten its prosperity. So the founder and leader of the Lega, Giuliano Bignasca, argued, for example, in 2000: "the agreement on the free movement of people is impossible, especially in a border canton such as Ticino, because it would be catastrophic for the economy and the social structure. ... Do you want to risk losing your job because your employer considers you too expensive and points out that the guy coming from nearby Lombardy has the same qualifications as you but is willing to work for half your salary?" (Bignasca 2000: 6, author's translation). In short, while cross-border workers from Italy were perceived to contribute to Ticino's economic development and prosperity up to the 1990s, European integration, by undermining protection measures for the local workforce, helped transform Italian workers into a perceived threat to Ticino's prosperity.

Conclusions

A small majority of Swiss voters expressed opposition to the EEA in 1992, but a clear majority has been supportive of the bilateral agreements that followed. However, this support varies depending on some socio-cultural and economic factors across the country, but also across cantons. As we have seen, one of the cantons where opposition to European integration has been at its highest is the Italian-speaking Canton of Ticino. The main thesis advanced in this chapter is that, in this canton, unlike elsewhere in Switzerland, the centre–periphery cleavage and Euroscepticism have become intertwined. In the southernmost canton Euroscepticism has become more prominent than in all the other regions of Switzerland, as nationalist claims against the EU have been conflated with a regionalist protest. This is the main reason why this canton suddenly eschewed its traditional openness in foreign policy and has turned itself into a champion of Euroscepticism since the 1990s.

This is a configuration that had never previously occurred in Ticino, although the canton has always had a peripheral status from a geographic, linguistic, and economic point of view. Regionalism arose in the 1990s, when a profound socio-economic crisis was successfully framed by the Lega dei Ticinesi, a new regionalist party founded in 1991 that went on to become not only the dominant party in the cantonal government, but also the main political opponent of European integration in Ticino. Generally speaking, once the EU is at stake, it is not only a matter of opposing the EU but also of politicising the socio-economic concerns of a region seen as vulnerable in the face of European integration, Italy, and globalisation. For Switzerland, as a whole, closer European integration brings about deep socio-economic changes. Reactions across cantons, however, have not been uniform. They depend on specific legacies and resources, as well as the evolution of the cantonal party system. In the case of Ticino, one crucial aspect is the fragility of the prosperity model that emerged in the post–World War II period. Since the

1990s, growing socio-economic uncertainty has created opportunities for political entrepreneurs to exploit Ticino's peripherality to demand more autonomy, protection, and resources from Berne.

The case of Ticino is also of interest from a comparative European perspective: it confirms the role played by specific forms of attachment to the nation and perceptions of foreign reality in explaining Euroscepticism (Hooghe and Marks 2009; De Vries 2018). Territorial variation in attitudes to European integration has often been noted and this has certainly been true in the case of Brexit. Voting studies on Brexit have often stressed, for example, the significance of the rural–urban cleavage and uneven economic development (e.g. Goodwin and Heath 2016; Alabrese et al. 2019). The case of Ticino highlights in particular the complex connections between regionalism and minority nationalism, on one side, and Europhilia or Europhobia on the other. As Dardanelli's chapter in this volume discusses, these connections are clearly prominent in the UK, where Scotland's and Northern Ireland's attitudes to Europe have been profoundly shaped by their relations with London (and, in Northern Ireland's case, with Dublin). Above all, the case of Ticino illustrates the role played by party competition between a regionalist challenger and its mainstream rivals. This, once again, finds clear echoes in Scotland and – to a somewhat lesser extent, given that the mainstream UK parties do not operate there – Northern Ireland in the UK context, but also sheds light on competition at the state level between UKIP/Brexit Party and the Conservatives.

12 Learning from Switzerland after Brexit

More barriers than breakthroughs

Clive H. Church

Asking what insights Switzerland offers for post-Brexit Britain may sound like a simple question. In fact, it is doubly problematic. First, it raises technical queries such as what do we mean by "insights", who is offering or seeking them and are they likely to be acted upon? All these can have contradictory answers. Second, it is a question which emerged a few years ago and has rather been left behind by fast-changing events in the UK. Here the rise to political dominance of increasingly radical Brexiteers has seemingly ruled out most ideas of learning from outsiders.

Insights in this context are, more often than not, rarely specific instructions to be followed. At best they are inspirations, suggestions or parallels and that is how they are mainly treated here. In any case, they are very rarely offered by the Swiss authorities and not all that often by the Swiss in general. Indeed, the latter are often prone to warn against attempts at copying them. Moreover, they can themselves seek lessons from the United Kingdom just as the European Union can learn from its own dealings with Switzerland. Many would-be lessons are offered up by British academics, journalists and enthusiastic Brexiteers, although the last can have doubts. Nonetheless, such lessons are usually meant for the UK government and other British decision makers.

However, the Johnson government seems increasingly unlikely either to act on insights or to care about parallels. There are three reasons for this. The first is that the insights available to Britain can be contradictory. Moreover, they often overlook areas where many may think Switzerland has something to offer. Second it is because, despite flashes of interest in Switzerland, much Brexit thinking more and more seems to preclude taking lessons from anyone. From claiming that Brexit would be easy and lead to the maintenance of most of the UK's advantageous links with the EU, supporters of non-membership have, more and more, moved to a position where only unsullied sovereignty and independence count so that the UK has to distance itself from the EU in all dimensions, whatever the costs. This stance now presents a major barrier to adopting ideas from outside. Such stress on "taking back control of money, laws and borders" does not, of course, stop Brexiteers from doing things which the Swiss experience may suggest, to an outsider, were ill-advised. This is despite the view of some observers claiming that Switzerland is again becoming relevant as the UK seeks to negotiate a new relationship with the EU as a non-member (Connelly 2019: 11). Third, it is because the question arises after a period in which the British have, for non-Brexit related reasons, become increasingly unfamiliar with Switzerland. Culturally and generally, Switzerland has lost the place it used to have in British thinking. All these things conspire to prevent any real breakthroughs in terms of Swiss influence on the post-Brexit process in the UK.

To explore these barriers to taking lessons from Switzerland requires an examination of the patchy and spasmodic story of changing British attitudes to Switzerland in the Referendum era, looking at what was sought from Switzerland, what was ignored and how Leavers then rather turned against Switzerland. This leads to a consideration of what the country could offer the UK in the new circumstances, whether immediately in terms of trade negotiating or through longer-term political lessons, both international and domestic, which the UK might learn. Finally, the chapter shows that such post-Brexit reservations are the latest manifestations of this well-established British turning away from Switzerland. All this means that Switzerland is unlikely to be an inspiration or a warning for tomorrow's footloose and fancy-free Britain.

The evolution of British attitudes to Switzerland

While, in recent decades, Switzerland had rarely figured in British political debate, things changed in the run up to the 2016 referendum. There was a certain enthusiasm in anti-EU circles for being like the Swiss. For some, exit offered the possibility of creating a new outer tier of the EU in which the UK and Switzerland might happily exist, enjoying the single market but free of the worst elements of the EU. Hence, Boris Johnson talked of creating a "Britzerland" future for the UK (Gimson 2012; Stephens 2016). Moreover, many in the Leave campaign advocated rejoining EFTA (e.g. Hannan 2012). More common was the way would-be Leavers were encouraged by Switzerland's semi-detached relationship with the EU. They liked the way Switzerland was said to stand up to the EU and rejected the idea of entry (Ashcroft 2016). Moreover, like British Europhobes, the Swiss challenged the very principles of the EU and not just its effects (Glencross 2015). This distance from the EU was often seen as the essential cause of the country's much envied prosperity.

Essentially then, Switzerland was esteemed by Brexiteers because it provided evidence that a country could have a successful life outside the EU, providing justification and encouragement for their hopes. In other words, if Switzerland could resist the EU so could the UK. Such self-interested ideas were clearly British-made. For a minority, however, Switzerland also meant something more, a source of democratic inspiration for a reconstruction of UK politics (e.g. Hannan and Carswell 2008). When the referendum went the Brexiteers' way, interest changed direction. The victors initially thought more in terms of allying with Switzerland than of copying its pattern of relations with the EU. Hence, they sought new links, especially with Swiss Europhobes. Thus, Eurosceptic MPs such as Bill Cash visited the other country, formed a new parliamentary association, and shown considerable enthusiasm for a joint UK-Swiss trade deal with Brussels (BC 2016). Even the Swiss Banking Association hoped that it may be able to set up a financial axis with the City, Hong Kong, and Singapore (Atkins 2016).

Brexiteers, however, took little part in the wider discussion of the "Swiss model" which began to flourish in academic circles and the mainstream press (Bradley 2018). What was referred to as the "Swiss model" was the structure of Swiss dealings with Brussels. Thus, a leader in *The Times* was encouraged by EU openness to Switzerland's adoption of "locals first" employment policies in the aftermath of the 2014 votation (Times 2016).

However, such borrowings were soon rather blocked off by Mrs May's frequent declarations that she wanted a bespoke arrangement and not any hand-me-down copied from another country. This was hammered home in her Lancaster House and Florence speeches and by other ministers (PMO 2017a, b). The increasing tendency of hardline Brexiteers to seek a "no deal" solution, largely reliant on WTO rules, was a further reason why the Swiss option did not figure more prominently in debate. The Scottish Parliament also briefly explored the EFTA option.

One other exception here was the growing interest in Swiss border practices. With the UK initially seeking to maintain frictionless trade after leaving the EU, the apparent lack of formalities and friction involved in entering Switzerland attracted attention. The Northern Ireland Committee thus visited Switzerland to see for itself, while the head of the Swiss customs service was invited to London to give evidence. Other witnesses were quizzed on the subject by the Commons Exiting the EU committee (HOCCEXEU 2018). However, this proved to be something of a dead end. Hence government statements on Switzerland gave a deadpan description of Swiss trade relationships. So, when the *Daily Express* enthusiastically claimed that the outcome of a Chatham House seminar was that the "Swiss model offers UK a BREXIT BLUEPRINT [*sic*] for dealing with EU, say experts", it was out of line both with the conventional wisdom as well as the detail of its own report (McGrath 2018).

Interestingly, much that might have been useful to the UK did not figure in post-Brexit discussion. On the one hand, the debate wholly ignored the fact that Brexit affects third parties such as Switzerland, whose interests should be considered in British policy making. It focussed totally on what the UK should and could do. This is likely to affect post-Brexit British relations with many more states than Switzerland alone. On the other, it rarely took into account that, like Switzerland, the UK was eventually going to be a third country where the EU was concerned and that it needed to prepare for this, especially if there was a limited, or no deal.

This failure to consider the Swiss experience may help to explain why, as time went on, hardline Brexiteers began to actually regard the Swiss "model" as damaging to their cause. Firstly, this was a reflection of the self-radicalisation of Brexit thinking with its growing preference for an absolute break with the EU without any kind of structured deal. There were two other Swiss-based concerns behind this change of mind. First, there seemed to be a specific problem with Swiss agreements with the EU because some of these were subject to a trip-wire (or guillotine) mechanism which meant that failure to maintain one element automatically meant that all other deals would lapse, something British critics referred to as "the Swiss Trap". Seen from the Brexiteer perspective this makes it too costly and damaging to resign from, forcing Switzerland to accept too much unwanted EU regulation (McTague 2017). In fact, the extent of the trip-wire clause is much more limited than many observers claimed.

Second, more general doubts about Swiss closeness to the EU have emerged. These were encouraged when the Swiss Parliament was forced, late in 2017, to evade the requirements of the 9 February 2014 votation on "Against mass immigration" in order to avoid being forced to cancel the country's agreements with the EU, which, worryingly, had led to the freezing of Switzerland's membership of educational and scientific programmes (Schwok and Lavenex 2015; Glencross and McCourt 2018: 10–11). Many Leavers therefore concluded that Switzerland was more in the EU than out, and this they did not want to copy. More recently, such doubts would have been confirmed by the obligation to conform to EU rules and jurisdiction contained in the draft Framework Agreement of December 2018 (DFAE 2018a). The way the Swiss Stock Exchange was penalised for not moving on this was seen as a warning in London. Similarly, a Swiss research report showing how acceptance of EU rules was effectively eroding Swiss sovereignty worried some Brexiteers (Perring 2019).

All this meant that Switzerland came to be seen as too dependent on the EU and so not a fit model or ally. There could also have been an awareness that the Swiss relationship with the EU was not working all that well (King 2018; Read 2020). Even Nigel Farage, despite having once claimed Switzerland's stance as the inspiration for Brexit, added to the criticism, arguing that the country's direct democracy was implicitly threatening, because it could open the way to new – potentially frivolous – votes on Brexit (Adedokun 2019; Farage 2020). This more jaundiced view typifies the way Brexiteer thinking was hardening.

British Brexiteer reticence about Switzerland was paralleled by the decline of Swiss hopes that it could, in turn, learn from Brexit. Although benefiting from David Cameron's attempt to secure EU reforms had proved a forlorn hope (Agnew 2016), the 2016 vote was rapturously welcomed in Swiss anti-European circles, the SVP calling on the government to sign a trade deal at once. However, as it became increasingly clear in Switzerland that Brexit was more a problem than a gain, such hopes died away (Werly 2018).

In fact, some began to think that Brexit was a warning of the difficulties that could face the country in its relations with Europe. Such concerns led the Swiss to launch their "Mind the Gap" strategy to ensure good Swiss–British relations after Brexit. In fact, the Swiss rather took the lead in reminding the British of Switzerland's economic importance to the UK, and then negotiating contingency agreements with the latter. Further deals followed in 2019 (DFAE 2020). Through all this, many Swiss continued to advise the British not to view them as a model (Blatter 2017; Allemand 2018).

Nonetheless, the actual launching of negotiations in March 2020 encouraged the Swiss to ask again if they could learn lessons from Brexit. Thus, there was renewed enthusiasm for Brexitism amongst Swiss Europhobes with *Weltwoche* publishing a rhapsodic review of David Frost's argument that independence and control of one's own laws was the raison d'être of Brexit (Heumann 2020). This was contrasted with the supine behaviour of the Swiss government, allegedly always willing to compromise so as to maintain access to the single market. This sacrificed Swiss sovereignty in a way that the UK was, apparently, not going to do.

However, it is likely that other Swiss would be alarmed by this increasingly aggressive British stance. The EU's behaviour suggests that it has learned rather different lessons from its dealings with Switzerland. In sum, the anti-European approach to mutual learning from Brexit had rather dried up. However, this does not mean that there are no useful parallels between what the Johnson government is about to try and do and Swiss experiences and practices.

Three relevant areas of Swiss experience?

Indeed, despite earlier reticence, the initial British negotiating brief of March 2020 shows some awareness of aspects of Switzerland's relationship with the EU, re-opening the possibility of lessons being learned (HMG 2020). The British have, in fact, drawn on one of three possible areas where Switzerland may be of use to them. This is the trade and institutional relations dimension, although what the Swiss enjoy is less ambitious than what the UK and the EU started out by talking about. Given the emerging signs that overall relations could well be somewhat acrimonious, in a way which Switzerland's relations with the EU have rarely been, a Swiss negotiating style could also be considered.

Such issues are likely to be the most significant in the short term. Yet, beyond this, there are two other longer-term areas where the free-standing UK could well learn from Switzerland, especially if there is "no deal". One is, as already suggested, how to be a third-party state having to relate to decisions taken by the EU which may affect you, whether you like it or not. The other area concerns domestic politics where Switzerland has potential lessons both on holding together a country divided over the EU and on developing a better system of direct democracy. Equally, its experience points to the importance of underlying Europeanisation, something influential but hardly ever directly considered by Brexiteers. However, the likelihood is that the present British government is unlikely to see these as lessons it should learn.

Trade and institutional deals

As the UK formally left the EU and set about negotiating a longer-term relationship with the EU, most attention was focussed on trade. If this were all that was involved then the Swiss experience would have been highly relevant. In fact, although this was not always appreciated in the UK, the latter was expected, as the Political Declaration makes clear, to achieve something wider and more demanding. Indeed, the EU's mandate actually offers the UK a quite unique and privileged form of partnership (EC 2020a).

What the EU had in mind, according to the 440-page draft treaty of 13 March with its six titles and a plethora of annexes and protocols, is a new partnership (EC 2020a). This would cover economic regulation, trade, security (both domestic and international), inclusion of the UK in EU programmes (including a non-voting seat on the European Research Council), institutional arrangements, and other provisions. The assumption was that this was feasible because it built on shared interests, security considerations, and values. There are also separate proposals for foreign policy cooperation, although the EU recognises that the UK does not want to negotiate on this (EC 2020a). The British position in approaching its negotiations with the EU is that things like foreign policy and security do not need an institutionalised form as the EU mandate implies. This no doubt is partly a reflection of the "unwritten" nature of British political culture and constitution. More importantly, such formal relations, whether or not in a partnership, clash with the Brexiteers' desire for the UK to be an independent, and pro-active, state. Politically a partnership could reduce the UK to being a dependant.

Despite its legal requirements, which have dominated discussion in the UK because they contained references to the increasingly demonised CJEU, this was a generous vision. Admittedly, it still requires harmonisation and a level playing field while also talking of sanctions, but nonetheless it is "ambitious and comprehensive". In fact, it offers the UK a unique position, reflecting its importance and its geographical proximity. And it ties the EU down to work with the UK and accept decisions emanating from the partnership institutions. Here there could be a Joint Partnership Council with 16 sub-committees. This goes well beyond the framework agreement currently being considered by the Swiss. In fact, it would endow the UK with rather more than the loose association agreement enjoyed by the Ukraine, to which Michel Barnier, the EU negotiator, once referred (EU 2014; Baczynska 2020).

However, the UK's response has adopted a very different tone, taking its lead from the unusually personal and pugilistic speeches of David Frost, its lead negotiator (Frost 2020; Wright 2020). The initial British position paper is concerned above all with political sovereignty. Addressed as much as to an internal audience as to the EU, the paper justifies itself by the 2019 Conservative manifesto, and looks for a distant, and probably frosty, relationship, not a partnership (HMG 2020). Hence, it regularly snipes at EU regulation and the CJEU while making much of appealing to the WTO and international best practice. It also tries to use existing EU trade deals with Japan, Canada, and others as precedents, while simultaneously vaunting its own world leading roles. It pointedly refuses to submit many of the most sensitive issues to any arbitration mechanism which may emerge.

Although the paper is quite wide ranging, it falls somewhat short of what is suggested in the Political Declaration, something which many think the UK is trying to dodge, along with the Irish protocol. Nonetheless, the potential for cooperation still goes beyond what the Swiss have and, if followed up (as the EU will want to do), would demand long and difficult negotiations. Hence, if something along those lines does emerge, there is a limit to what lessons the Swiss can actually offer the Brexiteers who, increasingly, have moved away from the ambitious visions of 2016 towards merely a clean break (HMG 2019a, b).

Moreover, developments in March 2020 suggested that the UK was moving in a very different direction from Switzerland, using tactics which the Swiss have largely avoided, and would probably counsel against if asked. Thus, on the one hand, its opening statement adopts a very different tone from that used in most Swiss negotiations. Indeed, it reads very much as a mandate dictated by the SVP would probably read. And it envisages a very different atmosphere for post-deal relationships, prickly and willing to make considerable economic sacrifices to maintain pure sovereignty and legal autonomy. Consequently, the paper is very executive oriented, making no provision for parliamentary involvement. It also seeks to move at a very different pace from the Swiss, seeking action by June and September 2020, and threatening to leave on 31 December 2020 with no deal.

On the other hand, it has since gone beyond its initial stance in a number of ways. Thus, it has made it plain that it does not intend to be bound by the European Convention of Human Rights, nor does it want to be involved in either European Air Safety collaboration or the European Medicines Agency. It is also refusing many forms of programmatic cooperation such as REACH. Both steps contrast with the pragmatism shown by Switzerland, which has been very willing to use the Council of Europe as a counterbalance to the EU. Switzerland also seeks to co-operate with most EU policies. Moreover, the increasing British stress on the necessity of border controls from 2021, despite opposition from business, is also very different from Switzerland's utilitarian and consensual approach. So far the British have not, as they had promised, published a draft treaty incorporating these points, confining themselves only to provide four papers on transport, trade, nuclear cooperation, and aviation and hinting that the full proposals will published when it is convenient for the UK to do so. This combination of reticence and uncertainty simply adds to the barriers to learning from Switzerland.

The promised British draft treaty has sometimes been described as being a free trade agreement (with protocols) together with several other proposed accords, not to mention a number of non-treaty-based consultation processes. This throws up a problem where Swiss experience is significant. The UK may want a series of deals, each symbolising an exercise of sovereignty. However, the EU wants a single, all embracing, document, such as its draft published on 19 March. It is also probably aware that the sectorial bilateralism now being pursued by the Johnson government may look attractive but it comes with a high political price (Blatter 2017; Legge 2019).

Switzerland's experience is that the EU will insist on this unity. In fact, it has already rejected a British request for a rapid, separate deal granting equivalence to the financial services industry. It does not want what has been called a "litigious muddle and an 'unruly jumble'" (Duff 2020: 1; Fleming 2020). The EU is said to be keen to avoid the constant negotiations it has had to endure with Switzerland (Rachman 2020). Here, it seems that it is the EU, rather than the UK, which is learning from its experience with Switzerland.

The EU's version of a treaty builds on the suggestions of the Political Declaration and establishes a Partnership Council which would meet in differing configurations, thus allowing for summits and ministerial groups (EC 2020a). It would be assisted by 15 specialist committees. The Council's decisions would be binding and reported to a Parliamentary Partnership Assembly. There would also be popular involvement through domestic advisory groups and a civil society forum.

Although there is also to be an arbitration mechanism not dissimilar to that set out in the framework agreement with Switzerland, these proposals go far beyond what has been agreed in the latter. The framework agreement proposal has only a joint horizontal committee and sectorial sub-committees which can only make recommendations. Implementation is left to each side. The thought arises that the UK might prefer such an arrangement to what the EU is offering, in order to fit in with its intransigent conception of sovereignty. However, in both cases, the EU controversially requires that all questions reflecting on the application of EU law should be decided by the CJEU. The framework agreement also allows for revision and denunciation as well as providing a two-year period for Switzerland to amend its constitution to changes in EU legislation. Interestingly, Switzerland has not produced an alternative framework document because the existing agreement was the result of long drawn out negotiations and was, more or less, agreed by both sides.

The British approach also conflicts with Switzerland's practice of negotiating its deals in other ways, which the Brexiteers may be well advised to learn. The Swiss have found that it is a long, complex, and difficult process. Delaying, or imposing rigid deadlines, as the Johnson government is doing, rarely works. In fact, as the COVID-19 crisis is engulfing the UK and calls for an extension multiply (Cowburn 2020; Zuleg 2020), Brexiteers like the European Research Group, the *Daily Express*, and *Independence Daily* remain insistent on persevering with the deadlines, often arguing both that the crisis makes leaving more than ever justified (Maddox and Williamson 2020) and that there are no reasons for postponing the negotiations. In Switzerland, by comparison, the whole topic has been dropped and even the SVP approved the delaying of the 17 May anti-EU votation (eventually held on 27 September 2020).

Another difference is that the Swiss have found that the EU has clout, tends to play hard, and it means most of what it says. Brexiteer opinion is that the EU is both fallible and is convulsed by its own crises so that it will not resist British demands. Equally the Swiss have found that it is wise not to tackle basic EU principles head on. Doing so in spades is, of course, written into Brexiteers' DNA and still dominates their discourse. All this contrasts with the more measured Swiss approach. Given that the Swiss export 20 times as much per head to the EU than they import from it, they are aware that embarking on a British style policy, where the default seems more and more to be no deal, would be disastrous for them.

The initial British paper did, however, review Switzerland's experience, seeking to emulate its relations with the EU on carbon pricing and data exchange. On the latter, it notes approvingly the related role of an arbitration process which excludes the CJEU. Equally, the paper seeks a relationship with the Schengen SIS system like that of Switzerland, to come into effect from 2021. All this is somewhat transactional and limited, it is not a breakthrough.

Moreover, the Swiss experience also raises two other technical questions which will need to be addressed by the UK whatever the scope of any final deal. One is whether or not the resulting agreement is to be a mixed one in EU legal terms, to be approved by both institutions and member states. This would add to uncertainty as some regional parliaments would have to consent and they have a history of querying such deals. It should be remembered that an UK–EU deal will have far more implications for third parties than that between the EU and Switzerland. They may expect a voice when coming to any final settlement.

This does not exclude the possibility that a basic trade deal may be all that can be achieved by December 2020, leaving other side deals to be negotiated later, even though this would risk creating another uncoordinated situation which the EU may think needed to be addressed by some sort of framework agreement. Indeed, Barnier has suggested that although there could be parallel negotiations on a variety of topics, they would concentrate on a basic free trade agreement, fisheries, and competition issues such as the "level playing field". It would therefore be rather more complicated a document than that signed by the Swiss half a century ago (EEC 1972).

Questions of security, foreign policy, and defence cooperation would come later. Where key questions like access to ERASMUS and HORIZON 2020 would be phased in, assuming the Brexiteers are willing to embrace them, is unclear. This is because, as has been shown, the UK paper suggests that the Johnson government is looking for very limited links, far below what many academics have suggested.

The other question concerns the longevity of any deal. The implication of the negotiations seems to be that the deal will be based on things as they are. Dynamic alignment is not mentioned but, as the Swiss have been made well aware, the EU is very concerned that deals with third parties should evolve in line with its *acquis communautaire*. Equally, there will need to be measures to cope with the inevitable British divergences in the future. There is also the question of whether all the agreements should be linked by a trip-wire clause, meaning that rejecting one would nullify them all, as is the case with the first set of bilateral agreements signed with Switzerland. Although British negotiators will not like such a clause, Switzerland's experience suggests that such issues will require much attention, which they have yet to receive.

International roles

Although, so far, Brexiteers' attention has been focussed on getting a trade agreement with the EU, leaving the latter actually raises difficult questions about the UK's wider international role post-2021. Thus there are questions about its wisest approach to Europe as a whole. Linked to this is its role in NATO and other security organisations. And finally it has to resolve its relations with other countries across the world. Swiss precedents are unlikely to be helpful here even if they were to be offered.

Whatever the deal reached with the EU, the UK will still have to decide how to react to developments in Europe. On the one hand, it will have to decide whether to work constructively or to develop the extreme Brexiteer line of trying to bring the EU down and "liberate its nations". There will probably be the same tension between government pragmatism and extremist pressures as there are in Switzerland. A lot will depend on how the UK's departure reshapes the EU itself (Oliver 2016). In any case, relations will have to be re-established with individual states such as Switzerland. At the same time, there is the question of developing relations with NATO and the USA where post-Brexit Britain could find itself pulled in two directions. This will be an open question whereas in Switzerland it has always been under the surface.

Beyond these two questions, there is the matter of what strategy to adopt in the wider world. While there has been much talk of a "Global Britain", according to which the UK would play an activist role worldwide, whether this will actually be the case is far from certain. On the one hand, other countries may not welcome it and will certainly seek to exploit the UK's weaknesses to their own advantage. On the other, Timothy Garton Ash believes that some Brexiteers would actually prefer the UK to follow the Swiss model, eschewing a global role and concentrating on becoming peaceful and, especially, rich (Garton Ash 2019). The interests of the former Labour voters who carried both the 2016 referendum and the December 2019 election are also primarily internal, looking to resolution of concerns about immigration and being "left behind". Such things do not require an activist foreign policy to achieve. Indeed, they could need a more defensive stance if the ravages of globalisation are to be reversed.

Switzerland does not have a lot to offer in all this partly because of its very different geographical situation and partly because of its historical and strategic orientation, focussed on its neutrality. It has never had to face the same demands as the UK does so its experience is not really relevant. Admittedly, it is very unlikely that Switzerland would ever embark on so risky an overall strategy as the Brexiteers seem to want to do. The Swiss have much more experience of being a smallish state in the wake of larger formations but the British situation and Brexit thinking do not suggest it would be willing to come to terms with being a minor third party in the way that Switzerland does. Indeed, going global for the UK could mean ignoring countries such as Switzerland. Hence, it has been Switzerland which has led the way in arranging for arrangements with the UK should a no deal Brexit materialise.

What has already happened between Switzerland and the UK is significant in another way. This is because the Swiss have been amongst the first non-EU countries not just to be aware that the UK's departure from the EU has implications for them, but, as already noted, to take action on such issues. So far this has not been taken on board by most Brexit thinking. The latter has been, and still is, so focussed on establishing the UK's own rights and replacing existing links with the EU by new trade deals, that it has rarely considered the impact of its actions on third parties and the likelihood of causing collateral damage to them, not to mention disappointing their expectations (Glencross and McCourt 2018: 10–11). Ironically, the new Foreign Office task force on bilateral relations is directed at EU member states not outsiders such as Switzerland.

Brutally breaking with half a century's understandings and practices is, of course, always likely to be unsettling. And, as recent discussions about closer relationships between Switzerland and the UK suggest, this has implications for the UK's wider international role. The Brexiteers' assumption has always been that third countries would be falling over themselves to trade with free Britain. In fact, other third countries approached for new deals may be more demanding and willing to exploit the UK's obvious needs, to extract benefits for themselves, politically as well as economically. All this suggests that, in developing the much-needed over-arching vision for foreign policy after 2021, the UK will have to think about far more things than being equidistant between Europe, the US, and China.

In any case, before HMS Brexit can set sail for the, (probably stormy), open seas, its officers have to solve relational questions closer to home. Thus, the UK has already signalled its apparent willingness to accept commitments and deals which seem to preclude a buccaneering role. On the one hand, these include what are described as global matters, including environment, health and pollution. On the other, they include, as is already clear, security and foreign policy partnerships. If these go ahead, they will clearly limit the UK's freedom of action, calling into question the reality of "taking back control". Here the Swiss experience suggests that seeking to evade EU supra-nationality will be difficult (Gabriel 2020). Hence Switzerland offers more of a warning than a positive lesson to be followed. Conversely, talk in Switzerland about getting the UK to join EFTA or act as an ally seems likely to be rejected because it would be counter to the Brexit "Great Power" project (Bluewin 2019; Bondolfi 2020). Moreover, should the UK attempt to agree such deals fail, leading to acrimony, this too would constrain British foreign policy in general. In other words, it will be difficult for Britain to follow Switzerland in being a happy third country should it ever wish to do so.

Domestic lessons?

Equally, Brexiteers have failed to see that the UK could learn something from Switzerland about dealing with the political fallout of divisions over Europe. Switzerland offers long lasting examples of how to hold a divided country together, of how to cope with an entrenched opposition and of how to utilise direct democracy successfully. It is also a warning about how deeply a country can become Europeanised even when not an EU member. Some British observers think there are things to be learned in this respect (Williams 2016; Knott 2019). They point out that the two countries share opposition to immigration, concerns about academia, and an identity crisis. They also have historical hang-ups, the Swiss with their origins and *Sonderfall*, the British – or, rather, English – with the

Empire and World War II. However, so far, Brexit thinking has given little attention to such domestic questions.

To begin with, the Johnson government occasionally talks of bringing the country together after the bitterness of the last four years. So far, there has been little sign of this. Coming together seems implicitly to mean supporters of closer links with the EU dropping their beliefs and rallying to support the Leavers' line. The latter are swift to jump on any Remainer hopes, denying that these now have any validity or rights. The Swiss example of providing institutional ways for the Catholic conservatives, defeated in the 1847 civil war, to integrate into, and influence, mainstream Swiss political society, may be a more positive approach. The adoption of the generally less confrontational and polemical tone of Swiss politics would also help.

The problem will be most acute where the UK itself is concerned. Recent events have increased the alienation of Northern Ireland and Scotland while there is also dissidence in Wales. So far the Johnsonian response has been to ignore the first and stamp down on the second. But this, especially after the 2020 Irish election, could well prove self-defeating and face the UK with a massive challenge. Coming to terms with fuller understandings of federalism and creating a properly decentralised polity would be a better way forward. Here the Swiss experience with the Jura, which was allowed free expression, could help.

Equally, the Swiss have also had much experience of polarisation, given the long battle of the SVP and its allies in AUNS against links with the EU, but pragmatic Euroscepticism has usually won out against outright Europhobia (Church 2009b). In the UK, the situation is now likely to be reversed with Brexiteers dominant in government, the media, and the electorate. Yet they are likely to be faced with a large and unreconciled Remainer body of opinion, which one day, may find its Blocher. Maybe the new Brexiteer elite can learn from the way the Swiss have managed to keep common sense afloat and partially blunt populism (Knott 2019). So far, there is no sign of this breaking through.

When it comes to direct democracy some Swiss have been happy to offer lessons. Kaufman and others have argued that the 2016 referendum was no true direct democratic act. It was a "so called and highly faulty referendum" (Kaufman 2018). This was because it was imposed from the top for self-interested motives by the Cameron government (meaning it was a plebiscite rather than an initiative) and asking an unclear, ill formulated question. It was also based on poor information and decided on a franchise which excluded a million people. Others went further and called it "drivel" or a "mischief" (Bondolfi and Stephens 2018). It could also be suggested that ignoring the Scots and Northern Irish votes stands in stark contrast to the Swiss requirement to have a cantonal majority, for such votes to succeed.

Moreover, the use made of the referendum in the UK is totally out of line with Swiss practice. Whereas the Swiss system allows repeat votes on the same subject as with women's suffrage and maternity allowances, Brexiteers have erected the 2016 referendum into a golden calf, the greatest ever democratic expression of opinion which trumps all else. Hence the bitter, but successful, resistance to a second referendum on the terms of exit (and indeed on Scottish independence). The introduction of the right of popular initiative and perhaps the separation of referendums from government policy, as is the case in Switzerland, would help to change British practices and stop one side pulling the ladder up after they had won a vote, as now seems to be the case. Equally, the ability of Switzerland's Federal Court to overrule votations on the grounds of imperfect information, as happened with a recent Christian Democrat proposition on the taxation of married couples, could well have been used with the claims made on their bus and elsewhere by the Leave campaign. But, as Farage has made plain, such ideas would be anathema to most Brexiteers, who have a very different attitude to direct democracy.

Another advantage of the Swiss system is that votations are often focussed on changes to the constitution. This leads to more detailed questions (and something of their implications) being put before the people rather than relying on what are essentially sound bites in the UK. The impasse of 2016–2019 had encouraged ideas of a codified constitution in the UK but the chances of this have dwindled since the election. However, the Johnson government seems likely to bring in more piecemeal changes of its own, designed to close the judicial and other avenues which were so skilfully used by Remainers in recent years.

One final facet of the Swiss experience which seems relevant to the UK is the strange way in which the long-standing SVP opposition to political links with the EU has gone in tandem with increasing Europeanisation, understood as both the direct and strategic effects of European rules on economy and society through formal accords and more indirect tactical effects of interactions with the EU (Church 2016: 67–8). These can involve legislation, where since 1988 all bills have had to have a European compatibility clause, and where Switzerland has often autonomously adopted EU laws and aligned its policies on those of Brussels. Existing deals are also sometimes updated by joint committees. However, this must be anathema to Brexiteers.

The EU dynamic can also affect administrative and political behaviour and structures, increasing their focus on the EU and changing their balance. For many, Europeanisation thus means a strengthening of the executive and technical services at the expense of representative politics. However, party politics and parliament are themselves affected, as are the media (Sciarini et al. 2014). All this brought Switzerland much closer to the EU even as the likelihood of entry continually diminished.

Strangely, neither the process nor its individual elements has been seriously queried by the SVP which prefers to focus on symbolic political issues and not on more routine and detailed adjustments even though these have major effects on Swiss relations with Europe. Indeed, for some Brexiteers they have deprived Switzerland of sovereignty (Perring 2019). Brexiteers will need to be alert to this possibility especially as the UK will be starting out from the position of a largely aligned member state. Even if rules are regularly repealed and attempts made to diverge from EU stances, it is likely that the influence of the EU will continue to affect the UK, especially when there is a strong Remainer lobby in both economy and politics. Anything like the partnership offered would intensify this tendency. At some stage, Brexitism will have to face this question. However, it is far from certain that it will be looked at in the light of Switzerland's experience.

Explaining British reticence

So why do the British pay so little attention to Switzerland? The key reason clearly comes from the Brexiteer stress on regaining sovereignty and control, a stance which does not obviously open many doors to learning from others, especially from a country which often does things which conflict with Brexiteer ideals (Contisguglu and Cooper 2019). However, longer-term factors also play a part. In fact, since World War II, Switzerland has lost its traditional place in British affections and concerns.

Although hostility to EU membership has a long history in the UK, it has not been distinguished by deep thought about what would happen if the UK were no longer in the EU. Once upon a time Teddy Taylor MP would have vaunted the merits of EFTA but this idea has long since been left behind. The circumstances of the referendum, and the Leavers' unexpected victory, also worked against thinking beyond British rights and the present. The way that immigration into provincial England played such a large role in the referendum increased the narrowness and insularity of Brexit thinking.

So Brexitism was an over-simple concept, implying that it was something which could be done by the British themselves, ignoring the need for negotiation with the EU and the outside world. One outsider has said that the UK has become self-obsessed, unable to look at the EU through any prism but its own, something which makes it hard for it to take seriously the interests of other nations, whether EU member states such as Ireland or non-members such as Switzerland (McRedmond 2020). Moreover, the concept of Brexit has changed over time, moving from a claim that a close relationship was desirable and available within a non-member status to a demand for a no-deal exit and maximum autonomy, whatever the economic and other price to be paid for this. In other words, the overwhelming desire to take back control and become a great power again prevents positive learning from a small country. Indeed, Leavers seem to be coming to see Switzerland as a warning against things they should not do.

To an extent, in failing to pay much attention to Switzerland, Brexiteers were following in the footsteps of British society in general. Whereas in the 19th century Switzerland had figured largely in British thinking, this began to change after 1945 (Church 2009a). In the century before last mountains and winter sports gave Switzerland a special place in upper-middle-class affections. There was also a notable interest in the new state with its emerging democratic institutions. This continued, albeit to a declining extent, in the inter-war years.

After 1945 both countries changed. Switzerland became increasingly successful, self-reliant and expensive while Britain was poorer and less middle class. Tourism fell off as flights to the sun replaced winter sports in holiday makers' minds. The perceived difficulty of Switzerland's languages also failed to appeal to a society becoming increasingly monoglot. Hence academic interest waned, as did that of the press. The continuing disdain of a once great power for small states also played a part in this (Szent-Ivenyi 2019: 20). All of this predisposed Brexiteers to overlook or misinterpret Switzerland, further limiting the possibility of breakthroughs.

Conclusions

Interest may well decline further in the 2020s given the tendencies of the Johnson government and the likely concentration on negotiations with the EU and on the search for replacement trade deals with larger English-speaking states. Given its escape from the EU and the parliamentary imbroglio which preceded the last election, post-Brexit decision makers are unlikely to recognise that Switzerland is going through a similar process which could teach it something. In any case, they do not seem to want to learn from anybody else. In particular, they are likely to regard Switzerland as too close to the EU, too constrained in its actions, and too complaisant towards Brussels norms to want to learn from it. Moreover, they will be aware of developments in Switzerland's own relations with the EU which suggest problems for British financial and other interests. The UK's very different political system and culture, not to mention hardening Brexit ideology, as it moves from Euroscepticism to Europhobia, also make it difficult for lessons to be learned.

Brexitism, in fact, inclines the UK to avoid some of the lessons which Swiss politics offer. Thus, there is a need for them to maintain the sanctity of the 2016 referendum and not follow the Swiss openness to full direct democracy. Equally, the whole purpose of Brexitism is to develop an openly anti-EU line rather than Swiss discretion and pragmatism. And Brexiteers are much more radical and better placed to influence policy than their Swiss equivalents. In any case, many of the possible lessons are not without their problems. This helps to explain why the Swiss themselves are as likely to urge the UK not to follow their example as to urge the UK to try to be more like Switzerland. In fact, it is often not very well-informed Brits who urge Brexit Britain to follow the Swiss road, even when there are few realistic possibilities of the UK doing this.

Nonetheless, even if there are limits to what Switzerland can offer the post-Brexit UK, there are still things in the Swiss experience which are worth considering. Thus, on the one hand, there are questions about the shape of any agreement which the British have yet to appreciate. This is also true of the likely ongoing problem of Europeanisation. On the other hand, many would say that Swiss practice in consensus politics, diplomacy, and direct democracy could well prove helpful to the UK. Nonetheless, there is a case for taking notice of attitudes in Switzerland as these are often better informed about the UK than the latter are informed about continental countries (Ader-Nissen et al. 2017).

Obviously, whether any of this is accepted depends in part on the way British politics develops after the impact of the coronavirus. Internally, things seem uncertain. Externally, we have also to ask, for instance, how will British strict "sovereignists" respond to the emerging general awareness of the need for more global cooperation to prevent further pandemics and depressions? And will other countries respond as automatically and warmly to what Brexiteers think is their right and reward?

Here, it is possible that, in future, the UK may need Switzerland, given that it is already the former's fourth largest market, ahead of China. Moreover, if the UK loses sales in the EU because of the new barriers Johnson is willing to accept, Switzerland could become more important. Equally, a "no-deal" scenario would drive Switzerland to interact more with London. Switzerland might also become more relevant should the UK's negotiations in 2020–2021 result in a bitty deal which resembles that which currently prevails between Berne and Brussels. Conversely, should the EU decide to develop some kind of outer circle of non-member allies then the two countries might again find they have things in common (Sandbu 2019). However, the likelihood of such structural reconstruction, as initially canvassed by Leavers, seems unlikely. Even if it does, Brexiteers – as evidenced by the government's refusal to accept an invitation to join the EU's bulk purchase scheme for medical equipment purchases – would most likely refuse it. It is hard to imagine Swiss pragmatism doing the same.

Finally, perhaps we should note the lessons Switzerland is now drawing from the Brexit crisis. One suggestion (Schmitz 2019) is that it shows that, despite saying that this is the "last and only deal", the EU will shift as it did when accepting Johnson's revised Withdrawal Agreement. However, this came at a high price given that it could potentially lead to Irish re-unification. It is not clear what sacrifices Switzerland might have to make if this happened. The Brexit crisis might also be taken to suggest that things improved once the British decided what they wanted, rather than allowing consultations to drag on. In other words, there are still questions about the nature of lessons and how they might be learned. Yet, the balance of the evidence suggests that the barriers of Brexitism are likely to prevent the British from trying to do this.

13 Conclusions

Insights from Switzerland's experience

Paolo Dardanelli and Oscar Mazzoleni

At first sight, Switzerland and the United Kingdom have moved in opposite directions in their relations with the European Union. While Switzerland has moved closer and closer to the EU, the UK has left the Union and, in the wishes of many, is seeking to move as further away from it as possible. Yet the two countries find themselves in a strikingly similar situation: they are both negotiating an overarching bilateral agreement with the EU. Such an agreement, they hope, would enable them to benefit from desirable aspects of European integration while minimising the latter's negative effects. From a longer-term perspective, this is nothing new. Since the early days of European integration after World War II, the two countries have displayed many similarities in their attitudes to Europe. Their joint founding of EFTA, as an alternative to the integrationist path pursued by the EEC, offered a clear illustration. From this perspective, it was the UK's abandonment of EFTA to join the EEC in the early 1970s that appeared "anomalous". Brexit has closed the chapter of EU membership for the UK and brought it in line once again with Switzerland's situation. While the two countries thus find themselves in a similar situation today, the main difference between them is that, for the UK, at least as far as the current generation is concerned, this is a new and unfamiliar situation whereas in Switzerland's case the present situation is the product of an evolution that has lasted almost 30 years. Over the course of these 30 years, Switzerland has accumulated an extensive experience of dealing with the EU as a non-member. It is fair to say that no third country has had closer interactions with the EU than Switzerland. There is thus potentially a lot to be learned from Switzerland's experience to illuminate the prospects facing the UK.

In the spirit of seeking to draw insights from the Swiss experience, the preceding chapters have explored several key aspects of Switzerland's relationship with the EU over the last 30 years and identified parallels and contrasts with the UK. In this concluding chapter, we try to weave these different threads together and distil some key insights. We proceed in five steps. First, we outline the nature of the fundamental choices the two countries have to make vis-à-vis the EU, which we characterise as trade-offs. Second, we consider to what extent the legal-institutional architecture of Swiss–EU relations could offer a more attractive model for the UK compared to the one currently being pursued and alternative arrangements. Third, we discuss the domestic impact of these relations, focussing on political parties, the labour market, and the system of territorial governance, and the possible responses called for. Fourth, we review the determinants of public attitudes and voting behaviour on EU matters and what they teach us about the political dimensionality of Europe. Lastly, we assess the likelihood that the UK will indeed be open to learn from the Swiss experience in charting its own future relations with the EU. By so doing we aim to summarise the main takeaways the book offers.

Fundamental trade-offs

The choice that Switzerland and the UK have faced vis-à-vis European integration can be described as a fundamental trade-off pitting the gains to be derived from integration, primarily of an economic nature, against the losses supranational decision-making implies for national autonomy, which are quintessentially political.

The terms of the trade-off have long been similar for the two countries on the negative side of the scales. For a host of reasons, both Switzerland and the UK have been highly protective of their sovereignty and autonomy. A long history of independence that unfolded along a somewhat distinct path from that followed by most other Western European countries has nurtured a widespread perception in each country of being to a degree special. This perception has been reinforced by their international outlook. In both cases, albeit for different reasons, the World War II experience deepened the perceived difference with the European mainstream, notably vis-à-vis Germany. More widely, Switzerland's attachment to neutrality and the UK's close links with the US and the Commonwealth have contributed to the feeling of being different from the rest of Europe.

On the positive side of the trade-off, though, the terms have differed more significantly, both between Switzerland and the UK and over time. Key factors here are the size and the geographical location of the two countries, and their respective economic trajectories. In the early phase of integration both countries concluded that the economic gains from integration would not outweigh the loss of national autonomy, hence they opted not to join the EEC and set up EFTA instead. Switzerland's assessment has since remained broadly consistent whereas the UK's has varied considerably. Within a year of the founding of EFTA the UK changed its mind and applied to join the EEC, only to be prevented from doing so by France's veto. A second application in 1967 was again vetoed by France. The fact that Switzerland's economy continued to grow strongly in the 1960s whereas the UK's was falling behind the growth rate of Continental Europe (e.g. Lamfalussy 1963; Vonyó 2008: 234) played a significant role in the different path taken by the two countries. When the UK entered the EEC, the latter's importance for Switzerland's economy increased significantly and led, as Rossi and Vallet in this volume show, to the signing of the first trade agreement in 1972. The attractions of the EEC/EU market accelerated further in the late 1980s–early 1990s with the drive to achieve a single market. The UK strongly supported the single market programme, while Switzerland applied to join the EEA and, eventually, the EU itself. The completion of the single market, based on extensive harmonisation of regulations and being accompanied by greater use of majority voting, also deepened the EU's reach into national legislation thus raising the potential losses for national autonomy. The objective of monetary union raised these even further. While the UK successfully negotiated an opt out from monetary union, the eurozone crisis eventually dealt a blow to the country's commitment to EU membership. On the Swiss side, as Rossi and Vallet point out, the desire to retain the competitive advantage afforded by the Swiss franc has been an important factor in the country's attitude to EU membership. Following Brexit, the terms of the trade-off for the UK are once again very similar to those Switzerland is facing and essentially pit the economic gains to be had from access to the vast EU single market against the constraints deriving from acceptance of the EU regulations and the role of the CJEU in policing them.

If the trade-off is broadly similar, there are nonetheless significant differences between Switzerland and the UK that affect the actual terms each faces. Four appears to be most consequential. The first and most obvious is size. The much larger size of the UK makes UK–EU relations less unbalanced than Swiss–EU relations, notably in the extent to which each country is dependent on the EU as an export market. A second clear difference is the geographical location of the two countries, where the UK's situation as an archipelago to the north-west of the European landmass affords it a degree of physical separation from the EU whereas Switzerland's location at the heart of the continent makes it an "island" entirely surrounded by EU territory. The third main difference, perhaps less commonly appreciated than the previous two, is the economic model of the two countries. Switzerland is a high-wage economy that poses less of a competitive threat to the EU than a potentially more low-wage, low-regulation UK. The last difference is in what we could call the wider "support network" the two countries have. Switzerland's tradition of neutrality makes it a more "solitary" country in the world, without natural allies. Moreover, because of deep cultural links, Switzerland would always want to retain close relations with Austria, Germany, France, and Italy. The special relation with the US and the rest of the Anglosphere, by contrast, means that the UK can more easily afford to emancipate itself from the EU. Size, geographical location, and "support network" all make the UK less dependent on the EU, hence potentially increase the former's bargaining leverage vis-à-vis the latter. They don't make the imbalance between the two sides disappear, however, and the potential competitive threat the UK poses to the EU, at least in the eyes of many, make the latter warier of making concessions to the former. Because of this perceived competitive threat, so-called "regulatory alignment" has become a central bone of contention between the two sides. Here, its experience of dealing with Switzerland has made the EU particularly sensitive to risks that concessions to the UK might provide a back door through which the regulatory integrity of the single market would be undermined.

It is in the nature of trade-offs that any choice based on them implies compromising between equally desirable goals. Choices optimising the trade-off tend to be located close to the middle of the policy spectrum rather than its extremes.

They are thus bound to prove controversial to those focussing on either one of those goals – in this case economic benefits versus the protection of national autonomy – and calling for maximalist solutions. One of the lessons Switzerland offers in this respect is the importance of making clear to citizens what the nature of the trade-off is and how best it can be optimised.

How to manage bilateral relations?

The economic benefits to be derived from having preferential access to the large EU market, as discussed above, have led Switzerland first and now the UK to seek an agreement with the EU that would grant them as much access as possible while sacrificing as little as possible of their political autonomy. As Schwok discussed in his chapter, Switzerland has done so via a bilateral and sectoral approach, consisting of individual agreements covering a wide range of areas, of which some are legally linked to each other. While on the whole this bilateral approach has served Switzerland well over the years, it is likely to have reached the limits of what it can achieve. The EU's insistence on signing an IFA seems to indicate as much.

For the UK the bilateral approach pursued by Switzerland over the last 30 years appears to offer two main attractions. First, it would give it better access to the EU market than a free trade pact modelled on the EU–Canada agreement. Given the much greater importance of the EU as an export market for the UK, this would be a significant attraction. Second, unlike a customs union, it would leave the UK free to conclude trade agreements with other countries, as well as greater leeway to diverge from EU regulations and less of a financial burden than EEA membership. It would not address, however, two questions that have bedevilled Swiss–EU relations for a long time and that in all likelihood will prove equally contentious in the negotiations with the UK. The first is the question of regulatory alignment with the EU and how to maintain such alignment up to speed with evolving EU legislation. Throughout the history of bilateral agreements with Switzerland, the EU has always made clear that regulatory alignment is the essential quid pro quo for preferential access to its internal market. To maintain such alignment, Switzerland has been expected to adapt its legislation whenever the EU's changed. This expectation of so-called "dynamic alignment" will be even more central in the negotiations with the UK given the higher competitive challenge the latter poses in the eyes of the EU. The second is the nature of the dispute resolution system adopted and the role the CJEU would play in such a system. On this issue, too, the EU's demand that the agreements be policed by the CJEU has been difficult to accept for Switzerland and would be equally so for the UK. The fact that these two issues are the main stumbling block to a successful conclusion of the negotiations on a Switzerland–EU IFA underline the limitations of the "Swiss model".

Nor does the Swiss model, of course, offer a solution to the question of free circulation and immigration. As Jenni shows in her chapter, the linkage between market access and free circulation has been an intimate and controversial one in Swiss–EU relations. Given the role played by immigration in the politics of Brexit, it is not surprising that both sides have implicitly agreed that any agreement between the UK and the EU would not include a Swiss-style free circulation provision. Nevertheless, this issue may rear its head again in UK–EU relations in the future.

Switzerland's experience of bilateral agreements thus highlights some crucial aspects of negotiating relations with the EU but does not appear to provide a ready-made model that would be viable for the UK. Both sides, though, are likely to keep the Swiss experience in mind when negotiating their future relations, albeit for different reasons. The European Commission negotiating mandate of February 2020 appears to suggest that the EU envisages an arrangement that would be de facto fairly close to the Swiss bilateral and sectoral model, save for the free circulation provisions. The British government on the other hand, as Church discusses in his chapter, appears to regard the "Swiss model" as something to be avoided. The current focus of the UK government, as outlined in its negotiating mandate, is on some sort of "Canada plus" option, i.e. a free trade agreement limited to the abolition of customs duties, as opposed to the removal of non-tariff barriers, and granting the UK virtually unlimited freedom to diverge from EU regulations. Rather ironically, this would be quite similar to the agreement that Switzerland had concluded with the EEC in 1972, i.e. before the onset of the "Swiss model" as we have come to know it.

Domestic impact of "integration without membership"

The preceding chapters have highlighted how deep and far-reaching the domestic impact of Europe is. Here we discuss three areas in particular: the impact on parties and the party system, on patterns of immigration and the labour market, and on the system of territorial governance.

As Fontanellaz and Dardanelli show, Europe has had a profound impact on the Swiss parties and party system. Two aspects of this impact seem to be especially consequential. The first is that the challenge European integration poses to national autonomy has helped provide saliency and coherence to an oppositional stance rooted in identity, sovereignty, and tradition. Riding such a stance has helped the Swiss People's Party grow dramatically in the 20 years following the 1992 EEA referendum, from being the smallest of the four governmental parties to being the largest. We can observe clear parallels in the UK, where opposition to the deepening of European integration fuelled the rise of UKIP first, which recorded the largest number of votes in the 2014 European election, and later spilled over into votes for the Conservative party, in the process significantly changing the latter's support basis.

The second, and broader, aspect is that support–opposition to European integration is a new axis of competition that tends to cut across the left–right divide that has traditionally structured most West European party systems. Long established parties, particularly those in the moderate section of the spectrum, thus face difficult choices in their strategies. The two centrist parties in Switzerland, for instance, have often found it difficult to take clear stances on occasion of popular votes on European issues, thus suffering a loss of visibility and "issue ownership" vis-à-vis their more sharply profiled rivals on the left and the right. Even the Socialist party, for long the most vocally pro-EU of the Swiss parties, has found it difficult to maintain its customary stance, in the face of the threats the draft IFA is perceived to pose to the country's ability to shield its workforce against competition from EU workers.

The disruptive potential of the European question is arguably even more significant for a less fragmented party system such as the UK one. This is because the Conservative and Labour parties, as traditional "broad churches" bringing together quite heterogenous constituencies, have less scope than the comparatively more "niche" Swiss parties to articulate a coherent position on European issues. Mirroring the predicament of the Swiss Socialists, the challenge appears to be particularly severe for the Labour Party, which is trying to reconcile the largely pro-EU metropolitan, highly educated, and service-sector electorate and the strongly anti-EU small-town, low-education, and working-class constituency. If some may hope that this disruptive effect will fade away post-Brexit, Switzerland's experience suggests otherwise. As the UK will inevitably need to maintain close relations with the European Union, the difficult choices it will face will continue to pose severe challenges to its political parties. While the Swiss experience does not necessarily provide an answer as to how these challenges may be best addressed, at least it points to the need to acknowledge their effects.

Europe has had an equally significant impact on patterns of immigration and labour market dynamics. As Jenni shows, the signing of the free circulation agreement with the EU has led to a profound transformation of the patterns of immigration into Switzerland, whereby job-seekers moving to the country are now overwhelmingly EU citizens. She also shows that this influx has not had a discernible negative impact on the Swiss labour market as a whole. This is because the kind of labour supplied by EU immigrants, which tends to cluster at the low end and the high end of the skill set distribution, tends to complement that of Swiss citizens rather than being in direct competition with it. While this is true for the nationwide labour market, however, the picture looks different in specific regions of the country such as the border cantons of Basel City, Geneva, and Ticino. In these areas, the influx of cheaper EU labour, often in the form of cross-border commuting, has put considerable pressure on the local job market.

These dynamics are broadly echoed in the UK. Following the 2004 enlargement of the European Union, the UK decided to open up its labour market to workers from the new member states without restrictions from the outset. This stance contrasted with that adopted for instance by Germany, which maintained restrictions for the maximum period allowed of seven years. Many workers from these new EU members seized the opportunity to move to the UK and start a career there, far outstripping the numbers that had been expected to migrate. An estimated 1 million people moved to the UK from Poland alone. Like in Switzerland, and for similar reasons, this large influx of workers did not have a negative impact on the labour market as a whole, which recorded a record high employment rate of 75% in the last quarter of 2019 (OECD 2020). But in the UK, too, the overall picture hides significant variation across localities (e.g. McCann 2016). In rural and/or declining areas, the influx of workers from the rest of the EU has been perceived as undue competition by the local labour force and has contributed to making immigration a politically salient issue in the run up to the 2016 referendum.

In this light, there are two key lessons to be drawn from Switzerland's experience. The first is a reminder that the free movement of labour is one of the fundamental "four freedoms" – alongside the free movement of goods, capital, and services – on which the EU single market is founded. In the eyes of the EU, therefore, the free movement of labour is an inescapable counterpart to the other three freedoms, and third countries that seek a preferential access to its market should be prepared to accept labour movement as a necessary quid pro quo. Given the UK's intention not to grant any preferential immigration rights to EU citizens post-Brexit, the country should not expect the EU to offer it particularly favourable market access terms. The second is that, in assessing the domestic impact of relations with the EU either ex ante or ex post, it is important to pay attention to its localised effects, not just the aggregate one. Although the UK circumstances are different, if the Swiss experience is any guide, these far-reaching and highly differentiated effects will continue to manifest themselves under the new type of relations with the EU post-Brexit. Specific measures targeted to areas that perceive themselves to be negatively affected by EU relations thus have a lot to recommend themselves as an effective way of dealing with the uneven domestic impact we have highlighted.

Territorial governance is a third important area where the domestic impact of integration has made itself felt. While at first sight Switzerland and the United Kingdom have experienced a very different impact in this area, a closer analysis reveals subtle parallels and, more importantly, suggests a similar policy response. In Switzerland, as Dardanelli's chapter shows, closer integration with the EU has had a predominantly centralising effect, exacerbating some long-standing internal dynamics of the same nature. The roots of this effect lie in the disconnection between the fact that Swiss–EU relations often touch upon matters of cantonal competence while the cantons' face obstacles in making their voice heard in the country's European policy. While the structural nature of these obstacles makes it difficult to remove them completely, a series of measures could be, and by and large have been, adopted to minimise the negative impact on the cantons. These include a new constitutional provision and federal legislation, an inter-cantonal forum for coordination and representation, and provisions for regular consultation and a degree of co-decision between the cantons and the federal government in European policy. While not entirely satisfactory, these measures have gone a long way in allaying cantons' fears and have been instrumental in securing the latter's broad support for the country's European policy. While fears that European integration would threaten Switzerland's cherished federal system are regularly cited by Eurosceptics as one of the grounds for their opposition to the EU, it is instructive that the cantons actually support membership as a long-term goal.

The early phase of post-1992 Swiss–EU relations, however, showed another effect of integration on the domestic system of territorial governance. In contrast to the one that prevailed later, discussed above, this was a potentially disintegrative effect. It was rooted in the sharp differences in voting behaviour on occasion of the 1992 EEA referendum between German-speaking Switzerland and the French-speaking *Suisse romande.* As highlighted by several chapters in this book, the EEA was rejected by a majority of German speakers whereas it was endorsed by a majority of French speakers. This divergence led many to fear that attitudes to European integration would create a chasm between the two communities and potentially alienate the French-speaking minority (e.g. Steiner 2003). Subsequent popular votes, and the scholarly analyses that have accompanied them, have consistently shown that French speakers have a more positive attitude than their German- and Italian-speaking compatriots (see chapters by Sciarini, Mueller, Theiler, and Mazzoleni, in this volume, in particular). Yet, the sharpness of the divide has somewhat faded over time and the feared alienation of the *Suisse romande* has not manifested itself. While a degree of convergence in attitudes and voting behaviour has played its part, the cautious path followed by the Swiss federal government and the sensitive handling of linguistic and regional sensitivities have also been important.

As the UK faces its own disintegrative Brexit fallout, the lesson to be drawn from Switzerland's experience is two-fold. First, that it would be wise to acknowledge the strength of feelings in Scotland and Northern Ireland at being dragged out of the EU against their will, and try to assuage their respective concerns. This could be done by pursuing a less extreme form of Brexit that many in England seem willing to contemplate (although, as Church's chapter in this volume argues, there are precious little signs of the UK government's intending to do so) and by paying particular attention to Northern Ireland's predicament (e.g. Blick 2020). Second, and more broadly, that it is important to develop inter-institutional channels of dialogue and coordination between Westminster and the devolved governments and legislatures so as to give the latter a more effective voice in the formulation of the country's European policy and in managing the domestic impact of relations with the EU.

Determinants of public attitudes and voting behaviour

Perhaps the richest source of insights in the attempt to drawn lessons from the Swiss experience is the determinants of public attitudes to European integration and corresponding voting behaviour. The preceding chapters highlight several key findings worth emphasising. The most general is the high level of stability of the predictors of voting behaviour across all the popular votes on Europe held in the last 30 years. This seems to suggest the existence of deep-seated factors and processes, impervious to short-term manipulation. Were the trajectory observed in Switzerland to replicate itself in the UK, we can then expect the patterns that governed the 2016 Brexit referendum to endure for the foreseeable future.

Revisiting the campaign for the pivotal 1992 referendum on the EEA, Kreis contrasts the appeals to identity and sovereignty made by the No supporters with the more pragmatic and economy-focussed arguments deployed by those advocating ratification of the agreement. This finds parallels in the campaign preceding the Brexit referendum, when Leave supporters also stressed the threats EU membership posed for British identity and sovereignty whereas Remainers emphasised the economic costs of leaving the EU (e.g. Curtice 2017; Clarke et al. 2017). Given the role played by emotions in voting decisions (e.g. Clarke et al. 2017: 445), these parallels between the EEA vote in Switzerland and the Brexit vote in the UK point to the importance for proponents of integration to engage their opponents also on the terrain of emotions and symbolism, not just on that of a cost-benefit calculus.

In his aggregate analysis of voting behaviour across nine popular votes since 1992, Sciarini finds two groups of factors to be the most important: socio-demographic characteristics and political attitudes and values. Among the former, the level of education and urban/rural location have the strongest predictive power, whereby highly educated persons and those living in cities are significantly more likely to vote in favour of closer relations with the EU compared to people with a low level of education and/or resident in rural areas. Among the latter, beyond expected factors such as partisanship and orientations towards openness versus isolation, left–right ideology and trust in government also emerge as prominent drivers of voting behaviour. These findings find clear echo in the analyses of the 2016 Brexit vote in the UK and suggest three main points. First, both the socio-demographic characteristics and some of the value orientations are consistent with a "winners versus losers of globalisation" explanatory framework (Kriesi et al. 2008). If so, a policy response aimed at maintaining openness but at the same time adopting compensatory measures to address the grievances of the "losers" appears to be the most promising way of navigating the politics of EU relations. Second, the overlap between left–right orientations and pro/anti-EU attitudes may continue to grow, thus providing additional fuel to the re-alignment of the British party system into a pro-EU Labour Party facing the anti-EU Conservatives (Curtice 2020). Third, in spite of the powerful role played by structural factors, voting behaviour is also shaped by variables such as trust in government, which are more amenable to short-term changes. It is likely that, other things being equal, such a variable would prove itself even more significant in a majoritarian parliamentary system such as the UK, compared to the more consensual and non-parliamentary Swiss system. If this is the case, future UK governments would be well advised to foster voters' trust in their steering of the country if they wish to carry the electorate with them in EU matters.

The "winners versus losers" framework finds further support in Mueller's analysis. He argues that beyond the general pattern of urban residents being more favourable to integration and rural residents being more sceptical, location in border areas has an important independent effect, particularly so when combined with lower socio-economic status. Peripheral location and social deprivation thus emerge as powerful determinants of attitudes and behaviour in this sphere.

This dovetails with evidence that support for Leave in the Brexit referendum was strongest in so-called "left behind" areas (e.g. Goodwin and Heath 2016; Becker et al. 2017) and, once again, reinforces the case for policies directed at tackling such forms of territorial and social disadvantage.

Theiler points to additional factors that play an important role in shaping attitudes to Europe, namely the cultural roots of these attitudes and their interaction with political support structures. He contends that the perception of European integration as a German-driven cultural threat to German-speaking Switzerland is a key mechanism fuelling Euroscepticism in the latter, particularly so because the *Deutschschweiz* lacks political institutions of its own. He posits a stimulating analogy with England's situation within the UK, where analyses of the 2016 referendum vote have found that not only was Brexit more strongly supported in England than elsewhere but also that English identity – i.e. primary identification with England rather than with the UK – was a significant driver of the Leave vote (e.g. Henderson et al. 2017). Some form of English devolution may thus be a way, perhaps counterintuitively, of reconciling English identifiers with Europe whereby facilitating the pursuit of closer relations with the EU in the future.

Last, but not least, Mazzoleni explains the puzzle of the particularly strong Euroscepticism in the Italian-speaking canton of Ticino by highlighting the role played by the conflation of attitudes to Europe – in this case primarily represented by Italy – and regionalist grievances vis-à-vis the federal government. Acting as a "political entrepreneur", the regional party Lega dei Ticinesi has portrayed Ticino as a vulnerable periphery that needs better protection by Berne from the threat posed by the EU/Italy. By whipping up the political saliency of the European question, the Lega dei Ticinesi has established itself as a major political force in the region, in the process making the latter the most Eurosceptic part of Switzerland. The dynamics of Euroscepticism in Ticino present a mirror image of the evolution of attitudes to the EU and to the UK in Scotland, where positive attitudes to integration have been sustained by a perception of the EU as a counterweight to London. This reminds us of the interaction between domestic centre-periphery relations and attitudes to European integration.

While the findings discussed above all point to broad parallels between the experience of Switzerland and the emerging patterns in the UK, there is an intriguing difference between the two countries of potentially far-reaching consequences for their future trajectory: the role of age. Age did not emerge as a strong predictor of voting behaviour in Sciarini's analysis, but there is some indication that support for EU membership is positively correlated with age in Switzerland (Szvircsev Tresch et al. 2019: 310). If this is indeed the case, it is in stark contrast to the UK pattern, where there is a strong negative correlation between age and pro-EU orientations (e.g. Curtice 2017: 15). Assuming this is a cohort rather than an age effect, it could prove to be a significant factor in the medium to long term, potentially pushing the UK closer to, and even raising the prospect of it rejoining, the EU (on which see e.g. Glencross 2020; Rose 2020).

Learning from Switzerland?

As we have attempted to summarise in this concluding chapter, there are many valuable insights that can be drawn from Switzerland's experience to shed light on the future trajectory of UK–EU relations. How likely, though, is the UK to be willing to learn from the Swiss experience? Church argues that the likelihood of the UK doing so is not very high. This is so for two main reasons. The first is that the Brexit ideology has been narrowly focussed on "getting out" rather than on what would follow exit. Brexiteers have thus emphasised the goal of regaining total sovereignty and autonomy from the EU, whatever the costs, economic and otherwise, of doing so. Such a focus has not predisposed the UK leaders to learn lessons from other countries, particularly those, such as Switzerland, wishing to maintain close links with the EU. The COVID-19 pandemic, by increasing uncertainty and exacerbating the economic challenges, may further complicate UK–EU negotiations and increasingly hold Switzerland–EU negotiations on the IFA hostage to the former (e.g. Steinworth and Schmutz 2020). The second reason is that knowledge and interest in Switzerland, for reasons unrelated to Brexit, have declined in the UK over the last few decades, with the result that the country has become increasingly unfamiliar to the British. This has also meant that the true nature of Swiss–EU relations has often been misunderstood by UK observers. Our hope is that this volume would go some way towards making Switzerland–EU relations better known and appreciated, thus offering a positive contribution to the debate on the UK's future in Europe.

References

Adedokun, N. 2019. Farage Sets Red Line for Second Referendum in 10 Years: "I Don't Want To Be Switzerland!" *Daily Express*, 5 December. https://www.express.co.uk/news/uk/1213637/nigelfaragebbcandrewneilinterviewsecondreferendumbrexitpartyelectionlatest.

Ader-Nissen, R, C Galpin and B Rosamond. 2017. Performing Brexit. How a Post-Brexit World is Imagined Outside the UK. *British Journal of Politics and International Relations* 9 (3): 573–91.

Afonso, A. 2005. When the Export of Social Problems Is No Longer Possible: Immigration Policies and Unemployment in Switzerland. *Social Policy and Administration* 39 (6): 653–68.

Afonso, A. 2014. How to Please Voters Without Alienating Friends? Parties, Organised Interests and Advocacy Coalitions in Swiss Immigration Policy. *Comparative European Politics* 12 (6): 568–83.

Afonso, A, M-C Fontana and Y Papadopoulos. 2014. The Europeanisation of Swiss Decision-Making in Comparative Perspective: From Outlier to Normal Case? *Swiss Political Science Review* 20 (2): 246–51.

Afonso, A and M Maggetti. 2007. Bilaterals II: Reaching the Limits of the Swiss Third Way? In CH Church (ed.), *Switzerland and the European Union – A Close, Contradictory and Misunderstood Relationship*. London: Routledge.

Agnew, H. 2016. Swiss-Style Deal for the UK Not Feasible. *Financial Times*, 3 September.

Alabrese, E, SO Becker, T Fetzer and D Novy. 2019. Who Voted for Brexit? Individual and Regional Data Combined. *European Journal of Political Economy* 56: 132–50.

Albertazzi, D. 2006. The Lega dei Ticinesi: The Embodiment of Populism. *Politics* 26 (2): 133–9.

Allemand, A. 2018. If You Believe in the "Swiss Model" for Brexit, I Need to Give You a Reality Check from Switzerland. *The Independent*, 14 November. https://www.independent.co.uk/voices/brexitlatestswissmodeltheresamayswitzerlandsecondreferendumeua8633416.html.

Almond, G. 1950. *The American People and Foreign Policy*. New Haven, CT: Yale University Press.

Altherr, H. 2020. *Federalism and the COVID-19 Crisis: An Interim Perspective from Switzerland*. Ottawa, ON: Forum of Federations. http://www.forumfed.org/wp-content/uploads/2020/04/SwitzerlandCOVID.pdf.

Anderson, B. 1983. *Imagined Communities – Reflections on the Origin and Spread of Nationalism*. London: Verso.

Anson, J and O Cadot. 2004. Par-delà le "Röstigraben": L'électorat suisse partagé face à l'UE. *Schweizerische Zeitschrift für Volkswirtschaft und Statistik* 140: 171–206.

Ashcroft, M. 2016. We Can Live Without Europe. *Lord Ashcroft Polls*, 22 March. https://lordashcroftpolls.com/2016/03/wecanlivewithouteuropethereistherestoftheworldoutthe rebelgradezurich/.

Atkins, R. 2015. Swiss Eye Gains from EU Reform Push. *Financial Times*, 15 November.

Atkins, R. 2016. SBA Proposes Financial Alliance with UK. *Financial Times*, 8 July.

Aughey, A. 2010. Anxiety and Injustice: The Anatomy of Contemporary English Nationalism. *Nations and Nationalism* 16 (3): 506–24.

Baczynska, G. 2020. EU's Barnier Eyes Loose Association Deal as Basis for New British Ties. *Swissinfo*, 29 January. https://uk.reuters.com/article/ukbritaineubarnier/eusba rniereyeslooseassociationdealasbasisfornewbritishtiesidUKKBN1ZS1P1.

Balassa, B. 1961. *The Theory of Economic Integration*. Homewood, IL: R.D. Irwin.

Baldoni, E. 2003. The Free Movement of Persons in the European Union: A Legal-Historical Overview. PIONEUR Working Paper. https://www.academia.edu/21816300 /The_Free_Movement_of_Persons_in_the_European_Union_A_Legal-historical_O verview.

Baldwin, RE. 2006. Multilateralising Regionalism: Spaghetti Bowls as Building Blocks on the Path to Global Free Trade. *The World Economy* 29 (11): 1451–1518.

BBC. 2019. Switzerland Gun Control: Voters Back EU Regulations. *BBC News*, 19 May. https://www.bbc.com/news/world-europe-48328867.

BBC. 2020. Immigration. BBC Briefing. *BBC News*. http://news.files.bbci.co.uk/include/ newsspec/pdfs/bbc-briefing-immigration-newsspec-26148-v1.pdf.

BC. 2016. Is the Swiss Model Suitable for PostBrexit UKEU Relations? *Brexit Central*, 25 September. https://brexitcentral.com/swissmodelsuitablepostbrexitukeurelations/.

Becker, S, T Fetzer and D Novy. 2017. Who Voted for Brexit? A Comprehensive District-Level Analysis. *Economic Policy* 32 (92): 601–50.

Beglinger, M. 2016. Le lundi noir. *Neue Zürcher Zeitung*, 2 March.

BfS. 1982. *Statistisches Jahrbuch der Schweiz. Herausgegeben vom Eidgenössischen Statistischen Amt*. Basel: Birkhäuser Verlag.

BfS. 2014. *Statistik der Bevölkerung und der Haushalte 2010–2014*. Neuchâtel: Bundesamt für Statistik.

BfS. 2018a. *Auslandschweizerstatistik 1993–2017*. Neuchâtel: Bundesamt für Statistik https://www.bfs.admin.ch/bfs/de/home/statistiken/bevoelkerung/migration-integration /auslandschweizer.assetdetail.4883376.html.

BfS. 2018b. *Statistical Data on Switzerland 2018*. Neuchâtel: Bundesamt für Statistik.

BfS. 2018c. *Amtliches Gemeindeverzeichnis der Schweiz: Angekündigte Änderungen – Gemeindestand per 01.01.2018*. Bundesamt für Statistik. https://www.bfs.admin.ch/ bfs/de/home/statistiken/regionalstatistik/regionale-portraets-kennzahlen/gemeinden.gn pdetail.2017-0538.html.

BfS. 2020. *Ausländische Bevölkerung*. Bundesamt für Statistik. https://www.bfs.admin .ch/bfs/de/home/statistiken/bevoelkerung/migration-integration/auslaendische-bevoelk erung.html.

Bignasca, G. 2000. Firmate il referendum contro gli accordi bilaterali. *Il Mattino della Domenica*, 9 January.

BK. 2020a. *Volksabstimmungen*. Berne: Bundeskazlei. https://www.bk.admin.ch/bk/de/ home/politische-rechte/volksabstimmungen.html.

BK. 2020b. *Volksinitiativen*. Berne: Bundeskanzlei. https://www.bk.admin.ch/bk/de/ home/politische-rechte/volksinitiativen.html.

Blatter, J. 2017. Britain Cannot and Should Not Imitate the Swiss Model of Sectoral Bilateralism with the EU. *LSE Blogs*, 27 November. https://blogs.lse.ac.uk/brexit/2017/11/27/britaincannotandshouldnotimitatetheswissmodelofsectoralbilateralismwiththeeu/.

Blick, A. 2020. Constitutional Options for Northern Ireland: A Discussion. Blog post. The Federal Trust. https://fedtrust.co.uk/constitutional-options-for-northern-ireland-a-discussion/.

Blöchliger, H. 2005. *Baustelle Föderalismus*. Zurich: Neue Zürcher Zeitung Verlag.

Bluewin. 2019. Switzerland is Promoting EFTA Membership for the UK. *Bluewin*, 29 August. https://ch.de/news/die-schweiz-will-grossbritannien-einen-efta-beitritt-nach-dem-brexit–vorschlagen-292540-292540.html.

Bochsler, D. 2017. Lo stemperamento dei contorni politici dei Cantoni svizzeri. In S Mueller and A Giudici (eds), *Il federalismo svizzero – Attori, strutture e processi*. Locarno: Armando Dadò.

Bond, R, C Jeffery and M Rosie. 2010. The Importance of Being English: National Identity and Nationalism in Post-Devolution England. *Nations and Nationalism* 16 (3): 462–8.

Bondolfi, S. 2020. Brexit Year Could Be Key for Berne-Brussels Relations. *SwissInfo*, 31 January. https://www.swissinfo.ch/eng/switzerlandeuropeanunion_brexityearcouldbekeyforbernbrusselsrelations/45527430.

Bondolfi, S and T Stephens. 2018. The Brexit Vote Wasn't Direct Democracy – It Was Drivel. *SwissInfo*, 30 May. https://www.swissinfo.ch/eng/directdemocracy/swisscriticism_thebrexitvotewasntdirectdemocracy--it-was-drivel-/44155278.

Bondy, C, D O'Sullivan, C Whiddington and E Colin. 2020. *Brexit Negotiations in the Midst of the COVID-19 Crisis: Is the Challenge Still Feasible?* London: Steptoe & Johnson LLP.

Bornschier, S. 2010. Integrating the Defense of Traditional Communities into the Libertarian-Authoritarian Divide: The Role of the Swiss People's Party in the Redefinition of Cultural Conflicts. In S Hug and H Kriesi (eds), *Value Change in Switzerland*. Lenham, MD: Lexington Books.

Bornschier, S. 2015. The New Cultural Conflict, Polarization, and Representation in the Swiss Party System, 1975–2011. *Swiss Political Science Review* 21 (4): 680–701.

Bornschier, S and M Helbling. 2005. Stabilität und Wandel von Parteiensystemen und Konfliktlinie zwischen Öffnung und Abgrenzung: Der theoretische Ansatz. In H Kriesi, R Lachat, P Selb, S Bornschier and M Helbling (eds), *Der Aufstieg der SVP – Acht Kantone im Vergleich*. Zurich: NZZ Verlag.

BR. 1988. *Bericht über die Stellung der Schweiz im europäischen Integrationsprozess*. Bern: Bundesblatt. III 249.

BR. 1990. *Bericht über die Stellung der Schweiz im europäischen Integrationsprozess vom 26. November 1990*. Berne: Bundesrat.

BR. 1992. *Bericht über den Beitritt der Schweiz zur Europäischen Gemeinschaft vom 18. Mai 1992*. Berne: Bundesrat.

BR. 1994. *Bericht über die Aussenpolitik der Schweiz in den 90er Jahren anhang: Bericht zur Neutralität Vom 29. November 1993*. Berne: Bundesblatt. I 153.

BR. 2015. Bericht des Bundesrates in Beantwortung des Postulats Keller-Sutter [13.4022] *Freihandelsabkommen mit der EU statt bilaterale Abkommen*. Berne: Beantwortung eines Postulats.

BR. 2020. Coronavirus: Die eidgenössische Volksabstimmung vom 17. Mai 2020 wird nicht durchgeführt. Press release of 18 March 2020. Berne: Bundesrat. https://www.bk.admin.ch/bk/de/home/dokumentation/medienmitteilungen.msg-id-78485.html.

Bradley, S. 2018. British Interested in Swiss Model to Save Europe Ties. *SwissInfo*, 28 June. https://www.swissinfo.ch/eng/postbrexitsolutions_britishinterestedinswissmodeltosaveeuropeties/42258826.

Braun, D. 2009. Constitutional Change in Switzerland. *Publius: The Journal of Federalism* 39 (2): 314–40.

Brown, H. 2017. Post-Brexit Britain: Thinking about "English Nationalism" as a Factor in the EU Referendum. *International Politics Reviews* 5 (1): 1–12.

Brunetti, A, M Jaggi and R Weder. 2000. Duplik zum Beitrag von Klaus Armingeon: "Oekonomische Erklärungen des Verhaltens bei aussenpolitischen Abstimungen: Eine Kritik der Analyse von Aymo Brunetti, Markus Jaggi und Rolf Weder". *Schweizerische Zeitschrift für Volkswirtschaft und Statistik* 136: 215–22.

Brunetti, A, M Jaggi and R Weder. 1999. *Die Schweiz in der europapolitischen Zwickmühle: Wirtschaftliche Umverteilung als entscheidender Faktor in der Aussenpolitik*. Zurich: Verlag Neue Zürcher Zeitung.

Brunner, M and P Sciarini. 2002. L'opposition Overture-Traditions. In S Hug and P Sciarini (eds), *Changements de valeurs et nouveaux clivages politiques en Suisse*. Paris: L'Harmattan.

Bühler, S. 2018. Mario Gattiker: "Der Anreiz wird kleiner, auszuwandern". *NZZ am Sonntag*, 14 January. https://nzzas.nzz.ch/schweiz/mario-gattiker-der-anreiz-wird-kleiner-auszuwandern-ld.1347267.

Butler, D. 1996. *The 1975 Referendum*. Basingstoke: Macmillan.

Cansin, A, J-C Dumont, Z Kone, Y Moullan, C Ozden, C Parsons and T Xenogiani. 2015. *A New Profile of Migrants in the Aftermath of the Recent Economic Crisis*. Paris: OECD Publishing. doi: 10.1787/5jxt2t3nnjr5-en.

Cappelletti, F. 2017. La perequazione finanziaria: Tra concorrenza e solidarietà. In S Mueller and A Giudici (eds), *Il federalismo svizzero – Attori, strutture e processi*. Locarno: Armando Dadò.

Cassidy, A and P Loser. 2015. *Der Fall FDP – Eine Partei verliert ihr Land*. Zurich: Rotpunkt Verlag.

CCG. 2004. *Europe, un défi pour le federalisme*. Berne: Conférence des gouvernements cantonaux. https://kdk.ch/fileadmin/files/Themen/Europapolitik/5_etat_des_lieux_du_12_mars_2004.pdf.

CCG. 2007. *Position des gouvernements cantonaux en politique européenne*. Berne: Conférence des gouvernements cantonaux. https://kdk.ch/fileadmin/files/Themen/Europapolitik/4_etat_des_lieux_du_23_mars_2007.pdf.

CCG. 2010. *Etat des lieux en politique européenne des gouvernements cantonaux*. Berne: Conférence des gouvernements cantonaux. https://kdk.ch/fileadmin/files/Themen/Europapolitik/3_etat_des_lieux_du_25_juin_2010.pdf.

CCG. 2011. *Réformes intérieures visant à consolider l'organisation étatique fédérale et démocratique dans le cadre de la politique européenne du Conseil fédéral – Prise de position des gouvernements cantonaux*. Berne: Conférence des gouvernements cantonaux. https://kdk.ch/fileadmin/files/Themen/Europapolitik/2_prise_de_position_du_24_juin_2011.pdf.

CCG. 2012. *Vereinbarung über den politischen Dialog Bund-Kantone zu Europafragen*. Berne: Konferenz der Kantonsregierungen. https://kdk.ch/fileadmin/files/Themen/Europapolitik/1_vereinbarung_ueber_den_politischen_dialog_bund-kantone_zu_europafragen.pdf.

CCG. 2019. *Accord institutionnel Suisse-UE – Prise de position du 29 mars 2019*. Berne: Conférence des gouvernements cantonaux. https://www.fdfa.admin.ch/content/dam/de

a/fr/documents/bericht_konsultationen_insta/stellungnahmen/KdK-Stellungnahme-InstA_fr.pdf.

Chavagneux, C. 2017. Qui va récupérer le business de la City? *Alternatives économiques* 15 December. https://www.alternatives-economiques.fr/va-recuperer-business-de-city/00082200.

Christen, H. 1998. Convergence and Divergence in the Swiss German Dialects. *Folia Linguistica* 32 (1–2): 53–68.

Christin, T, S Hug and P Sciarini. 2002. La mobilisation des clivages lors des votations populaires. In S Hug and P Sciarini (eds), *Changements de valeurs et nouveaux clivages politiques en Suisse*. Paris: L'Harmattan.

Christin, T and AH Trechsel. 2002. Joining the EU? Explaining Public Opinion in Switzerland. *European Union Politics* 3 (4): 415–43.

Church, CH. (ed.). 2007. *Switzerland and the European Union – A Close, Contradictory and Misunderstood Relationship*. London: Routledge.

Church, CH. 2009a. Swiss History Through Anglo-Saxon Eyes. In M Oeri von Auw and AJ Crouz-Tornare (eds), *Clio dans tous ses états – Mélanges pour Georges Andrey*. Geneva: Editions Infolio/Editions de Penthes.

Church, CH. 2009b. Setting Limits to Europhobia? Recent Developments in Swiss Euroscepticism. In Krisztina Arato and Petr Kaniok (eds), *Euroscepticism and European Integration/Euroskepticizam i europske integracije*. Zagreb: Political Science Research Centre/Forum CPI Library 6.

Church, CH. 2016. *Political Change in Switzerland – From Stability to Uncertainty*. Abingdon: Routledge.

CJEU. 2018. Judgment in Case C-33/17 Čepelnik d.o.o. v Michael Vavti. Press release, 13 November. Court of Justice of the European Union. https://curia.europa.eu/jcms/upload/docs/application/pdf/2018-11/cp180170en.pdf.

Clarke, HD, M Goodwin and P Whiteley. 2017. Why Britain Voted for Brexit: An Individual-Level Analysis of the 2016 Referendum Vote. *Parliamentary Affairs* 70 (3): 439–64.

CoEU. 2012. Council Conclusions on EU Relations with EFTA Countries. 3213th Transport, Telecommunications and Energy Council Meeting. Press release, 20 December. Council of the European Union. http://www.consilium.europa.eu/uedocs/cms_data/docs/pressdata/en/trans/134523.pdf.

CoEU. 2014. Council Conclusions on a Homogeneous Extended Single Market and EU Relations with Non-EU Western European Countries. Press release, 16 December. Council of the European Union. https://www.consilium.europa.eu/uedocs/cms_data/docs/pressdata/en/er/146315.pdf.

CoEU. 2016. Council Conclusions on a Homogeneous Extended Single Market and EU Relations with Non-EU Western European Countries. Press release, 13 December. Council of the European Union. https://www.consilium.europa.eu/en/press/press-releases/2016/12/13/conclusions-homogeneous-extended-single-market/.

CoEU. 2017. Council Conclusions on EU Relations with the Swiss Confederation. Press release, 28 February. Council of the European Union. http://www.consilium.europa.eu/en/press/press-releases/2017/02/28/conclusions-eu-swiss-confederation/pdf.

CoEU. 2019. Council Conclusions on EU Relations with the Swiss Confederation. Press release, 19 February. Council of the European Union. https://www.consilium.europa.eu/en/press/press-releases/2019/02/19/council-conclusions-on-eu-relations-with-the-swiss-confederation/.

Cohen, AP. 2013. *Symbolic Construction of Community*. London: Routledge.

Connelly, T. 2019. Talks: Goodbye Canada, Hello Switzerland? *RTE*, 11 January. https://www.rte.ie/news/brexit/2020/0110/110566-brexit-talks/.

Contisguglu, C and C Cooper. 2019. The UK May not Like Swiss Advice on the Post-Brexit Future. *Politico*, 19 April. https://www.politico.eu/article/brexitukswitzerlandfinancialservicesjeremyhuntukmaynotlikeswissadviceonpostbrexitfuture/.

Cottier, T and A Kopse (eds). 1998. *Der Beitritt der Schweiz zur Europäischen Union – Brennpunkte und Auswirkungen*. Zurich: Schulthess.

Cowburn, A. 2020. "Deeply Inappropriate": Boris Johnson Facing Mounting Demands to Suspend All PostBrexit Trade Talks During Coronavirus. *The Independent*, 25 March.

CS. 1999. *Accord entre la Confédération suisse, d'une part, et la Communauté européenne et ses Etats membres, d'autre part, sur la libre circulation des personnes*. Berne: Confédération suisse. https://www.admin.ch/opc/fr/classified-compilation/19994648/index.html#_blank.

Curtice, J. 2017. Why Leave Won the UK's EU Referendum. *Journal of Common Market Studies* 55 (1): 19–38.

Curtice, J. 2020. Brave New World: Understanding the 2019 General Election. *Political Insight* 11 (1): 8–12.

Dafflon, B. 2006. *Fiscal Federalism in Switzerland: A Survey of Constitutional Issues, Budget Responsibility and Equalisation*. Working paper No. 278. Université de Fribourg. http://www.thomasfleiner.ch/files/categories/IntensivkursII/FiscalFederalismCH.pdf.

D'Amato, G. 2008. Historische und soziologische Übersicht über die Migration in der Schweiz. *Schweizerisches Jahrbuch für Entwicklungspolitik* 27 (2): 177–95.

Dardanelli, P. 2011. Multi-Lingual but Mono-National: Exploring and Explaining Switzerland's Exceptionalism. In F Requejo and M Caminal (eds), *Federalism, Plurinationality, and Democratic Constitutionalism – Theory and Cases*. Abingdon: Routledge.

Dardanelli, P. 2017. *Restructuring the European State – European Integration and State Reform*. Montreal, QC: McGill-Queen's University Press.

Dardanelli, P and S Mueller. 2019. Dynamic De/Centralization in Switzerland, 1848–2010. *Publius: The Journal of Federalism* 49 (1): 138–65.

Dauner, M, I Kramer, A Hassel and B Wagner. 2018. Reform der Entsenderichtlinie: Schutz gegen Sozial- und Lohndumping oder Einschränkung des Binnenmarkts? *ifo Schnelldienst* 71 (3): 3–12. https://www.econstor.eu/bitstream/10419/175160/1/ifosd-v71-2018-i03-p03-12.pdf.

De Lauretis, M and B Giussani. 1992. *La Lega dei Ticinesi – Indagine sul fenomeno che ha sconvolto il Ticino politico*. Locarno: Dadò editore.

De Vries, C. 2018. *Euroscepticism and the Future of European Integration*. Oxford: Oxford University Press.

De Winter, L and M Gomez-Reino. 2002. European Integration and Ethnoregionalist Parties. *Party Politics* 8 (4): 483–503.

Deloitte. 2015. Switzerland Remains Number 1 in International Private Wealth Management. *Deloitte Switzerland*, 1 February. https://www2.deloitte.com/ch/en/pages/financial-services/articles/international-wealthmanagement-centre-rankings-2015-press.html.

DFAE. 2018a. *Accord facilitant les relations bilatérales entre l'Union européenne et la Confédération suisse dans les parties du marché intérieur auxquelles la Suisse participe*. Berne: Département fédéral des affaires étrangères. https://www.dfae.admin.ch/dam/dea/fr/documents/abkommen/Acccord-inst-Projet-de-texte_fr.pdf.

DFAE. 2018b. *Le relazioni Svizzera-UE*. Berne: Dipartimento Federale degli Affari Esteri. https://www.eda.admin.ch/missions/mission-eu-brussels/it/home/politica-svizzera/in-cifre.html.

DFAE. 2020. *Switzerland–UK Relations Post Brexit*. Swiss Government, Department of Foreign Affairs. https://www.fdfa.admin.ch/dea/en/home/verhandlungenoffenethemen/offenethemen/brexit.

Diez Medrano, J. 2003. *Framing Europe – Attitudes to European Integration in Germany, Spain, and the United Kingdom*. Princeton, NJ: Princeton University Press.

Duff, A. 2020. Brexit: Getting It Done. Discussion Paper, 9 January. Brussels: European Policy Centre. https://www.epc.eu/en/Publications/BrexitGettingitdone~2df5a0.

Dupont, C and P Sciarini. 2001. Switzerland and the European Integration Process: Engagement without Marriage. *West European Politics* 24 (2): 211–32.

Dupont, C and P Sciarini. 2007. Back to the Future: The First Round of Bilateral Talks with the EU. In C Church (ed.), *Switzerland and the European Union – A Close, Contradictory and Misunderstood Relationship*. London: Routledge.

EC. 2020a. *Recommendation for a Council Decision Authorising the Opening of Negotiations for a New Partnership with the United Kingdom of Great Britain and Northern Ireland*. Brussels: European Commission, 3 February. https://ec.europa.eu/info/sites/info/files/communicationannexnegotiatingdirectives.pdf.

EC. 2020b. *Commission Postpones Application of the Medical Devices Regulation to Prioritise the Fight against Coronavirus*. Brussels: European Commission. Press release. https://ec.europa.eu/commission/presscorner/detail/en/ip_20_589.

Economist. 2006. Capital City. *The Economist*, 19 October. http://www.economist.com/node/8058157.

EEC. 1972. Agreement between the European Economic Community, of the One Part, and the Swiss Confederation, of the Other Part. *Brussels*, 31 December.

Elias, A. 2008. From Euro-Enthusiasm to Euro-Scepticism? A Re-Evaluation of Minority Nationalist Party Attitudes towards European Integration. *Regional and Federal Studies* 18 (5): 557–81.

Engeli, I and A Tresch. 2005. *Analyse VOX des votations fédérales du 5 juin 2005*. Geneva/Berne: Université de Genève/gfs.bern.

English, R. 2011. *Is There an English Nationalism?* London: Institute for Public Policy Research.

Epiney, A. 2018. Der Entwurf des Institutionellen Abkommens Schweiz-EU – Überblick und erste Einschätzung. *Jusletter*, 17 December.

Epiney, A and N Gammenthaler. 2008. Marktzugang in der EU und in der Schweiz: Rechtsquellen, Tragweite der Grundfreiheiten und des Personenfreizügigkeitsabkommens. In A Epiney, N Gammenthaler and I Hochreutener (eds), *Marktzugang in der EU und in der Schweiz – Zur Grenzüberschreitenden Mobilität von Personen und Unternehmen im EU-Recht und dem Personenfreizügigkeitsabkommen*. Zurich: Schulthess Juristische Medien.

Epiney, A and L Hehemann. 2019. Die Tragweite Des Institutionellen Abkommens Im Bereich Der Arbeitnehmerentsendung. *Jusletter*, 8 April.

Epiney, A, A Meier and A Egbuna-Joss. 2007. Schengen/Dublin. In D Thürer, RH Weber, W Portmann and A Kellerhals (eds), *Bilaterale Verträge I & II Schweiz-EU – Handbuch*. Zurich: Schulthess.

Epiney, A, B Metz and B Pirker. 2012. *Zur Parallelität der Rechtsentwicklung in der EU und in der Schweiz – Ein Beitrag zur Rechtlichen tragweite der "Bilateralen Abkommen"*. Zürich: Schulthess.

Erk, J. 2008. *Explaining Federalism – State, Society and Congruence in Austria, Belgium, Canada, Germany and Switzerland.* London: Routledge.

Essletzbichler, J, F Disslbacher and M Moser. 2018. The Victims of Neoliberal Globalisation and the Rise of the Populist Vote: A Comparative Analysis of Three Recent Electoral Decisions. *Cambridge Journal of Regions, Economy and Society* 11 (1): 73–94.

EU. 2014. Association Agreement between the European Union and its Member States, of the One Part, and Ukraine, of the Other Part. *Brussels*, 29 May. https://trade.ec.europa.eu/doclib/docs/2016/november/tradoc_155103.pdf.

Eurostat. 2019. Share of Non-Nationals in the Resident Population. 1 January 2018 (%). https://ec.europa.eu/eurostat/statistics-explained/index.php?title=File:Share_of_non-nationals_in_the_resident_population,_1_January_2018_(%25).png&oldid=424544.

Farage, N. 2020. Switzerland Was "Inspiration" for Brexit, Says Farage. *Swissinfo*, 17 January. https://www.swissinfo.ch/eng/eurelations_switzerlandwas-inspiration-for--brexit--says-farage-/45499628.

Farrand, B. 2017. Bold and Newly Independent, or Isolated and Cast Adrift? The Implications of Brexit for Intellectual Property Law and Policy. *Journal of Common Market Studies* 55 (6): 1306–21.

Feddersen, A. 2011. *Clivages et démocratie directe – Analyse de la mobilisation des anciens et nouveaux clivages lors des votations populaires de 2002 à 2008.* Unpublished paper. Département de science politique et relations internationales, Unversité de Genève.

Federal Council. 2016. *Rapport sur la politique extérieure 2015.* Berne: Federal Administration, 13 January.

Federal Customs Administration and Federal Department of Finance. 2020. *Monnaies de facturation.* Berne: Federal Customs Administration, 27 February.

Felber, R. 1988. Europas Zukunft darf uns nicht gleichgültig lassen. Prioritäten der schweizerischen Europapolitik. *Badener Tagblatt*, 19 November.

Ferraro, F. 2013. Schengen Governance after the Lisbon Treaty. Library of the European Parliament. Library Briefing. http://www.europarl.europa.eu/eplibrary/Schengen-governance-after-the-Lisbon-Treaty.pdf.

Fischer, A. 2005. *Die Auswirkungen der Internationalisierung und Europäisierung auf Schweizer Entscheidungsprozesse – Institutionen, Kräftverhältnisse und Akteursstrategien in Bewegung.* Zurich and Chur: Verlag Rüegger.

Fischer, A. 2007. Internationalization of Swiss Decision-Making Processes. In U Klöti, P Knoepfel, H Kriesi, W Linder and Y Papadopoulos (eds), *Handbook of Swiss Politics.* Zurich: NZZ Libro.

Fischer, A. 2015. Looking Beneath the Surface: Differences in Decision-Making Structures across Processes. In P Sciarini, M Fischer and D Traber (eds), *Political Decision-Making in Switzerland – Challenges to Consensus Politics.* London: Palgrave Macmillan.

Fischer, A and P Sciarini. 2013. Europeanization and the Inclusive Strategies of Executive Actors. *Journal of European Public Policy* 20 (10): 1482–98.

Fischer, A and P Sciarini. 2014. The Europeanization of Swiss Decision-Making Processes. *Swiss Political Science Review* 20 (2): 239–45.

Fischer, M, P Sciarini and D Traber. 2010. The Silent Reform of Swiss Federalism: The New Constitutional Articles on Education. *Swiss Political Science Review* 16 (4): 747–71.

Fleming, S. 2020. With UK Deal, EU Wants to Avoid Another Swiss Mess. *Financial Times*, 23 January. https://www.ft.com/content/37e458003ddf11eab232000f4477fbca.

Fontanellaz, B. 2019. *Entre Sonderfall et intégration – Les partis politiques suisses à l'épreuve de l'Europe (1989–2014).* Louvain-la-Neuve: Academia/L'Harmattan.

Fontanellaz, B and F Saint-Ouen. 2019. *Suisse – Union Européenne, les débats autour de l'accord institutionnel*. Geneva: Centre de compétences Dusan Sidjanski en études européennes de l'Université de Genève.

Fontanellaz, B and F Saint-Ouen. 2020. Suisse – Union Européenne, quel avenir? *Revue de l'Union européenne* 636: 153–5.

Foster, P, M Dickie and J Pickard. 2020. Boris Johnson Sets Up Clash with Scotland and Wales over State Aid. *Financial Times*, 12 July. https://www.ft.com/content/af238d8a-f7b5-4e7a-bddd-b5244305e92e.

Fowler, B. 2020. A New Normal? Parliament after Brexit. *Political Insight* 11 (1): 41–3.

Franklin, M, M Marsh and L McLaren. 1994. Uncorking the Bottle: Popular Opposition to European Unification in the Wake of Maastricht. *Journal of Common Market Studies* 32 (4): 455–72.

Freiburghaus, D. 2009. *Königsweg oder Sackgasse? Sechzig Jahre schweizerische Europapolitik*. Zurich: NZZ-Libro.

Frost, D. 2020. David Frost Speech in Full: Britain's Brexit Position. *Reaction*, 18 February. https://reaction.life/davidfrostspeechinfullbritainsbrexitposition/.

Gabel, M and HD Palmer. 1995. Understanding Variations in Public Support for European Integration. *European Journal of Political Research* 27 (1): 3–19.

Gabriel, JM. 2020. Great Britain and Switzerland: Circumventing EU Supranationality? *La Suisse en Europe*. https://suisseeneurope.ch/wpcontent/uploads/2020/01/GBandCHPDFfinal.pdf.

Gallagher, J. 2012. Intergovernmental Relations in the UK: Co-operation, Competition and Constitutional Change. *The British Journal of Politics and International Relations* 14 (2): 198–213.

Garton Ash, T. 2019. Interview. *Tages Anzeiger*, 21 December. https://www.tagesanzeiger.ch/ausland/europa/derbrexitwirdschlimmerfuereuropaalsfuerengland/story/27673466.

George, S and D Haythorne. 1996. The British Labour Party. In J Gaffney (ed.), *Political Parties and the European Union*. London: Routledge.

Germann, R and U Klöti. 2004. The Swiss Cantons: Equality and Difference. In U Klöti, P Knoepfel, H Kriesi, W Linder and Y Papadopoulos (eds), *Handbook of Swiss Politics*. Zurich: Neue Zürcher Zeitung Publishing.

Germann, RE. 1990. Bundesverfassung und "Europafähigkeit" der Schweiz. *Jahrbuch zur Staats- und Verwaltungswissenschaft*. Lausanne: Institut des hautes études en administration publique.

Germann, RE. 1994. La diplomatie référendaire de la Suisse dans l'Europe transnationale. In Y Papadopoulos (ed.), *Présent et avenir de la démocratie directe – Actes du colloque de l'Université de Lausanne*. Geneva: Georg.

Geser, H. 2004. The Communes in Switzerland. In U Klöti, P Knoepfel, H Kriesi, W Linder and Y Papadopoulos (eds), *Handbook of Swiss Politics*. Zurich: Neue Zürcher Zeitung Publishing.

Gimson, A. 2012. Boris Johnson in Britzerland. *The Guardian*, 21 December. https://www.theguardian.com/commentisfree/2012/dec/21/borisjohnsoninbritzerland.

Giudici, A. 2017. Una centralizzazione passata dalla porta di servizio? Il federalismo scolastico svizzero: origini, evoluzione e sfide contemporanee. In S Mueller and A Giudici (eds), *Il federalismo svizzero – Attori, strutture e processi*. Locarno: Armando Dadò.

Giugni, M and P Sciarini. 2009. Polarisation et politisation en Suisse. In C Suter (ed.), *Rapport social 2008*. Zurich: Seismo.

Glencross, A. 2015. Why a Brexit Referendum on EU Membership Will Not Solve the Europe Question. *International Affairs* 91 (2): 303–17.

Glencross, A. 2020. Why the UK Might Re-Join the EU. *Political Insight* 11 (1): 36–7.

Glencross, A and D McCourt. 2018. Living Up to a New Role in the World. *Orbis*, 13 November. https://www.fpri.org/article/2018/11/livinguptoanewroleintheworld thechallengesofglobalbritain/.

Gmür, H. 2018. Der Bundesrat steckt beim Rahmenabkommen in der Zwickmühle. *Neue Zürcher Zeitung*, 28 November.

Goetschel, L. 1994. *Zwischen Effizienz und Akzeptanz – Die Information der Schweizer Behörden im Hinblick auf die Volksabstimmung über den EWR-Vertrag vom 6. Dezember 1992*. Berne: Haupt.

Goetschel, L. 2007. The Wider Setting of Swiss Foreign Policy. In CH Church (ed.), *Switzerland and the European Union – A Close, Contradictory and Misunderstood Relationship*. London: Routledge.

Goetz, E. 2017. Brexit: Comprendre le passeport financier en 5 questions. *LesEchos.fr*, 18 January. https://www.lesechos.fr/18/01/2017/lesechos.fr/0211703941616_brexit---comprendrele--passeport-financier--en-cinq-questions.htm.

Golder, L, C Jans, P Huth, S Tschöpe and N Herzog. 2017. KMU-Territorium und internationale Drehscheibe – Die Schweiz sucht ihr Verhältnis zu Europa. *Credit Suisse*. https://www.credit-suisse.com/media/assets/corporate/docs/news-and-expertise/articles/2017/11/europabarometer.pdf.

Goodwin, MJ and O Heath. 2016. The 2016 Referendum, Brexit and the Left Behind: An Aggregate-Level Analysis of the Result. *The Political Quarterly* 87 (3): 323–32.

Gould, CA and A Messina (eds). 2014. *Europe's Contending Identities – Supranationalism, Ethnoregionalism, Religion, and New Nationalism*. Cambridge: Cambridge University Press.

Gstöhl, S. 2002. *Reluctant Europeans – Norway, Sweden and Switzerland in the Process of Integration*. Boulder, CO: Lynne Rienner Publishers.

Gubler, M. 2014. Carry Trade Activities: A Multivariate Threshold Model Analysis. Swiss National Bank Working Paper, No. 6.

Guerber, T. 1995. *Nationale Oppositionsstrategien gegen eine Annäherung der Schweiz an Europa – Eine vergleichende Untersuchung zur Strategie und Wirkung europäischer Opposition in der Schweiz am Beispiel der Abstimmungskämpfe über das Freihandelsabkommen mit der EWG (1972) und den EWR-Vertrag (1992)*. Master's thesis. Europainstitut Basel.

Guilluy, C. 2014. *La France périphérique – Comment on a sacrifié les classes populaires*. Paris: Flammarion.

Guilluy, C. 2016. *No Society – La fin de la classe moyenne occidentale*. Paris: Flammarion.

Haas, W. 2000. Die deutschsprachige Schweiz. In R Schläpfer and H Bickel (eds), *Die Viersprachige Schweiz*. Aarau: Sauerländer.

Häcki Buhofer, A and T Studer. 1993. Zur Entwicklung von Sprachdifferenzbewusstein und Einstellung zu den Varianten des Deutschen in der Deutschen Schweiz. *Bulletin CILA* 58: 179–99.

Hägi, S and J Scharloth. 2005. Ist Standarddeutsch für Deutschschweizer eine Fremdsprache? Untersuchungen zu einem Topos des sprachreflexiven Diskurses. *Linguistik Online* 24.

Hannan, D. 2012. Switzerland and Norway Prove We Can Leave the EU. *London Loves Business*, 14 September. https://londonlovesbusiness.com/danhannanswitzerlandand norwayprovewecanleavetheeu/.

Hannan, D and D Carswell. 2008. *The Plan: Twelve Months to Renew Britain*. London: Lulu.

Hausherr, R. 1980. Die schweizerische öffentliche Meinung zur Frage EWG oder EFTA in den Jahren 1957–1963. Unpublished paper. University of Berne.

Hayward, K and M Murphy. 2018. The EU's Influence on the Peace Process and Agreement in Northern Ireland in Light of Brexit. *Ethnopolitics* 17 (3): 276–91.

Heidbreder, E, E Thomann, I Stadelmann-Steffen and F Sager. 2018. EU Referendums in Context: What Can We Learn from the Swiss Case? *Public Administration* 97 (2): 370–83.

Helbling, M. 2011. Why Swiss-Germans Dislike Germans: Opposition to Culturally Similar and Highly Skilled Immigrants. *European Societies* 13 (1): 5–27.

Helbling, M, D Hoeglinger and B Wuest. 2010. How Political Parties Frame European Integration. *European Journal of Political Research* 49 (4): 495–521.

Henderson, A, C Jeffery, R Liñeira, R Scully, D Wincott and R Wyn Jones. 2016. England, Englishness and Brexit. *The Political Quarterly* 87 (2): 187–99.

Henderson, A, C Jeffery, D Wincott and R Wyn Jones. 2017. How Brexit Was Made in England. *The British Journal of Politics and International Relations* 19 (4): 631–46.

Hepburn, E. 2010. *Using Europe – Territorial Party Strategies in a Multi-Level System*. Manchester: Manchester University Press.

Heumann, P. 2020. Vorbild Boris Johnson. *Weltwoche*, 4 March. https://www.weltwoche.ch/ausgaben/2020-10/kommentare-analysen/vorbild-boris-johnson-die-weltwoche-ausgabe-10-2020.html.

Hirter, H and W Linder. 2001. *Analyse des votations fédérales du 4 mars 2001*. Berne: Université de Berne/Institut de recherche GfS, Analyse VOX No 73.

HMG. 2018. *The Future Relationship between the United Kingdom and the European Union*. Cm 9593. London: HMSO. https://assets.publishing.service.gov.uk/government/uploads/system/uploads/attachment_data/file/725288/The_future_relationship_between_the_United_Kingdom_and_the_European_Union.pdf.

HMG. 2019a. *Agreement on the Withdrawal of the United Kingdom of Great Britain and Northern Ireland from the European Union and the European Atomic Energy Community*. London: HMSO.

HMG. 2019b. *Political Declaration Setting Out the Framework for the Future Relationship between the European Union and the United Kingdom*. London: HMSO.

HMG. 2020. *The Future Relationship with the EU – The UK's Approach to Negotiations*. CP211. London: HMSO.

Hobolt, SB. 2016. The Brexit Vote: A Divided Nation, a Divided Continent. *Journal of European Public Policy* 23 (9): 1259–77.

Hobolt, SB. 2009. *Europe in Question: Referendums on European Integration*. Oxford: Oxford University Press.

HOCCEXEU. 2018. House of Commons Exiting the European Union Committee "The Future UK-EU Relationship'. Fourth Report of Session 2017–19, 29 March. https://publications.parliament.uk/pa/cm201719/cmselect/cmexeu/935/935.pdf.

Hooghe, L and G Marks. 2007. Sources of Euroscepticism. *Acta Politica* 42 (2–3): 119–27.

Hooghe, L and G Marks. 2009. A Postfunctionalist Theory of European Integration: From Permissive Consensus to Constraining Dissensus. *British Journal of Political Science* 39 (1): 1–23.

Hooghe, L and G Marks. 2018. Cleavage Theory Meets Europe's Crises: Lipset, Rokkan, and the Transnational Cleavage. *Journal of European Public Policy* 25 (1): 109–35.

Hug, S., and P. Sciarini. 2000. Referendums on European Integration: Do Institutions Matter in the Voter's Decision? *Comparative Political Studies* 33(1): 3–36.

Hutter, S, E Grande and H Kriesi (eds). 2016. *Politicising Europe – Integration and Mass Politics*. Cambridge: Cambridge University Press.

Ichijo, A. 2003. The Uses of History: Anglo-British and Scottish Views of Europe. *Regional and Federal Studies* 13 (3): 23–43.

Ignazi, P. 1992. The Silent Counter-Revolution. *European Journal of Political Research* 22 (1): 3–34.

Inglehart, R. 1971. Public Opinion and European integration. In L Lindberg and SA Scheingold (eds), *European Integration*. Cambridge, MA: Harvard University Press.

Jenni, S. 2014. Europeanization of Swiss Law-Making: Empirics and Rhetoric Are Drifting Apart. *Swiss Political Science Review* 20 (2): 208–15.

Jenni, S. 2016. *Switzerland's Differentiated European Integration – The Last Gallic Village?* Basingstoke: Palgrave Macmillan.

Jenni, S. 2018. Which Future for EU-Swiss Relations? A Citizens' Perspective. *TEPSA Briefs*. http://www.tepsa.eu/wp-content/uploads/2018/09/TEPSA-Brief-Sabine-Jenni .pdf.

Jenni, S. 2019. Switzerland's Sectoral Access to the EU's Single Market. *Efta-studies.org* . https://c3043ae8-097a-4505-aad71df308fd935f.filesusr.com/ugd/15fad1_8cf07b6 bd3ac4126948565c56e4d59e6.pdf.

Jenni, S. 2020. Switzerland's European Policy after the Election Year – Same Positions, New Urgency. *EFTA-Studies.org*. https://www.efta-studies.org/post/switzerlands-eur opean-policy-after-the-election-year.

Jolles, PR. 1992. Die Kontinuität der schweizerischen Europapolitik. *Schweizer Monatshefte* 11: 883–96.

Jolly, SK. 2015. *The European Union and the Rise of Regionalist Parties*. Ann Arbor, MI: University of Michigan Press.

Johnson, B. 2020. PM Speech in Greenwich. 3 February. https://www.gov.uk/government/ speeches/pmspeechingreenwich3february2020.

Jost, HU. 1999. *Europa und die Schweiz 1945–1950 – Europarat, Supranationalität und schweizerische Unabhängigkeit*. Zurich: Chronos.

Kaddous, C and M Jametti Greiner (eds). 2006. *Accords bilatéraux II Suisse UE et autres accords récents*. Basel: Helbing & Lichtenhahn.

Kaufmann, B. 2018. Let the British People Decide the Outcome of Brexit. *Swissinfo*, 16 November. https://www.swissinfo.ch/eng/opinion_let-the-british-people-decide-the -outcome-of-brexit/44549646.

Keating, M and L Hooghe. 2006. Bypassing the Nation-State: Regions and EU Process. In JJ Richardson (ed.), *European Union – Power and Policy-Making*. London: Routledge.

King, I. 2018. Why Swiss Struggles Do not Bode Well for Brexit. *Sky News*, 29 November. https://news.sky.com/story/whytheclockistickingforswissineutreatytalks11565976.

Knott, P. 2019. A Swiss Solution to Calm the Populist Surge. *The New European*, 18 February. https://www.theneweuropean.co.uk/topstories/paulknottaswisssolutiontoc almpopulistsurge15883337.

Knüsel, R. 1994. *Plurilinguisme et enjeux politiques – Les minorités ethnolinguistiques autochtones à territoire: l'exemple du cas helvétique*. Lausanne: Payot.

Kobach, K. 1994. Switzerland. In D Butler and A Ranney (eds), *Referendums around the World – The Growing Use of Direct Democracy*. Washington, DC: The AEI Press.

Kreis, G. 1995. Der lange Weg des Staatsvertragsreferendums. Schweizerische Aussenpolitik zwischen indirekter und direkter Demokratie. *Basler Schriften zur europäischen Integration* No. 12.

Kreis, G. 2012. Der hastige Aufbruch nach Europaland. In D Freiburghaus and G Kreis (eds), *Der EWR – verpasste oder noch bestehende Chance?* Zurich: NZZ Libro.

Kreis, G. 2018a. *Fremde Richter – Karriere eines politischen Begriffs*. Baden: Hier & Jetzt.

Kreis, G. 2018b. Konkurrenz oder Kooperation? Zur Entwicklung der parlamentarischen Zuständigkeit in der Aussenpolitik, 1920–1992. *Traverse* 3: 60–70.

Kriesi, H. 1998. The Transformation of Cleavage Politics: The 1997 Stein Rokkan Lecture. *European Journal of Political Research* 33 (2): 165–185.

Kriesi, H. 1999. Introduction: State Formation and Nation Building in the Swiss Case. In H Kriesi, K Armingeon, H Siegrist and A Wimmer (eds), *Nation and National Identity – The European Experience in Perspective*. Zurich and Chur: Verlag Rüegger.

Kriesi, H. 2005. *Direct Democratic Choices – The Swiss Experience*. Lanham, MD: Lexington Books.

Kriesi, H, E Grande, M Dolezal, M Helbling, D Höglinger, S Hutter and B Wüest. 2012. *Political Conflict in Western Europe*. Cambridge: Cambridge University Press.

Kriesi, H, E Grande, R Lachat, M Dolezal, S Bornschier and T Frey. 2008. *West European Politics in the Age of Globalization*. Cambridge: Cambridge University Press.

Kriesi, H, R Lachat, P Selb, S Bornschier and M Helbling. 2005. *Der Aufstieg der SVP – Acht Kantone im Vergleich*. Zürich: NZZ Verlag.

Kriesi, H, C Longchamp, F Passy and P Sciarini. 1993. *Analyse de la votation fédérale du 6 décembre 1992 (EEE)*. Genève/Berne: Université de Genève/Institut de recherche GfS, Analyse VOX No 47.

Kriesi, H and A Trechsel. 2008. *The Politics of Switzerland*. Cambridge: Cambridge University Press.

Kriesi, H, B Wernli, P Sciarini and M Gianni. 1996. *Le clivage linguistique: Problèmes de compréhension entre les communautés linguistiques en Suisse*. Berne: Office fédéral de la statistique.

Krugman, P. 1991. The Move toward Free Trade Zones. *Federal Reserve Bank of Kansas City Economic Review* 76 (6): 7–25.

Kübler, D. 2014. Agglomerationen. In P Knoepfel, Y Papadopoulos, P Sciarini, A Vatter and S Häusermann (eds), *Handbuch der Schweizer Politik / Manuel de la politique suisse*. 5th ed. Zurich: NZZ Verlag.

Kugler, P and B Weder. 2002. The Puzzle of the Swiss Interest Rate Island: Stylized Facts and a New Interpretation. *HWWA Discussion Paper*, No. 168.

Lamfalussy, A. 1963. *The United Kingdom and the Six – An Essay on Economic Growth in Western Europe*. London: Macmillan.

Lampart, D, E Baselgia and F Bender. 2018. *Arbeitnehmende und Löhne schützen! Personenfreizügigkeit, Flankierende Massnahmen und Migration*. Berne: Schweizerischer Gewerkschaftsbund. https://www.uss.ch/fileadmin/user_upload/Dokumente/Broschueren__Buecher/BroschuereFlaM2018_deutsch_web.pdf.

Langejürgen, R. 1993. *Die Eidgenossenschaft zwischen Rütli und EWR*. Chur: Rüegger.

Laponce, JA. 1987. *Languages and Their Territories*. Toronto, ON: University of Toronto Press.

Laurent, A and G Vallet. 2014. La construction progressive de l'avantage compétitif financier suisse (1914–1936). *Revue d'économie financière* 113: 259–73.

Lavenex, S. 2006. Switzerland: Between Intergovernmental Co-Operation and Schengen Association. In M Caparini and O Marenin (eds), *Borders and Security Governance – Managing Borders in a Globalised World*. Münster: LIT.

Lee, N, K Morris and T Kemeny. 2018. Immobility and the Brexit Vote. *Cambridge Journal of Regions, Economy and Society* 11: 143–63.

Legge, S. 2019. The Upsides of Brexit: Key Lessons for Switzerland. *SwissInfo*, 26 March. https://www.swissinfo.ch/eng/opinion_theupsideofbrexit-key-lessons-for-switzerland/44852004.

Lindberg, LN and SA Scheingold. 1970. *Europe's Would-Be Polity – Patterns of Change in the European Community*. Englewood Cliffs, NJ: Prentice-Hall.

Linder, W. 2010. *Swiss Democracy – Possible Solutions to Conflict in Multicultural Societies*. Basingstoke: Palgrave Macmillan.

Linder, W. 2011. Europe and Switzerland: Europeanization Without EU Membership. In A Mach and C Trampusch (eds), *Switzerland in Europe – Continuity and Change in the Swiss Political Economy*. London: Routledge.

Linder, W. 2013. Switzerland and the EU: The Puzzling Effects of Europeanisation without Institutionalisation. *Contemporary Politics* 19: 190–202.

Linder, W. 2014. Swiss Legislation in the Era of Globalization: A Quantitative Assessment of Federal Legislation (1983–2007). *Swiss Political Science Review* 20 (2): 223–31.

Linder, W, C Bolliger and Y Rielle (eds). 2010. *Handbuch der eidgenössischen Volksabstimmungen 1848–2007*. Berne: Haupt.

Linder, W, O Hümbelin and M Sutter. 2009. *Die Entwicklung der eidgenössischen Gestezgebungstätigkeit 1983-2007: eine quantitative Analye*. Universität Bern, Institut für Politikwissenschaft.

Linder, W and S Mueller. 2017. *Schweizerische Demokratie*. 4th ed. Berne: Haupt.

Linder, W, R Zürcher and C Bolliger. 2008. *Gestpaltene Schweiz-geeinte Schweiz – Gesellschaftliche Spaltungen und Konkordanz bei den Volksabstimmungen seit 1874*. Baden: Hier+Jetzt.

Lippmann, W. 1922. *Public Opinion*. New York, NY: The Free Press.

Lowe, S. 2018. *The first Swiss Lesson for Brexit Britain*. Centre for European Reform. http://www.globalbusinessoutlook.com/thefirstswisslessonforbrexitbritainnegotiationsneverend/.

Maddox, D and D Williamson. 2020. Brexit Deal: Boris REJECTS Extension. *Daily Express*, 17 March. https://www.express.co.uk/news/politics/1255874/Brexittradedealextensioncoronaviruslatest.

Maiani, F and V Boillet. 2017. EU-Swiss Free Movement and "Stop Mass Immigration": Much Ado about Nothing? http://eumigrationlawblog.eu/eu-swiss-free-movement-and-stop-mass-immigration-much-ado-about-nothing/.

Marquis, L and P Sciarini. 1999. Opinion Formation in Foreign Policy: The Swiss Experience. *Electoral Studies* 18: 453–71.

Maurhofer, R. 2001. *Die schweizerische Europapolitik vom Marshallplan zur EFTA bis 1960 – Zwischen Kooperation und Integration*. Berne: Haupt.

Mazzoleni, O. 2008. *Nationalisme et populisme en Suisse – La radicalisation de la "nouvelle UDC"*. Lausanne: Presses polytechniques et universitaires romandes.

Mazzoleni, O. 2015. Oltre il consociativismo. L'evoluzione del sistema dei partiti e di governo del Cantone Ticino dagli anni '90 ad oggi. *Archivo storico ticinese* 157: 46–61.

Mazzoleni, O. 2017a. *Les défis du régionalisme politique en Suisse – Le Tessin et ses relations avec Berne*. Geneva: Editions Slatkine.

Mazzoleni, O. 2017b. A Regionalist League in Southern Switzerland. In O Mazzoleni and S Mueller (eds), *Regionalist Parties in Western Europe – Dimensions of Success*. London: Routledge.

Mazzoleni, O, P Ferragutti, M Stanga and A Pilotti. 2007. *L'Europa vista dal Ticino*. Bellinzona: Ustat.

Mazzoleni, O, M Pacella and A Plata. 2011. *Le elezioni cantonali ticinesi del 2011: Partecipazione e orientamento di voto fra lealtà, defezione, protesta*. Travaux de science politique, Université de Lausanne.

Mazzoleni, O and A Pilotti. 2015. The Outcry of the Periphery? An Analysis of Ticino's No to Immigration. *Swiss Political Science Review* 21 (1): 63–75.

Mazzoleni, O and C Ruzza. 2018. Combining Regionalism and Nationalism: The Lega in Italy and the Lega dei Ticinesi in Switzerland. *Comparative European Politics* 16 (6): 976–92.

McCann, P. 2016. *The UK Regional-National Economic Problem – Geography, Globalisation and Governance*. London: Routledge.

McGrath, C. 2018. Swiss Model Offers UK a BREXIT BLUEPRINT etc. *Daily Express*, 27 April. https://www.express.co.uk/news/politics/952236/brexitnewseuukswitzerlandswissmodelcustomsunion.

McRedmond, F. 2020. Britain Is Uncomfortable because Ireland Has the Upper Hand for the First Time. *The Irish Times*, 28 February. https://www.irishtimes.com/opinion/britainisuncomfortablebecauseirelandhastheupperhandforthefirsttime1.4187051.

McTague, T. 2017. Brexiteers Fear "Swiss Trap" Trade Deal. *Politico*, 17 October. https://www.politico.eu/article/brexiteersfearswisstrapdealforbritain/.

Mendez, F, M Mendez, and V Triga. 2014. *Referendums and the European Union: A Comparative Inquiry*. Cambridge: Cambridge University Press.

Menzi, B. 2010. Kaum Opposition gegen mehr Koordination im Bildungswesen. In W Linder, C Bolliger and Y Rielle (eds), *Handbuch der eidgenössischen Volksabstimmungen 1848 bis 2007*. Berne: Haupt.

Métral, G. 2001. *From National to Multi-Scale Identities*. Paper presented at the 29th ECPR Joint Session of Workshops, Institut d'Etudes Politiques de Grenoble, pp. 6–11.

Moore, P. 2016. How Britain Voted at the EU Referendum. *YouGov*. https://yougov.co.uk/topics/politics/articles-reports/2016/06/27/how-britain-voted.

Morgenthau, H. 1956. *Politics among Nations – The Struggle for Power and Peace*. New York: Knopf.

Morris, P. 1996. The British Conservative Party. In J Gaffney (ed.), *Political Parties and the European Union*. London: Routledge.

Mueller, S and P Dardanelli. 2014. Langue, culture politique et centralisation en Suisse. *Revue internationale de politique comparée* 21 (4): 83–104.

Mueller, S and A Heidelberger. 2020. Should We Stay or Should We Join? 30 Years of Sovereignism and Direct Democracy in Switzerland. *European Politics and Society* 21 (2): 182–201.

Muller, F. 2020. *Kleine Geschichte des Rahmenabkommens*. Zurich: NZZ Libro.

MW. 2014. A Summary History of Immigration to Britain. Briefing paper. *Migration Watch UK*. https://www.migrationwatchuk.org/briefing-paper/48.

Najy, CM and R Schwok. 2018. The Most Reluctant Country with Regard to European Integration. In P Moreau and B Wassenberg (eds), *European Integration and New Anti-Europeanism – Perceptions of External States on European Integration*. Stuttgart: Franz Steiner Verlag.

NZZ. 1992. Plädoyer für ein EG-Beitritt der Schweiz. *Neue Zürcher Zeitung*, 21 May.

Obinger, H. 1998. Federalism, Direct Democracy, and Welfare State Development in Switzerland. *Journal of Public Policy* 18 (3): 241–62.

OECD. 2020. *Employment Rate (Indicator)*. doi: 10.1787/1de68a9b-en (5 March 2020).

Oliver, T. 2016. European and International Views of Brexit. *Journal of European Public Policy* 23 (9): 1321–8.

Papadopoulos, Y. 1996. De Charybde en Scylla: Le système politique suisse entre crise de représentation et crise d'adaptation. In C Honegger, J Gabriel, R Hirsig, and J Pfaff-Czarnecka (eds), *Gesellschaften im Umbau – Identitäten, Konflikte, Differenzen/ Sociétés en construction – Identités, conflits, différences*. Zurich: Seismo.

Perring, R. 2019. Switzerland Loses Sovereignty to EU Despite Being Independent Nation-Shock Study. *Daily Express*, 1 August. https://www.express.co.uk/news/world/1160111/.

Pilotti, A and O Mazzoleni. 2014. *Il voto ticinese sull'iniziativa "contro l'immigrazione di massa" del 9 febbraio 2014*. Travaux de science politique, Université de Lausanne.

Pirker, B. 2019. Zum Schiedsgericht im Institutionellen Abkommen. *Jusletter*, 3 June.

PMO. 2017a. The Government's Negotiating Objectives for Exiting the EU. Prime Minister's Office, 17 January. https://www.gov.uk/government/speeches/the-governments-negotiating-objectives-for-exiting-the-eu-pm-speech.

PMO. 2017b. PM's Florence Speech: A New Era of Cooperation and Partnership between the UK and the EU. Prime Minister's Office, 22 September. https://www.gov.uk/government/speeches/pms-florence-speech-a-new-era-of-cooperation-and-partnership-between-the-uk-and-the-eu.

Quillian, L and D Pager. 2001. Black Neighbors, Higher Crime? The Role of Racial Stereotypes in Evaluations of Neighborhood Crime. *American Journal of Sociology* 107 (3): 717–67.

Rachman, G. 2020. Brexit Solved with the Sword of Damocles. *Financial Times*, 3 March.

Rapp, C, R Traunmüller, M Freitag and A Vatter. 2014. Moral Politics: The Religious Factor in Referenda Voting. *Politics and Religion* 7 (2): 418–43.

Read, C. 2020. EU Crisis: Switzerland to Hold Referendum as Country Prepares for Its Own "Brexit Moment". *Daily Express*, 13 February. https://www.express.co.uk/news/world/1241507/EUnewsswitzerlandreferendumschengenMaybrexitlatestborisjohnson.

Rennwald, L. 2015. *Partis socialistes et classe ouvrière – Ruptures et continuités du lien électoral en Suisse, Autriche, Allemagne, Grande-Bretagne et France (1970–2008)*. Neuchâtel: Editions Alphil.

Reynié, D. 2013. *Les nouveaux populismes*. Paris: Fayard.

Rhinow, R. 2006. Le fédéralisme suisse: L'approche juridique. In R Frey, G Kreis, G-R Plattner and R Rhinow (eds), *Le fédéralisme suisse – La réforme engagée. Ce qui reste à faire*. Lausanne: Presses polytechniques et universitaires romandes.

Riano, Y and D Wastl-Walter. 2006. Immigration Policies, State Discourses on Foreigners, and the Politics of Identity in Switzerland. *Environment and Planning A: Economy and Space* 38 (9): 1693–713.

Rokkan, S. 1999. *State Formation, Nation-Building, and Mass Politics in Europe – The Theory of Stein Rokkan.* Oxford: Oxford University Press.

Rosamond, B. 1993. National Labour Organizations and European Integration: British Trade Unions and "1992". *Political Studies* 41 (3): 420–34.

Rose, Richard. 2020. What Would It Take to Undo Brexit? *Political Insight* 11 (3): 32–3.

Rossi, S. 2015. L'economia ticinese nel contesto globale: problemi e prospettive. *Archivio storico ticinese* 157: 27–45.

Rossi, S. 2019. The Dangerous Ineffectiveness of Negatives Interest Rates: The Case of Switzerland. *Review of Keynesian Economics* 7 (2): 220–32.

Safi, K. 2010. Swiss Euroskepticism: Economically or Culturally Determined? In S Hug and H Kriesi (eds), *Value Change in Switzerland*. Lenham, MD: Lexington.

Sandbu, M. 2019. European Bloc's Way Forward Rests on Ties with Non-members. *Financial Times*, 18 December.

Sardi, M and E Widmer. 1993. L'orientation du vote. In H Kriesi (ed.), *Citoyenneté et démocratie – Compétence, participation et décision des citoyens et citoyennes suisses*. Zurich: Seismo.

Sarrasin, O, EGT Green, C Bolzman, EP Visintin and E Politi. 2018. Competition- and Identity-Based Roots of Anti-Immigration Prejudice among Individuals with and without an Immigrant Background. *International Review of Social Psychology* 31 (1): 1–12.

Sarrasin, O, T Kuhn and B Lancee. 2018. What Explains Increasing Euroscepticism in Switzerland? A Longitudinal Analysis. In R Tillmann, M Voorpostel and P Farago (eds), *Social Dynamics in Swiss Society – Empirical Studies Based on the Swiss Household Panel*. Cham: Springer.

SBA. 2015. *The Swiss Financial Centre – Ready for the Renminbi*. Basel: Swiss Bankers Association.

Schäfer, F. 2018. Die theoretische Trendwende bei den Asylzahlen. *Tages Anzeiger*, 21 November. https://www.tagesanzeiger.ch/schweiz/standard/die-theoretische-trendwende-bei-den-asylzahlen/story/16664331.

Schimmelfennig, F. 2017. *Differentiation and Self-determination in European Integration*. Euborders Working Paper 01.

Schläpfer, R. 1994. Das Spannungsfeld zwischen Standard und Dialekt in der deutschen Schweiz. In H Burger and A Häcki Buhofer (eds), *Spracherwerb im Spannungsfeld von Dialekt und Hochsprache*. Berne: Peter Lang.

Schmitz, C. 2019. Brexit-Deal. Was bedeutet er fur die Schweiz? *Neue Zürcher Zeitung*, 18 October.

Schnabel, J and S Mueller. 2017. Vertical Influence or Horizontal Coordination? The Purpose of Intergovernmental Councils in Switzerland. *Regional and Federal Studies* 27 (5): 549–72.

Schneider, N and G Vallet. 2019. The Green Light or the Green Line? Challenges Facing the Energy Choices in Switzerland. *Cahiers de recherché du CREG*, No. 3.

Schweizer, P. 1991. Federalism in Switzerland. *India International Centre Quarterly* 18 (4): 161–9.

Schwok, R. 2006. *Suisse–Union européenne – L'adhésion impossible?* Lausanne: Presses polytechniques et universitaires romandes.

Schwok, R. 2018. *Brexit, Swiss "Model", Pros and Cons in Comparative Perspective*. London: House of Commons, Exiting the EU Committee. https://www.parliament.uk/business/committees/committees-a-z/commons-select/exiting-the-european-union-committee/news-parliament-2017/eu-withdrawal-government-response-special-report-published-17-19.

Schwok, R and S Lavenex. 2015. The Swiss Way: The Nature of the Swiss Relationship with the EU. In EE Oddvar (ed.), *The EU's Non-members – Interdependence under Hegemony*. Abingdon: Routledge.

Sciarini, P. 1991. Le role et la position de l'Assemblée fédérale dans les relations avec la Communauté européenne depuis 1972. In Parlamentsdieste (ed.), *Das Parlament – "Oberste Gewalt des Bundes"?* Berne: Haupt.

Sciarini, P. 1994. *La Suisse face à la Communauté européenne et au GATT – Le cas-test de la politique Agricole*. Geneva: Georg.

Sciarini, P. 1999. La pratique de la démocratie directe en politique extérieure. In J-D Delley (ed.), *Démocratie directe et politique étrangère en Suisse*. Basel: Helbing et Lichtenhahn.

Sciarini, P. 2000. La formation des opinions dans les votations populaires de politique extérieure. *Revue suisse de science politique* 6 (1): 71–84.

Sciarini, P. 2005. Les cantons, tiraillés entre la volonté de coopération intercantonale et la tentation de faire cavalier seul. *Le Temps*, 16 February.

Sciarini, P. 2014. Eppure si muove: The Changing Nature of the Swiss Consensus Democracy. *Journal of European Public Policy* 21 (1): 116–32.

Sciarini, P. 2020. The Dilemma between Bilateral Agreements and Immigration Control: How Would Swiss Voters Decide? In R Careja, P Emmenegger and N Giger (eds), *The European Social Model under Pressure*. Berlin: Springer.

Sciarini, P, A Fischer and S Nicolet. 2002. L'impact de l'internationalisation sur les processus de décision en Suisse: Une analyse quantitative des actes législatifs 1995–1999. *Revue suisse de science politique* 8 (1): 1–34.

Sciarini, P, A Fischer and S Nicolet. 2004. How Europe Hits Home: Evidence from the Swiss Case. *Journal of European Public Policy* 11 (3): 353–78.

Sciarini, P, A Fischer and D Traber (eds). 2015. *Political Decision-Making in Switzerland – The Consensus Model under Pressure*. Basingstoke: Palgrave Macmillan.

Sciarini, P, S Hug and C Dupont. 2001. Example, Exception or Both? Swiss National Identity in Perspective. In L-E Cedermann (ed.), *Constructing Europe's Identity: The External Dimension*. Boulder, CO: Lynne Rienner.

Sciarini, P, S Lanz and A Nai. 2015. Till Immigration Do Us Part? Public Opinion and the Dilemma between Immigration Control and Bilateral Agreements. *Swiss Political Science Review* 21 (2): 271–86.

Sciarini, P and O Listhaug. 1997. Single Cases or a Unique Pair? The Swiss and Norwegian "No' to Europe. *Journal of Common Market Studies* 35 (3): 407–38.

Sciarini, P and L Marquis. 2000. Opinion publique et politique extérieure: Le cas de la Suisse. *International Political Science Review* 21 (2): 149–71.

Sciarini, P and S Nicolet. 2005. Internationalization and Domestic Politics: Evidence from the Swiss Case. In H Kriesi, M Kohli and Z-N Milad (eds), *Contemporary Switzerland – Revisiting the Special Case*. Basingstoke: Palgrave Macmillan.

Sciarini, P and A Tresch. 2009. A Two-Level Analysis of the Determinants of Direct Democratic Choices in European, Immigration and Foreign Policy in Switzerland. *European Union Politics* 10 (4): 456–81.

Sciarini, P and A Tresch. 2011. Campaign Effects in Direct-Democratic Votes in Switzerland. *Journal of Elections, Public Opinion and Parties* 21 (3): 333–57.

Sciarini, P and A Tresch. 2014. Votations Populaires. In P Knoepfel, Y Papadopoulos, P Sciarini, A Vatter and S Häusermann (eds), *Handbuch der Schweizer Politik/Manuel de la politique suisse*. Zurich: NZZ Libro.

Sciarini, P, A Tresch and M Fischer. 2014. Europeanization in Parliament and in the Press. *Swiss Political Science Review* 20 (2): 232–8.

SECO. 2017. 15 Jahre Personenfreizügigkeit. 13. Bericht des Observatoriums zum Freizügigkeitsabkommen Schweiz-EU – Auswirkungen der Personenfreizügigkeit auf den Schweizer Arbeitsmarkt. Staatssekretariat für Wirtschaft, Bundesamt für Migration, Bundesamt für Statistik, and Bundesamt für Sozialversicherungen, Schweizerische Eidgenossenschaft. https://www.seco.admin.ch/seco/de/home/Publikationen_Dienstl

eistungen/Publikationen_und_Formulare/Arbeit/Personenfreizuegigkeit_und_Arbeitsb eziehungen/observatoriumsberichte/13_Bericht_Observatoriums.html

SECO. 2018. 14. Bericht des Observatoriums zum Freizügigkeitsabkommen Schweiz-EU – Auswirkungen der Personenfreizügigkeit auf Arbeitsmarkt und Sozialversicherungen. Staatssekretariat für Wirtschaft (SECO), Schweizerische Eidgenossenschaft. https://www.seco.admin.ch/seco/de/home/Publikationen_Dienstl eistungen/Publikationen_und_Formulare/Arbeit/Personenfreizuegigkeit_und_Arb eitsbeziehungen/observatoriumsberichte/14_Bericht_Observatoriums_Freizuegig keitsabkommen_Schweiz_EU.html.

Seitz, W. 2014. *Geschicte der politischen Gräben in der Schweiz*. Zurich and Chur: Verlag Rüegger.

SEM. 2018. Visa Monitoring. Entwicklung der Visumerteilung durch Schweizer Auslandvertretungen. Jahresausgabe 2017. Staatssekretariat für Migration, Justiz- und Polizeidepartement, Schweizerische Eidgenossenschaft. https://www.sem.admin.ch/sem/de/home/publiservice/statistik/visamonitoring.html.

Senti, M. 2012. *Europapolitik – Treibstoff der Konservativen*. Zurich: Verlag Neue Zürcher Zeitung.

Siebenhaar, B and A Wyler. 1997. *Dialekt und Hochsprache in der deutschsprachigen Schweiz*. Zürich: Pro Helvetia.

Sieber, P and H Sitta. 1994. Zur Rolle der Schule beim Aufbau von Einstellungen zu Dialekt und Standardsprache. In H Burger and A Häcki Buhofer (eds), *Spracherwerb im Spannungsfeld von Dialekt und Hochsprache*. Berne: Peter Lang.

Stanga, M. 2013. Una minoranza non solo linguistica: Votazioni federali 1945–2013: quando in Ticino (e nel Moesano ?) si vota diversamente. *Dati, Statistiche e Società* 2: 19–33.

Steenbergen, MR, EE Edwards and CE De Vries. 2007. Who's Cueing Whom? Mass-Elite Linkages and the Future of European Integration. *European Union Politics* 8 (1): 13–35.

Steinberg, J. 2015. *Why Switzerland*. 3rd ed. Cambridge: Cambridge University Press.

Steiner, J. 2003. Continental Integration and Swiss Federalism: A New Openness to Europe? In H Lazar, H Telford and RL Watts (eds), *The Impact of Global and Regional Integration on Federal Systems*. Montreal, QC: McGill-Queen's University Press.

Steinworth, D and CG Schmutz. 2020. Intensive Beziehungen zu China sind im Interesse Europas. *Neue Zürcher Zeitung*, 29 June.

Stephens, T. 2016. Would the Swiss Model Suit a Post-Brexit Britain? *SwissInfo*, 3 May.

Swissvotes. 2020. Database of Swiss Referendums. https://swissvotes.ch/votes (27 March 2020).

Szczerbiak, A and P Taggart. 2008. *Opposing Europe? The Comparative Party Politics of Euroscepticism – Comparative and Theoretical Perspectives*. Oxford: Oxford University Press.

Szent-Ivanyi, B. 2019. The Visegrad Four. In A Glencross (ed.), *Renewing and Rethinking Bilateralism after Brexit*. Aston University. https://research.aston.ac.uk/en/publicat ions/renewing-and-rethinking-bilateralism-after-brexit.

Szvircsev Tresch, T, A Wenger, S De Rosa, T Ferst, M Giovanoli, E Moehlecke de Baseggio, T Reiss, A Rinaldo, O Schneider and JV Scurrell. 2019. *Sicherheit 2019 – Aussen-, Sicherheits- und Verteidigungspolitische Meinungsbildung im Trend*. Militärakademie (MILAK) an der ETH Zürich und Center for Security Studies, ETH Zürich. https://css .ethz.ch/content/dam/ethz/special-interest/gess/cis/center-for-securities-studies/pdfs/Si 2019.pdf.

Tanner, J. 1990. Die Schweiz und Europa im 20. Jahrhundert: Wirtschaftliche Integration ohne politische Partizipation. In P Bairoch and M Körner (eds), *Die Schweiz in der Weltwirtschaft (15.-20. Jahrhundert)*. Zurich: Chronos.

Thatcher, M. 1979. Press Conference after Dublin European Council, 30 November. Margaret Thatcher Foundation. https://www.margaretthatcher.org/document/104180.

Thatcher, M. 1988. Speech to the College of Europe, 20 September. Margaret Thatcher Foundation. https://www.margaretthatcher.org/document/107332.

The CityUK. 2014. Key Facts about the UK as an International Financial Centre. The CityUK Reports, June. https://www.thecityuk.com/assets/2014/Reports-PDF/ae6aa5bc78/Key-Facts-about-international-financial-and-related-professional-services-2014.pdf.

Theiler, T. 2004. The Origins of Euroscepticism in German-Speaking Switzerland. *European Journal of Political Research* 43 (4): 635–56.

Theiler, T. 2012. Does the European Union Need to Become a Community? *Journal of Common Market Studies* 50 (5): 783–800.

Thürer, D and M MacLaren. 2009. Swiss Confederation. In H Michelmann (eds), *Foreign Relations in Federal Countries*. Montreal, QC: McGill-Queen's University Press.

Times. 2016. Feel the Berne. *The Times*, 21 September.

Tobler, C. 2017. Homogenität im Rechtsbestand der Schengen- und Dublin-Abkommen: Übernimmt die Schweiz im Assoziationsrahmen nicht notifiziertes Asyl- und Datenschutzrecht der EU? *Swiss Review of International and European Law* 27 (2): 211–26.

Tobler, C and J Beglinger. 2020. Tobler/Beglinger-Brevier zum institutionellen Abkommen Schweiz-EU. http://www.eur-charts.eu/wp-content/uploads/2017/08/Tobler-Beglinger-Brevier-Institutionelles-Abkommen_2017-08.1.pdf.

Tobler, C, J Hardenbol and B Mellár. 2010. Internal Market Beyond the EU: The EEA and Switzerland. Briefing paper. European Parliament. https://www.europarl.europa.eu/RegData/etudes/note/join/2010/429993/IPOL-IMCO_NT(2010)429993_EN.pdf.

Tomkin, J. 2011. Citizenship in Motion – The Development of the Freedom of Movement for Citizens in the Case-Law of the Court of Justice of the European Union. In E Guild and P Minderhoud (eds), *The First Decade of EU Migration and Asylum Law*. Leiden: Brill.

Tonge, J. 2020. General Election 2019: Northern Ireland. *Political Insight* 11 (1): 13–5.

Toppi, S. 1998. L'economia: l'età delle incertezze (1975–1990). In R Ceschi (ed.), *Storia del Cantone Ticino – Il Novecento*. Bellinzona: Stato del Cantone Ticino.

Trechsel, A. 2007. Direct Democracy and European Integration: A Limited Obstacle? In CH Church (ed.), *Switzerland and the European Union*. London: Routledge.

Ueberwasser, S. 2013. Non-Standard Data in Swiss Text Messages with a Special Focus on Dialectal Forms. In M Zampieri and S Diwersy (eds), *Non-standard Data Sources in Corpus-Based Research*. Aachen: Shaker Verlag.

UFS. 2011. *Il nuovo censimento della popolazione*. Neuchâtel: Ufficio Federale di Statistica.

UFS. 2018a. Votazioni popolari (risultati al livello dei comuni dal 1981). https://www.pxweb.bfs.admin.ch/.

UFS. 2018b. *Statistica dei frontalieri*. https://www.bfs.admin.ch/bfs/it/home/statistiche/lavoro-reddito/rilevazioni/staf.html.

UFS. 2020. Various Data. https://www.bfs.admin.ch/bfs/it/home.html.

Universität Freiburg. 1989. *Die Schweiz vor der Herausforderung der Europäischen Gemeinschaft*. Freiburg: Universitätsverlag. Reihe Herausforderung und Besinnung No. 12.

Vahl, M and N Grolimund. 2006. *Integration without Membership – Switzerland's Bilateral Agreements with the European Union*. Brussels: Centre for European Policy Studies.

Vallet, G. 2010. La Suisse et la zone euro: Une zone monétaire optimisée? *Revue du Marché commun et de l'Union européenne* 543: 624–35.

Vallet, G. 2012. Should I Stay or Should I Go? Switzerland and the European Economic and Monetary Integration Process. *Journal of Economic Integration* 27 (3): 366–85.

Vallet, G. 2016. *Economie – Les grandes notions*. Paris: Ellipses.

Vasilopoulou, S. 2016. UK Euroscepticism and the Brexit Referendum. *The Political Quarterly* 87 (2): 219–27.

Vatter, A. 1994. Der EWR Entscheid: Kulturelle Identität, rationales Kalkul oder Struktureller Kontext? *Schweizerische Zeitschrift für Soziologie* 20 (1): 15–42.

Vatter, A. 2018. *Swiss Federalism – The Transformation of a Federal Model*. Abingdon: Routledge.

Vonyó, T. 2008. Post-War Reconstruction and the Golden Age of Economic Growth. *European Review of Economic History* 12 (2): 221–41.

Waterfield, B. 2017. Copy the Swiss Model, Schäuble Advises Britain. *The Times*, 23 January. https://www.thetimes.co.uk/article/copy-the-swiss-model-schaeuble-advises-britain-qt97sl7dj.

Weiss, S and S Blockmanns. 2016. The EU Deal to Avoid Brexit: Take It or Leave. Special Report. Brussels: Centre for European Policy Studies.

Wellings, B. 2012. *English Nationalism and Euroscepticism – Losing the Peace*. Vol. 1. Berne: Peter Lang.

Werlen, I. 1998. Mediale Diglossie oder asymmetrische Zweisprachigkeit? Mundart und Hochsprache in der deutschen Schweiz. *Babylonia* 1: 22–35.

Werly, R. 2018. Entre Berne et Bruxelles, le poison lent du Brexit. *Le Temps*, 3 June.

Widmer, J. 2004. *Langues nationales et identités collectives – L'exemple de la Suisse*. Paris: L'Harmattan.

Widmer, S. 1991. *Aufbruch aus der Verspätung. Unsere Zukunft – 78 Autoren im Gespräch*. Zürich: Weltwoche.

Williams, S. 2016. Britain after Brexit, Becoming More Swiss. *The Conversation*, 15 June. http://theconversation.com/britainafterbrexitsteadilybecomingmoreswiss61692.

Wright, O. 2020. You Are Equals of the EU, British Negotiators Told. *The Times*, 3 March.

Wüger, D. 2013. Das für die Schengen- und die Dublin-Assoziierung mass-gebliche Recht: Publikation und Zugang. *LeGes* 1: 63–87.

Wunderli, P. 2001. Destruktion eines Mythos: die viersprachige Schweiz. *Akademie-Journal* 2: 15–9.

Wyder, R. 1999. *Die Schweiz und der Europarat 1949–1971*. Berne: Haupt.

Wyman, O. 2016. The Impact of the UK's Exit from the EU on the UK-Based Financial Services Sector.Report commissioned by the CityUK. https://www.thecityuk.com/assets/2016/Reports-PDF/d0c6c84174/The-impact-of-the-UKs-exit-from-the-EU-on-the-UK-based-financial-services-sector.pdf.

Zbinden, M. 1992. Das EWR-Projekt: Eine Wiederholung des Assoziationsversuchs von 1961–1963. *Schweizerisches Jahrbuch für Politische Wissenschaft* 32: 221–48.

Zuleg, F. 2020. *The Need for a Longer Transition*. Brussels: European Policy Centre.

Zürcher, B. 2010. Das Wachstum der schweizer Volkswirtschaft seit 1920. *Die Volkswirtschaf – Das Magazin für Wirtschaftspolitik* 1 (2): 9–13.

Index

For Product Safety Concerns and Information please contact our EU
representative GPSR@taylorandfrancis.com
Taylor & Francis Verlag GmbH, Kaufingerstraße 24, 80331 München, Germany

www.ingramcontent.com/pod-product-compliance
Ingram Content Group UK Ltd.
Pitfield, Milton Keynes, MK11 3LW, UK
UKHW020007200926
475702UK00015B/2519
9780367498047